HAMPSHIRE BOY

Hampshire Boy

Douglas J. French

The Pentland Press Limited
Edinburgh · Cambridge · Durham · USA

© Douglas J. French 2001

First published in 2001 by
The Pentland Press Ltd.
1 Hutton Close
South Church
Bishop Auckland
Durham

British Library Cataloguing in Publication Data.
A catalogue record for this book is available
from the British Library.

ISBN 1 85821 842 X

Typeset by George Wishart & Associates, Whitley Bay.
Printed and bound by Antony Rowe Ltd., Chippenham.

*This book is dedicated to my wife,
Audrey, to the whole of my family,
sons, grandson, daughter-in-law,
nephews and nieces, to all my friends
and people of all nationalities.*

Contents

Medals and Clasps

Below are listed the medals which Douglas J. French was awarded during his service with the Royal Hampshire Regiment, otherwise known as The Tigers, between 1933-1947. He served in various Battalions:

2nd Battalion – Isle of Wight and Aldershot, Hants as a Private

1st Battalion – Pakistan, India, Palestine and Egypt as a Private, Lance Corporal and Corporal

5th Inflation – England, North Africa and Italy as a Sergeant, Quarter Master Sergeant and Platoon Commander.

1. India General Service Medal with clasp 1936-7

2. Palestine General Service Medal with clasp 1938-9

3. Africa Star 1st Army Clasp 1943

4. Italian Star (PC) 1944-45

5. Defence Medal 1939-45

6. Total War Star 1939-45

7. War Medal 1939-45

8. He was also awarded by the Comrades Association in commemoration of those men who took part in or were killed at the Battle of Cassino in Italy 1944-5 during which he was wounded on 4 March 1944.

Preface

To appreciate the enclosed story and to understand some of the writing, I would like you to read this Preface first as most of it refers to the Military life, and our ways of conversation are so much different from those of our civilian life.

So, here goes:-

Having finished these memoirs of mine, which have taken many years, I have managed to put it all into some respectable order and I thought that I would pick it up and read it properly and then give my own true opinion.

To start with, the reader must bear in mind that I am no true experienced writer, I write as things come to mind, admittedly I have tried to keep it in some sort of sequence of times and stories. Whilst going about this task, I wrote various stories that in my opinion were not good enough and so it meant destroying many pages and rewriting them to try and make it more interesting.

There have been times, I can tell you, when I have felt like giving it all up entirely, but then I thought that those who are left behind me would most likely want to know what went on in days gone by.

As I have said before, I think whoever reads this part first will then appreciate the way it is written. There are mainly two faces to it, one is of civilian life and one is of a military life; two entirely different ways of going about the organisation of one's life, one of civilisation, one of destroying the enemies of one's country.

The one that I wish to enlarge upon and explain is the military one. Those who have not experienced military life as a soldier, no matter what rank, may find it rather disturbing because from the beginning it is drummed into you that you are here to defend your country. You have given your life to us with that purpose in mind, if not, why are you here as a professional soldier? So, from beginning to end, this way of living is not an easy one and is all about discipline, obedience, ranks and promotion and for the individual to get what he can out of it. Also for the individuals, if they are interested in bettering themselves by obtaining promotion, the better quality of life i.e. not being pushed around by N.C.O.s etc, the only way is to join them, but not necessarily being the same nasty characters as they are. You find your own way of conducting your life. As I have said before, one cannot compare this life to civilian life and we know full well that providing you survive the soldiering, you have to return to the life of a civilian. You then have to change your ways and believe you me, it is not easy.

To start with your military life, ask someone with past experience what it entails, harsh discipline, doing as you are told, standing to attention to all above the rank of a private soldier and saluting officers. If you don't like the sound of it, don't join. Keep away.

For me, for some reason or other, it was to be a challenge, so I stuck it out for a few years (13 years 6 months) and only left because I was medically discharged. Does it change a man's character? To tell you the truth, yes, some ways for the good, some for the bad. Those of past military experience do infer that this strict discipline has been found virtually a necessity, especially during battles. The soldier will gain confidence in the proficiency of his leader or commander and he then takes his part as one of the team.

Those of you who have seen films relating to the Japanese soldier will see that their discipline was even harsher than ours. They devoted their lives to their Emperor and we thought that their discipline went beyond all human endurance, so try and appreciate the way this is explained.

Good reading.

Prologue

This is a story of an ordinary citizen of England. It is not often that we get the opportunity of reading such stories about the life of anyone of no great importance. It may fit in with thousands of others such as myself. I am not yet sure how to head it – either 'The Hampshire Boy' or 'Seven Gongs', this relates to my short service in the Army.

I was born in the town of Southampton in 1916 at 87 Wilton Avenue which is situated near The Dell where the Saints still play today. I am referring to their football team. In my own career as a professional soldier, I never did have the opportunity to reach any dizzy heights as regards to promotion, but nevertheless I held my own. I managed to earn a decent living, this also refers to my later life as a civilian.

At my age now, I can look back and think of the mistakes that I made, and if I was able to have that time back I would probably go about things in a different way. One learns by experience, so let's carry on and see what I can turn out that can be of some interest to people who were born in this County, or who had served in the ex Royal Hampshire Regiment.

Biography of Douglas John French, born at Southampton, Hants at 87 Wilton Avenue in January 1916.

This biography could be of interest to anyone in the County of Hampshire or who had some connection with the Royal Hampshire Regiment. Their sons may be mentioned in the story and it may include some information as to what happened to them during their service whilst overseas. If they wish to know more, providing I know, I am willing to oblige but it must be remembered that it is all so many years ago. However, in some cases my memory is still good.

Finished and signed this day Wednesday 7th May 1997
D.J. French (Douglas John French)

Prologue

CHAPTER ONE

Start of Life

I was born into a family that in those days would have been classed as 'lower middle class', but of course to me at that very early age it would not have meant much to me. It was what my own Father mentioned to me. He, my Father, was born in Whitby, Yorkshire. His profession was that of a Commercial Traveller in the food line. Our family consisted of one daughter and three sons of which I was the youngest. The eldest was my brother Roland, about seven years older than myself, then Norman, about three years and eight months older, and next came my sister, Lorna, eighteen months older than me. Then there was my half-sister from my Mother's second marriage. I don't call her half-sister as I don't like the word half. As far as I am concerned, she is my sister and we have had a long, friendly relationship during our lives. We will have more to say about Pamela later on in this story or as and when she comes into my mind.

We all had our education as children like many others in the Secondary Modern Schools, but were lucky enough to finish up in colleges of some sort which gave us a better start in life when we became adults, a little more advantage than those who did not have that opportunity. I was like many other youngsters, unable to remember much of my very early life, only from the age of about five years old. We, as kids, in those days used to make our own entertainment. For instance, at the lower end of our avenue, there was an old dump and we used to pick out odds and ends like bicycle parts and build ourselves some sort of a bicycle out of it. We would find an old frame and a couple of wheels without tyres, even without brakes, they were made with a piece of wood jammed in between the frame and the wheel. We also fixed up some sort of saddle, a real poor effort, some old rag tied around the area where it should be, wrapping some string around to hold it on. We would take it to the top of the avenue and freewheel down some 800 yards, we just hoped, that nothing was coming in our way. Another game that we got up to was to find an old wing from some old car, sit in it and slide down a slippery, muddy bank. We had great fun with all this, the dangers, well, we didn't see any, we just got on with it.

As I said from the beginning of this story, we may have been middle class, but I had no thought of that then, I didn't know what it meant, I used to go along with anyone that I got attached to. We made friends and that was that, and I know that they all turned out to be nice people.

Another prank that we used to get up to was down at the Pier near the docks. We used to amuse some of the people by diving into the sea to catch the coins that they threw into the water. We had to catch these before they got down too deep and as we had no pockets, the coins were put into our mouths. When our mouths were filling up with coins, we would go back to where our clothes were and conceal them, so that no one would take them. We would take turns in guarding our money, we were wise to all that.

As Southampton is a fairly large town, quite a lot used to be laid on as regards to sport for the younger people. That is where I learnt to roller skate and also ice skate, but for us kids, our main area for roller skating was from the back of the West Station down past Perelli's Cable Works reaching down as far as the Royal Pier. We were lucky in those days in respect of traffic, there was not so much of it about, so there was little danger for us, it was great fun.

On my first day of attending Junior School, I was foolish enough to get a hitch on the tail of a truck with the tailboard down. I was hanging onto this and did not let go of it soon enough. As it gathered speed, my legs could not keep up, I fell off and consequently ended up on the road, knocking myself out. I ended up in bed with the doctor looking at me. I had hurt not only my head but my back, I was given hot formentations on it which seemed to be the cure for it in those days. An idiotic thing for me to do, hanging onto the tail of a truck, so that was not repeated any more. How we learn the hard way!

The school that I attended in this area was at Western.

So ends our stay in this part of Southampton.

CHAPTER TWO

School Life

My Father, for his own reasons, decided to move to Netley Abbey and our address was 'Dunreath', Station Road. We were now about six miles out of the town, so it meant a bus or train to get there. But, to start with, I had to attend school at Butlocks Heath, one of these schools that one had to fight one's way in to as well as out of, more about that later.

My eldest brother Roland was in the Army, he joined the Royal Engineers and was stationed in Southampton at the London Road Ordnance Survey Department and so I did not see much of him in those days.

The school I attended was about three miles away and we had to walk that in all weathers. According to my Father, I was not making much progress, I had spent about two years here when he decided that I should attend a better school. I was then sent to Woolston Cooks College. I must have been about ten years old then, the school was also in College road. It all seemed to belong to the headmaster. I can see him now, in his mortar board hat and walking about with his long swishy cane, the cane that he used to discipline us with, so if you misbehaved, you had your punishment with that cane, and boy that hurt. So you tried to keep out of trouble. It certainly did us good for our future behaviour, it did not get us into trouble like the youngsters seem to get into today. There of course, were some misbehaved ones around, I suppose there always will be. This College was there not only for further education but also to try and make us young gentlemen and to learn to respect our elders. My journey was by bus from Netley each day. Black and dark green were our school colours. I was here for about another two years when my Father decided to get me nearer home, so

4

now it was to Victoria College, Station Road, Netley, not more than half a mile from our own house. It was a mixed school with boarders as well as a day school, this was a Convent College, so good behaviour was a must and treating young ladies with much respect.

It was here that I made some friends. One was Eric Woodsford, his father was the local Police Sergeant. We have kept in touch to this day and he is living in Christchurch, Hants. After serving in the Navy during the 1939/45 World War, achieving the rank of Petty Officer, he then joined the Local Constabulary and eventually arrived at the Rank of Chief Inspector, so he did well for himself. Then there was Eric Harris, who at that time lived nearly opposite us in Station Road. We saw more of each other because of this. He was also in my Scout movement, he was Second in my Patrol, as he was a little younger than me, we did a lot together in that movement. Eric Woodsford was also with us as a Patrol Leader, he had a Patrol of his own. Eric Harris was also in the war with us, but was in the Royal Engineers. I think he became a Sergeant and as a civilian he worked in some big business shop in Southampton, in hardware I think. I see him sometimes, but not so often, they are all too far away now. There were others at this school but they were not so close to me, I have lost track of them as time went on.

During my stay in this village of Netley, we all belonged to the Netley Hospital Choir, at least the boys did. It was during my stay in this choir, that for some reason I had a fight with another boy and I was being observed by one of the choir men who happened to be a Sergeant in the Royal Army Medical Corps and their Physical Training Instructor, he was also a boxer. He said to me, 'I was watching you fight that other boy and both of you got nowhere because neither of you have any idea of fighting. Would you like to learn the art of self defence? Your arms are flying about like windmills. How about coming along to the gymnasium and I will teach you to box properly?' I agreed, and went back and told my Father this and he agreed as well. After that, whenever I went to choir practice, I attended this boxing class afterwards. I kept this up for some time until he said, 'I think that you have now reached the standard to take care of yourself. If you have any more scraps, you can now box them properly and you will find that you have the advantage over them, if they haven't had any training,' I don't think that I had any more, at least not as a boy. I did some boxing when I was in the army and this I will tell you about later on.

My stay at Victoria College was soon coming to an end, firstly because I was approaching 16 years old and that was the age limit for this College. We all sat for our Oxford Examination, my friends as well as myself all passed, even though my effort was not all that good, but at least it was a pass, I was a late learner. Unfortunately I had to leave the College as my Father had to retire from his work, so was not in such a good financial position. I could have gone on for further education to a University but it was not for me. I think the reason why I passed my exams at this college was because it was not crowded and the teachers were a lot more patient with us, they had some sort of method that would make us concentrate a little more.

CHAPTER THREE

My Brothers and Sisters

What about my eldest Sister Lorna? She must have felt out of place with all these brothers around her. She and I got on very well together as there was not so much difference in our ages I suppose, we can only remember having a bit of a push around with one another. I was chasing her around the house for some reason and as she was in front of me she pulled the door behind her to keep me out and I got my head squashed in the doorway, so I, like a gentleman, kicked her in the stomach – not nice was it? No harm done really, we ended up the best of pals. Just a short story that I thought I would tell you.

Lorna attended a school in Woolston called 'Miss Ways Finishing School for Young Ladies'. When I was in College at Woolston I sometimes used to have to wait for her and the girls used to look at me and giggle, don't ask me why, perhaps it was my knees! The teachers there used to show the girls how to sit properly, by holding their skirts at the back and as they sat down the skirt was brushed with a forward movement so that it was all neat at the front and they had to make sure that their knees were together, all so lady like, not like it is today, they couldn't care less now. The other thing they had to do was to walk properly, with books on the top of their heads looking straight ahead and not letting the book fall. Let's not forget the speech, forming their mouths by saying 'prunes and prisms' no vulgar words, oh no, all so lady like, not forgetting the curtsy. I bet there are not many ladies about now who had to go through all that palaver.

When Lorna left school she obtained a job in one of town's big draper's stores as a shop assistant.

Then the day came for my sister to depart from us and go and live with my Mother, this must have been arranged with my Father and Mother who were divorced long ago. I suppose it was only right that a young lady should be brought up by a Mother and not quite right for a Father to bring up a daughter, at least that was the idea in those days. Lorna left me and I was out of touch with her for a long time.

Let's now have a word about my brother Norman, the second eldest brother. His finishing College was at Queens, London Road, a Commercial School relating to business. After that, he worked at some large wholesale grocers in Ogle Road, Southampton. He put up with that for a while, but suddenly shot off and joined the Royal Navy as a Writer, not as an Able Seaman. He served some of his time in Malta, in fact he got married out there around 1935, I think, they had a son born out there who eventually became an Air Vice Marshal, so he did well.

Norman was later returned to England and served in Lee on Solent. He rose to the rank of a Chief Petty Officer and did have an opportunity for a commission but for various reasons rejected it and decided to leave the Navy and join Civvy Street. He eventually became a Director with Hawkins Brothers who were a Firm of Builders and he was also a Secretary to a few other firms, there he stayed until retirement.

His first marriage came to an end for various reasons and he then married Brenda. They decided to settle down in Budleigh Salterton, Devon and they have both been very happy there.

Sadly for us, Norman has now died and we all miss him very much. He lived to a good age of 81 years. His favourite pastime and hobby was golf, apart from going on nice holidays with his lovely wife Brenda, but Audrey and I visit her at times as well as her driving up here to see us.

Seeing that I am still in the area of Netley let me say a few things about it. I have already mentioned the Military Hospital here, this was at one time a very large place, built during the Crimean War to take all the wounded Soldiers and Sailors. It was then used a great deal during the First World War and again during the Second World War, mainly then by the Americans who had a large number of men over here helping us fight. It was two storeys high and was a quarter of a mile long, the corridors were wide enough to take an American Jeep, they used to drive through them when bringing in their casualties. Let us not forget to give our thanks to the Americans because without them we would probably still be fighting that war. Maybe that is slightly exaggerating, because it has been over for fifty years, but I for one show my appreciation.

Not much was left of the building, only the centre part is there, which in my day was the church. This is now the museum showing bits and pieces from the First and Second World War of both British and American memories. The grounds themselves are open to the public for just sitting around and enjoying the scenery around them, probably more entertaining for people during the summer weather. There are a lot of people buried over the back part inside the woods, the graves are taken good care of, but that is all there is to show in memory of that place, which to me seems a shame. I dare say it was too far out of the town to have taken the hospital over for civilian use, that was why it was demolished. The village of Netley no doubt use it at times for various functions, but the whole place brings back pleasant memories to me to when I was a child and most likely to many others as well.

CHAPTER FOUR

Leaving School and onto Adult Life

The time came for me to leave school and to find some kind of employment. This was not easy in those days because of the mass unemployment and depression that the country was going through in the 1930s.

I left school in 1931 and was fortunate that my father, because of the nature of his work in the food line was well known in this area and found a job for me in one of the Southampton grocery stores. The firm was Williams Pink & Sons, situated in London Road, and that was where I started. I was employed as a Grocer's Assistant and worked behind the counter. I was on the provision side, all was much different in those days. I was responsible for serving the customers and taking the money with the use of the counter machine. At the end of the day the money had to be counted up and had to agree with whatever was on the paper roll account, if not in agreement we must have given the wrong change and if so one was in trouble. The packets of sugar, tea etc. all had to be weighed up, nothing was prepacked like it is today. I worked for them for about a year, I think for the big sum of 18 shillings and six pence per week, my Father had most of it and I only had the six pence. It was long hours for short pay, I worked from 8.00 a.m. to 5.00 p.m. week days and some Saturdays. At times it was 10.00 p.m. at night before I got home.

One of our jobs for the Junior Assistants each Friday was to have to prepack all these bits and pieces such as sugar, tea, rice, flour, currants, sultanas and many other things, and it had to be the exact weight, no shortages.

I must tell you this, because I got into my first trouble with the Assistant Manager. I had just finished weighing up my sugar from a hundredweight bag and I was sitting on the next bag along side of me having a short rest when he came along and gave me a shove. He did it harder than he intended I think because I went over backwards and hit my head on the concrete, not hard enough to draw blood but hard enough to raise my temper! I shot up and clouted him one in the face, this caused some confusion as I had knocked off his spectacles and hurt one of his eyes. I was sacked on the spot. I took off my shop apron, picked up my personal belongings and walked out of the shop. As I was walking down the pavement thinking of what my Father was going to say now that I had been sacked, I bumped into the manager, who just happened to be out when all this was going on, he said to me 'What are you doing out at this time of the day?' I said, 'I have been sacked by the Assistant Manager.' I told him what had happened. 'Right,' he said, 'You had better come back with me and we can have a talk about this.' So back I went with him, this made them all stare at us thinking, this is going to be a good show, but it wasn't, for them, because we all trooped into the Manager's Office and sorted it out. It ended up with the Assistant Manager taking some of the blame for pushing me, but he said that I should not have retaliated as I did, so I made an apology to him. He said he did not want me in his Department any more so the Manager put me over on the perishable side which was bacon, cheese etc. I then had to learn how to cut up a side of bacon, both green and smoked, this was quite an art as I found out. Anyhow I was reinstated with the firm which saved me a bit of explanation with my Father, I don't think that he ever found out about this affair. I carried on with this job for a while, until I saw a notice down the road a bit and opposite, in the shop window of David Greig Grocery Shop – 'Wanted Boy Shop Assistant, Wages 20 shillings'. I thought that's a bit more than I am getting here, so I walked in and applied for the job. The manager soon recognised me and he said, 'Why, you work across the road with Pinks don't you?' I said 'Yes, that is correct, but surely I can better myself if I try.' 'Alright I'll accept you, you give them one week's notice and you can start here the following Monday.' I went

11

back to Pinks and at the end of the day I told the manager that I wished to terminate my services, by giving him one week's notice. This was agreed.

CHAPTER FIVE

At my First Employment

So there I was, now with David Greigs, they are still around today in some towns.

The first morning that I arrived the Manager said to me, 'What are you like at patting butter?' I said to him, 'I have not even started that as yet.' He replied to me, 'Well now is the time to start.' So I was given some practice on this for a few hours and found it quite easy, in no time I became good at it. I was dressed up all in white top hat, coat and apron with black buttons and placed in a position of observation in the front window so that the public could watch me. As I patted the butter up in various weights I had to stamp it with the Scottish Thistle, this was a wooden stamp. In addition to this, I was an egg boy. I had to check each egg over a light which was enclosed in a box affair, to make sure that no dark patches showed up on the egg, if I found any of these they were thrown away and not to be eaten. There was another branch of David Greigs situated down in East Street below Bar Gate. This was an even busier shop, all around was the Docks area and there was a lot of unemployment in this area, so Saturday nights the poorer people used to come around to our shop to see if we had any surplus meat over. This happened at times, because in those days we did not have fridges, only coolrooms which were made up with ice blocks each day. So as not to have to throw this meat away we would sell if off very cheap, as well as eggs or broken biscuits. It was heart breaking to see these half starved kids hanging around the shop after ten o'clock at night, some had not seen any soap for weeks by the look of them. They also wore no shoes on their feet, terrible conditions at that time. I forgot to mention above, that this was the branch where they sent me to help, as they must have thought that I was good at my job, but even here I did not last so long as it was not meant for me. I got into trouble, not for fighting, but I was carrying out a hundredweight of butter from the store to the shop when I caught the side of the butter board on the side of the counter and the lot went splash onto the floor. The floors in those days were covered in sawdust and moistened to keep the dust down. Half of the butter had to be thrown away and the rest of it I was made to pay for gradually out of my wages. It was an accident, so I thought I should do something about this. My Father was not so happy about this either. It was not so much that the butter was heavy, but the distance and the awkwardness of it with too many corners to go round and obstacles in the way made it difficult, but no allowances were made for that.

In my lunch break time I used to take my sandwiches in the park nearby, especially in good weather. After eating them I would stroll around and at times I would pass a sign on a building advertising joining the Army and seeing the world.

At this particular time I was giving it some thought. I of course knew nothing at all about the Army and did not really know if I was making the right move. It was obvious that I was not too happy with what I was doing at the time being and could see very little for my future, so I took courage and went over to make some enquiries. I spoke to the Recruiting Sergeant there. First of all he said to me, 'How old are you?' I said, 'Eighteen years old.' I did know that one should be that age to join the Men's Service as it said that on the notice, but I was not that as yet. This was about the end of August 1933 and I would not be eighteen until January 1934 so I had five months to go, but he did not ask me for any Birth Certificate and accepted me as a recruit to start with. He said, 'You will have to have a small educational test to begin with.' It was about basic maths, history and geography. I did not let on that I had already passed my Oxford Exam, so I sat at a table nearby and wrote my answers on the form supplied, finished it and passed it on for his scrutiny. He studied it for a while, and then said, 'Well, that's alright sonny, no problems there. You will also have to have a medical later on but now let's sort out which Service you wish to join Navy, Army or Air Force.' I said, 'The Army.' 'Right,' he says. 'Which Department? There are many different branches you know.' So he went through a few which to me did not mean a lot, 'How about an active unit like the Infantry?' I said, 'Yes.' 'Well which Regiment?' he said to me. I did not know which one so he suggested, 'How about your County Regiment? You know which County you live in don't you?' I said, 'Yes, Hampshire.' 'Right then, it's the Hampshire Regiment. They are Heavy Infantry and their Depot for training is in Winchester,' the Recruiting Sergeant told me. As I have said all this about Regiments was something new to me, so I had a lot to learn. 'Well,' he said, 'you have passed to enter but you have yet to sign on the dotted line, in other words to be sworn into the Regiment. This will take place at Carlton Place which is near here some time next week. I'll let you know. Right now I see the Medical Officer has turned up so he will see you now.'

I then went in for a medical. I seemed fit enough but he said to me, 'You need fattening up, you are under weight, but no worry there, we will see to that once you are in the Regiment.'

I then returned home with all this news to give to my Father. I don't really remember really what his remarks were, I don't think we had any bad words on the subject. He was most likely pleased for me as it was one son less to have to take care of, although that might be a little unkind. I told him that I was waiting to hear from them as regards to the signing of my Attestation Papers and that it would take place at Carlton Place, Southampton.

So it was a farewell to my Father and his housekeeper, Miss Boot. He did eventually marry her and settled down in Basset and around Southampton.

CHAPTER SIX

Army Life

Along came the letter as promised for me to report to Carlton Place to be sworn in, on September 15th 1933, early morning. They gave me a travel warrant to take me to Winchester with my two shillings and sixpence for the day. So onto the bus, a short journey to Winchester, my first time in this city so I did not know my way around and I had to ask a man where this Depot was. He said, 'Right there,' and he pointed to the gates, just a few paces away. With my little suitcase and me still dressed in my school jacket I approached these gates and stood there for a while looking through the bars of this gate watching some young soldiers being drilled on the square. There was a Corporal standing there, I later found out that they were Regimental Police. He said to me, 'Who you waiting for sonny, your Father?'

I said, 'Oh no, I have just joined the Regiment for training.'

'Well,' he said, 'do come in, can't have you standing out there all shy can we?'

He opened the side gate for me and let me in. I probably thought to myself what have I let myself in for here. Where I stood, unknown to me, was the Guard Room, the place that we all get familiar with as time goes on.

He soon arranged for me to be picked up. I was then ushered up to the Orderly Room which was our Headquarters. I was taken to the Adjutant who is an Officer who works close to the Commanding Officer. He had a few words with me and then passed me onto a Junior N.C.O. (Non-Commissioned Officer) who took me to the Quarter Master's Store to pick up my blankets, white sheets and a few other things and then onto a room where I was to sleep, all on my own for a while, as I was the first recruit of a new squad to be formed called Wolfe Platoon, named after General Wolfe, (we had to learn all about him later on). He then took me to the Sergeant who was to train me in Wolfe Squad, his name was Sergeant Hogan. He again, put me wise to a few things relating to the Army such as recognising Officers, Sergeants and Junior N.C.O.s, who to salute to and who not to, who to stand to attention to, which seemed to be many. He told me as I was the first in this squad that in the meantime, until there were more recruits, I would start my training with Tiger Squad which was already in training. There was another Sergeant by the name of Johnson as well as a couple of full Corporals to help train us, Corporal Norman and Corporal Snooks.

This General Wolfe happened to be the first Colonel of the Regiment, then it was called the 37th of Foot which was formed in 1702. This we had to keep in mind for future examinations as well as many other things relating to the Regiment.

I was also marched up before the Regiment Sergeant Major who pointed out a few things for me to remember. It was here that I was given a number that you used for the rest of your service or even today for one's pension. I was then known as 5497129 – Private D.J. French and don't you forget it, as they said, you have made your bed so lie on it.

Talking about pensions, I'll now tell you how I earned it. Going back to my entry to this barrack room where I was all on my own, this N.C.O. said, 'Take your pick where you want to sleep, the choice is yours.' I looked around and decided to take the end place, which later turned out to be the right one. Up by the main door was not a good place to be, when a crowd of rookies had been out for an evening on the beer, or for when the Duty N.C.O. was looking for some fatigue wallers (Soldiers needed for some work to be done), so I can tell you I was pleased with my choice.

The next man who turned up was from Jersey Channel Isles by the name of Percy Andrews, we knew him as Curly, because he had curly hair. He became a buddy of mine for life, although we were separated for a while. He was posted to India before me, he went in 1935 but I did not go until early in January 1936. I shall most likely have a few more things to say about Curly later on.

We had not as yet started seriously to learn soldiering, we had things to learn first as regards to tidiness, how to make your bed up to look tidy during the day, it was up into a sitting position, as I called it. There were three blankets and a pair of sheets all folded the same size and placed on top of one another, with one blanket wrapped right around the lot. In fact nearly everything one had was sorted out and put out in uniformity, this was performed every day with the exception of Sunday.

As I arrived at midday I was in time for my first army meal. A bugle was sounded to indicate that this was so, there were many other calls that we all had to get used to hearing and one had to act on them sharply. There were words to most of them, like the call to meals 'Come to the cook house door boys, come to the cook house door.' Or reveille, 'Get out of bed you lazy b —, get out of bed, get your feet on the deck'. When meal time came you had to be ready with your knife, fork, spoon, plate and mug and that had to be clean or else, there could be a lightning inspection. We had to fall in outside and march to the cook house. I must say that I felt rather strange at first until the rest of the Wolfe Squad was formed. I and a few others were still attached to Tiger Squad so in a way we had a start on the ones that came on after us.

On arrival at the meal table I was welcomed by remarks like, 'What did you want to join this mad lot for?' 'You should have your head seen to', 'You will be sorry'. I guess I had an answer for them like, 'Well how come you joined this mad lot then? What are you doing here?' There were some unpleasant remarks as well but I won't mention those, I put it down to where they came from.

To get to the Mess Room you had to go up some iron steps to the large entrance of this very large room. It most likely seated about two hundred men and what a racket they made, all talking at once, until the Sergeant and the Orderly Officer came around. The Sergeant would shout out 'Silence!' then talking would stop at once, he was there to find out if you had any complaints about the meal. There was dead silence, no remarks were made, one had to be careful how one answered, if you said the wrong thing you could be pulled to pieces.

The menu, well I can't really remember much about that, but it was all edible and built us up with the exercises, probably what we called bangers and mash (sausages and potatoes), followed by rhubarb and custard and washed down with a large mug of tea. After a few months of this, I began to put on some weight. Of course, during the time that we were all eating the noise was less, and I was just about getting used to their language, bad English and swearing. They were new to me some of the swear words, I dared not seem surprised to hear such words, otherwise, I would be ridiculed. I did find out later that the use of these bad words was forbidden, if one said such words to the wrong person you could be on a charge. I must say that I steered clear of the swearing during my service and I never did permit the use of it in my platoon. When men were about to be posted to my platoon, they were warned not to use it in my presence, I thought it all unnecessary. We know full well that Officers and Sergeants did use it on occasions so these rules did get broken.

There was a further task that we had to perform after our meal and that was to wash our utensils. At the base of the steps there was a large bowl of hot water, there you had to wash these properly and dry them when you got back into your barrack room, with your towel, and put them away properly in your locker.

CHAPTER SEVEN

Enlisted Life in the Army as a Professional

About three weeks later the room began to fill up with new recruits, all about my age, some a little older and mainly from around this area of Hampshire.

So we began to train as killers in earnest. No good kidding ourselves, because that was what we were, but that word was very seldom used except by the Instructors. We were here to defend our country in case of war. We would always find some nation somewhere in this world who would want to have a go at us for some political reason, we just did not want to be dominated. I can say that we never entered into this kind of conversation, at least not in earnest, we all had our own particular reason for joining this man's army – I'll give you mine.

At that time I was bored with my job as a Grocer's Assistant, not enough action for me, too dull and I was getting nowhere. I wanted to see something of the world outside of the British Isles. I had visions that there was something better for me some place.

I had no knowledge of Army life whatsoever, so I came here and found it hard but I could take the discipline as long as it was justified. I used to get myself into trouble at times if I gave my opinion when something was not justified, but as time went on you could see the reason for such discipline, especially in battle. That was how I thought about it at that age.

Let me now get on with my story. I try at times to think of some of the names of men who were in my squad. The ones that I really got friendly with were, Sid Bourne, who came from Totton. I visited his home once but never saw him after I left them in the desert in late '39. Then there were Ted Russell and Bungee Thompson, from Basingstoke. Ted became the Commanding Officer, Silver Bugler in Rawlpindi, Pakistan and a good friend of mine for a long time. There was also Gerrish from Luggershaw, Lionel Baker, Jungle May, the tubby comedian, not to forget Curly Andrews. They were all good men who did their best to serve their Regiment. I often think about them and how they progressed through life, I can see a lot of faces, but I am not able to put names to them.

There were various characters and there was mickey taking at times that used to cause a fight, but it all ended up with the shaking of hands and if one or the other was getting the worst of the fight it was put a stop to. You could not afford to be too much of a weakling, or you found that you were being pushed around.

Let me now bring up the subject of cleanliness, not only were we made to shower or bath regularly, but also have a regular change of underwear, this was sent weekly to the laundry. We were issued with a printed ticket with the articles already printed on it, all we had to do was put a tick along side of the item, with your laundry mark so as to identify your own washing, on return. You did not want anyone else's washing, that was not on. Your Army number, rank and name were on the ticket and the washing was handed into the Quarter Master's Store. Our laundry for the future would be called 'dhobi', an Indian word for washing, brought back to England, to be used in the dictionary, like many other foreign words that drift back to this country.

So here we were all together, a time that would never again occur in our lifetime, going through this training to try and make us good soldiers. Some of us would make it, some of us would fall by the wayside, but at that age we were not as yet aware of it.

By then we had all drawn our full kit which included our Lee Enfield Rifle and Bayonet, that rifle, in case you do not know fired a .303 bullet and when fired by a good shot would reach one thousand yards with accuracy. I know this because I was sent on a Sniper Course in the area of Dagenham Docks. One had to have a score of ninety-nine out of one hundred and I did it, much to my surprise. At that time I was a Sergeant, so I had had plenty of practice.

So what did we do to try and make us all proficient? Well, starting early in the morning, reveille was at 06.00 hours, we were woken up by the usual bugle call. Within seconds the Duty N.C.O. would be around also to shout 'Right, out of those beds and on your feet, P.T. (Physical Training) in five minutes.' No matter what the weather, we had to fall in outside in our gym kit and up to the gymnasium to carry out our physical jerks. We had to go up on the wall bars, the wooden horse, horizontal bars and climbing rope that was attached to the ceiling. At times we had a tug of war, not forgetting the long jump outside, as there was a passing out test later on, we had to be able to jump at least 18 feet, which was not a bad jump for amateurs. After this performance we would have to fall in outside and double back to barracks, grab a mug and fall into a queue for a mug of gun fire (tea) all nice and steaming hot. Then back to the barrack room to drink it, then to the wash house for the usual wash and shave. This shaving lark I had not yet started, but on inspection by Training Sergeant Hogan, he spotted my chin and tickled it saying, 'What's that stuff on your chin? Do I have to get my cat down to lick it off for you? You had better make use of that shaving equipment that has been issued to you from now on.' So I started this, but it was not necessary every day, at least not for a while until it grew tougher.

CHAPTER EIGHT

Progress as a Private

Let's talk about the rifle for a while. According to the Sergeant Instructors, this was to be our best friend for some time if we took good care of it. This rifle had not changed much since the last war, and still fired a .303 bullet. It had to be kept clean at all times as we never knew when we would be pounced upon for a lightning inspection and it was most important that it was cleaned after firing on the range. It was fitted with a pull through, a piece of cord about 2 ft 6 inches long with a brass weight on the end, which was dropped through the barrel. On the end of the cord there was a loop on which we threaded a piece of flannelette, just large enough to fit tight in the barrel, this was soaked in some light oil and pulled through a few times to make sure that the barrel was cleaned. There were just no excuses for it being dirty and you were charged if it was found to be dirty. With regard to the oil part of it, there was also supplied a small brass oil bottle filled with the correct oil. We were responsible for making sure that there was always oil in it. Both this and the pull-through fitted into the butt of the rifle which had a trap built into it, this was made of brass as well, so that was something else to keep clean. There was a sling supplied to fit the rifle, which was made of webbing with a brass hook on both ends, these had to be kept polished. The sling was kept clean with a green webbing block, which was moistened and brushed on and allowed to dry a green colour. The woodwork on the rifle also had to be linseed oiled and rubbed in hard so that it ended up polished as well.

Then came the time to fire this rifle. This was not carried out until we had had some dummy practice at targets with dummy bullets. There was a rule, if I can remember it, so many years ago now, it went something like this, 'Get the tip of the foresight in the centre of the aiming mark and in line with the 'U' of the backsight, sight thus in line, focus the mark', something like that. The aim could be checked by an aiming target held to the eye of the Instructor, he could see through a small hole what you were aiming at to see if you were aiming straight. Once he was sure that you understood all about the rifle we would then set off to the range, these were set out about every 100 yards. We always started at the 100 yards first to have our rifle zeroed. When that happened, we always had an armourer with us so he would fix the sight that suited your aim. Firing a rifle is a technique that comes with practice. We are not all the same the way we go about it, that is why there are good and bad shots. Some make it and some don't. Maybe it's a question of holding one's breath, or holding the rifle in a comfortable position, or not dwelling on the aim too long, as I said, it all comes with practice. Like me, at the Depot I was to start with only a Second Class Shot, but when I joined the Second Battalion in the Isle of Wight I became a marksman both on the rifle, and machine gun, but with a pistol I was only First Class and at times Second only. I wore the marksman badges for the rest of my service, when I remembered.

The next part of our training was on the Barrack Square, learning to stand to attention and standing at ease and easy. Then we were to march off and keep in line, swinging our arms up to the level of the waist and at the same time keeping them straight, looking straight ahead and not to left or right unless told to. All basic drill but necessary for a smart appearance. You must qualify on this drill, if not, you were not allowed out until you had passed a standard. There were of course other drills to do with the rifle, sloping arms, marching the trail and presenting arms, this was needed for the purpose of saluting Officers above the Rank of a Captain up to and including a General or any other special occasion. Most of us had little difficulty in mastering this drill.

Then came the time when you were first allowed out into town. This was quite an occasion, your uniform had to be smart and your hat in order, that was, your chin strap was put on correctly, there was a special way of putting that on. In those days, we wore puttees, so those had to be put on in the correct manner. Your boots had to be polished so much so that you could nearly see your face in the toes and your belt had to be cleaned and polished. We did have mirrors to look in, long ones that were fixed to the walls. We used to stand in front of those mirrors for a few minutes to make sure that as far as we could see nothing was wrong with our dress. I must say that when we got to the Guard Room the N.C.O. there on duty had to inspect you before allowing you out, if there was something wrong he would not tell you what it was, he would just say, 'Go back and check yourself out.' So back we would go and have another look in the mirror and most likely get someone else to have a look as well. I was sent back once I know, and I could not see what was wrong but someone pointed out that my chinstrap was put on incorrectly so I altered it and returned to the Guard Room for another inspection and he said, 'Well, that's right now, so off you go.' So down towards the town I went and who did I see in front of me but the Regimental Police, and you bet your life they would give you the once over as you passed them so you marched past them in a smart and soldier like manner. They were probably having a grin to themselves as I passed by. But what did I do going round a corner? I slipped, so it was, pick yourself up and tidy yourself, feeling rather foolish after going to all that trouble to make sure that you were smart, but they said not a word. Some troops used to go out drinking beer but up to now I had not touched it. I don't know how they could afford it, on the poor salary that we received, maybe they received some other income. At this time in any case it had not as yet appealed to me to get drunk, it seemed rather stupid, but I dare say it's the company you keep and they eventually get you to try some of it. Anyhow, more on that later perhaps.

I can tell you now, if you were caught drunk you were in big trouble, because a soldier according to Military Law is supposed to be ready for duty twenty-four hours a day.

Talking about alcohol just now, it was my eldest brother

Roland who was in the Royal Engineers who introduced me to beer one day. When I was in Streatham, London I was out with him. I think we were off to a dance in the Locano Dance Hall. He said, 'Let's call in here and have a drink.' I said 'I haven't tasted it, what is it like?' He replied 'The best way to find out is to come on in and taste.' He of course bought me what I called a strong beer, barley wine, or some call it old beer. Well the first taste did not seem so bad, so I had another, but no more as there was no effect on me at all. We then went off to this dance, that was it, I had tasted it. Time to talk about the Sergeant's Mess later on.

Still at Winchester let's now say something about my running ability. This was not really discovered until we started cross country running at this depot. We first ran against the Winchester College boys, General Montgomery's son attended this College, not sure if he was there at that time. Once on the road I found it easy to keep up at the front, with what they called 'the cream'. They had a young man who was their best runner at all times, so I kept with him for many miles without much effort. I don't think he cared for my efforts, he was not annoyed, just anxious that I did not pass him. We were to cover about twelve miles I think, so getting towards the end of the run I let myself go and so did he. I pressed harder, in the end he gave up and I continued on in to win the race by quite a few yards. So this was the discovery that I had this running ability which stuck with me for most of my service. It may sound as if I am boasting but it is only the truth. I think if one is good at something why not express your ability? It gives you pleasure as well as other people who wish to challenge you and also to watch you.

I later developed other types of running on the track, such as the 200 yards (as it was called then). I had the equivalent of the world record in 1936 for the 200 yards, which was then 22.5 seconds, the Olympics at that time were held in Germany in the presence of Adolf Hitler. When I obtained this it was in India in the Army Championships. I used to enjoy my running ability. My brother Norman who was then in the Navy was also a very good runner, but we never did manage to meet, we would both have liked that because we always did rib one another about our abilities.

Well so much for the running side of it, I am now going to talk about my boxing ability, but first of all I will tell you how I managed to get involved. Fairly early on I got myself arrested for striking an N.C.O. The reason was this, each morning as I have already mentioned we had our exercises up in the gymnasium and returned to the barracks for our early morning mug of tea, still in our gym kit, shorts etc. There always was this Corporal Cook who stood at the head of the queue helping to pour out this tea. He sort of took a fancy to my legs and attempted to stroke them, but never did, as I prevented this. He would say something like, 'Well, I do like these lovely legs, nearly as nice as my wife's.' Well, this had been going on for a very long time now and I was just about getting fed up with his remarks each day. I was urged on by my fellow comrades to do something about it. One fellow said to me, 'Hey Doug, you are a boxer, aren't you? Why don't you slosh him one?' I said, 'Well if I do I shall be in the Guard House.' 'So what,' he said 'You will get off lightly, he is provoking you, isn't he?' Anyhow I did nothing about it that day, but gave it some serious thought during the day. I told the lads, 'If he does it tomorrow morning he is going to catch a wallop from me', so this was something that they were looking forward to. It came, we were in the queue as usual, with the Sergeant on the steps watching things as well. The Corporal was at it again, he was not ready for it, but I drove him a beauty right on the chin. It knocked him over the spare urn of tea and he was flat out. Then came what I expected, the Sergeant shouted to another Corporal, 'Arrest that man!' The Corporal detailed two men to escort me at the double down to the Guard Room, where I was greeted by the Regimental Police, who chased me around like some criminal, sayings things like, 'So you would strike a fellow N.C.O. would you?' and 'So scrub this and scrub that,' during my stay in this place. I was being punished even before I was tried. I don't think that N.C.O. liked me, he didn't even know why I had done it. I was still in my gym kit and was cold, but he didn't care about that.

It was not too long before my Training Sergeant came down and took me away. I don't think the staff in the Guard Room wanted me to go as they had not finished giving me the works but the Sergeant said, 'Right Corporal, let me have that man right away.' I was marched away back to my Barrack Room, made to wash, shave and get dressed. I was now under open arrest. I then had my breakfast and awaited Trial with the Commanding Officer at 10.00 hours.

I was marched into his Office with a lot of shouting of orders. The Sergeant read out the charge of striking an N.C.O. This the Commanding Officer took seriously and said to me, 'Now French, what have you to say? I will not stand junior soldiers striking my N.C.O.s. What have you to say in your own defence?' So I told him what had been going on for weeks regarding this N.C.O.'s behaviour, which was annoying me very much and asked him, 'What else could I do to stop it?' He then stated, 'You should have reported it to your Sergeant and he would have done something about it.' I said, 'And what sort of remarks would I have got from various men, if they knew that I had made such an appeal to my Sergeant? I would have been ribbed forever. I was provoked into this by his continual bad behaviour, so I had to show him that I would not put up with it any longer. I know that it was wrong to strike an N.C.O. and am willing to take my punishment.' He continued to reprimand me, but he had to mention that it was a pity that this had happened to me, as I had a good report all round. He stated, 'I am going to give you one day's detention and seven days C.B.' (Confined to Barracks), meaning that you are not allowed out and also you had to report to the Guard Room at 22.00 hours at night, also during the evening you would be given some extra work to do, or fatigues as we called it. So ended my first Charge in the Army. I did notice that as I was dismissed from the Commanding Officer's Office that the Corporal, was also up before the Commanding Officer and I heard that he was severely reprimanded for this behaviour, which did him no good for a long time. It stopped his further promotion, and later I passed him for promotion.

I did not spend any more time in the Guard Room as he said I would have to have one day's detention and I had already spent time in there, my Sergeant saw to that, which was fair enough, I had already had enough of that lot down there.

I will tell you now, whilst I am on the subject, that I did meet up with this Corporal five years on, as I was returned to England as an Instructor. I had gone on ahead as a Billeting Officer in a village called Doddington, in Kent. As I was strolling around this camp, I spotted a Corporal and I noticed he was the Corporal that I had struck when I was a recruit. He did not recognise me, as I had grown up somewhat and was now a Sergeant. So, I thought I would have a bit of fun with him. I called him over and said to him, 'Is it normal that a senior N.C.O. should walk about like you do, with your hands in your pockets?' He was absolutely flabbergasted and said, 'No, not normally Sergeant.' I said, 'How about standing to attention to a senior N.C.O.' I know, not a nice thing to do, but I was still having a go at him. He stood to attention then I started to question him, 'You don't recognise me now, do you?' 'No Sergeant, who are you?' he said. I did not answer his question right away and then said, 'I see you have not gained your third stripe as yet.' He then replied, 'That's right, it's a sore point. Why do you ask?' I answered him, 'Well you should not go round trying to stroke young soldiers' legs or passing remarks about them.' 'But how did you know about that?' I replied, 'Well I was the one who belted you in the nose for doing it.' Well, you should have seen his face, it was funny enough to make me laugh. He then said to me, 'Well it certainly did not stop you from going ahead, as you see, it did not do me much good.' 'I don't suppose you ever tried that again,' I said to him. 'Hardly, but I only meant it to be a bit of fun. Well, it's been a long time now so we can forget about that,' he replied. We shook hands and parted and I never did see him again. I will say no names, if he is about today, and reads this, he will know who he is.

The result of striking an N.C.O. was that I was automatically put into the Depot Boxing Team. I had already had some training in self defence, I would have been a light weight by then.

Just above our Barracks there were a couple of other Regiments in training, the Rifle Brigade and the K.R.R.'s (Kings Royal Rifles). It was a competition between us, one big happy family.

This boxing was taken very seriously, especially with the Senior Officers. They turned up each evening all dressed up in their best scarlet dress and were given a good seat at the front. I for one had about four fights in my weight and it all came as a surprise to me, to keep winning. The training that I had as a boy must have been good for me, because I was boxing and not scrapping, there is a difference. In those three or four nights I won all my fights. I was congratulated all round. We were not presented with any awards that final night but a few days afterwards by our General, Hakins, I think. All this was up on the Barrack Square, in front of all the troops, quite an affair. I was presented with a silver medal, which I still have today. I was never allowed to forget this in the future, I was put in to fight for the Battalion Boxing Team all the time, and I did not always win, got many a hiding. All this eventually came to an end as the Second World War started.

I must tell you, that at one time I fought a professional and beat him on points. It was Charity Bout in aid of a Senior Citizens' Dinner, somewhere in Kent in 1942. His manager asked me if I would take it on if the war finished soon. Well that was a silly suggestion as who knew when that was to be, he said he thought I was good at it, but that was my last bout of boxing.

Still at the Depot we were becoming partly trained soldiers, which was true we were only partly trained. We had yet to learn tactics and field craft, but this had to be carried out with one of our Battalions, the Second Battalion. Our First Battalion was out in India, that would come later for us. Leaving this Depot was a bit of a sad occasion for us, as we would never return. As I see it today it was a sad occasion indeed, it was empty and probably waiting to be demolished. I can see ghosts, running around the square in the form of young soldiers. It could be turned into flats because to me, it is a good solid building and what I would call substantial.

CHAPTER NINE

Moving on out of Depot Training

So we were off to the Second Battalion of the Hampshire Regiment, now that we had finished our first six months training as recruits. We were considered as part trained soldiers, with a lot more to learn. Albany Barracks, just outside Newport, at the back of us not too far away, is the prison for those that have misbehaved. Today, 1994, it is all one prison as they took over the barracks.

The Isle of Wight is not so easy to escape from because it is an island. We were sorted into various Companies, I was in 'Z' Company. Here we had to continue our education. I had already sat for one Certificate at the Depot, being the Third Class Certificate and passed that, the next would be the second Class Certificate. I started it there but finished it, and passed it, when I was in Pakistan late in 1936. Here at this Battalion we had a lot of training to do, including many hours on the firing ranges. It was here that I obtained my Marksman Badge on the rifle and Lewis machine gun. It meant more pay, as well as having to wear your Marksman Badges on your uniform, on the lower part of the left sleeve.

For our leisure hours there was the town of Newport, only about a mile away. This was quite an interesting town with a cinema.

Other pleasures that interested me were sports, I was still running for the Battalion but here I was not always first, there was one good runner already who had been established for some time. An older soldier than myself, once again his name does not come to me now, but I still used to run a good second. I was still good on the track and I also did a little boxing.

Another sport that agreed with me was hockey, I found I

shone at that, quite a bit. First of all I played for my Company and later on for the Battalion.

In this training I managed to get myself into trouble once again. It was not my fault, at least I did not think so. I was out training one day for cross country running when I accidentally ran through a squad of Junior N.C.O.s on a Cadre Course, as I turned a sharp corner in the Barracks I ran into them. I did no harm, but, instead of turning back, I ran straight through them. The Sergeant who was instructing them took a poor view of it and called me back and placed me under open arrest, for obstructing his training. When I appeared before my Company Commander he gave me seven days confined to Barracks. He had to administer punishment as the Sergeant had made the Charge, so I did not get away with it. It was not a Charge that remains on one's Record. It was quoted as minor, and he said something about, 'Owing to the fact that you were training for cross country, I am letting you off somewhat.' This did in fact affect my performance on the cross country running, I lost interest in performing well and it was noticed by the Sports Officer, he said to me one day, 'How come you don't put yourself out these days, you are running but have no interest anymore?' I said, 'It's only how I feel at the moment.' But I mentioned that I was charged for training a few days ago, and that I caused a bit of a nuisance by running through an Instruction Course by accident, and was given seven days punishment for doing so, which I thought unjust. He said, 'Not to worry, I'll have a word with the Company Commander about it and see that it is not put on permanent record.' So I put away that mood and got on with it again. For this punishment I had to do extra fatigues in the evening, mainly I helped out in the Officers Mess cleaning their silver. I did not mind that, as I received a nice supper from them.

During my stay here I was selected for a 'Rough Riders Course' in Bulford Camp, Wiltshire, so was back on the mainland for a few weeks, on Salisbury Plains attached with the Twenty First Lancers. I was there to learn all about horses. My way of dress changed somewhat, I had to wear riding breeches, you know, the ones with patches on the inside of the leg, which stopped rubbing on the legs when you were riding. We also wore the bandolier made of leather which in wartime carried ammunition in the pouches, this was across the chest. We also carried a short whip, mainly for dress, we never did hit the horse, we only used it as a guide, just a light tap here and there to indicate which way you wanted it to turn.

They gave us an excellent course, and it just about covered everything about horses. We started off for a couple of weeks in the Riding School, riding bare back, then with a blanket on the horse's back, followed by the saddle, teaching us how to ride at the walk, to canter and then onto a gallop. We were also taught how to set up a team of six horses all about seventeen hands, how to fix them up with all that complicated harness, this had to be kept smart at all times. These six horses had at times to be fixed up so they could pull the heavy gun carriage. We also had to learn how to ride these horses in various places in the team, either the front pair, middle pair or at the rear, and again, at various speeds. This was done by passing through wooden pegs fixed to the ground paced out to more or less the width of the gun carriage wheels. It took a bit of practice to pass through without knocking them over, you did not pass if you knocked them over on your final. Also as we were attached to the lancers we had to learn how to use the lance. We had to pierce a sack of straw which was placed on the ground, doing it at various speeds, all with as much accuracy as possible. In addition to all this we had to learn how to look after the horses. The horse always had priority over you, when you had finished with him for the day, you had to make sure that he was rubbed down, fed and watered, as well as having clean straw to lie on. All harnesses had to be taken off and hung up in the proper place. During the night they were looked after by a Picket, a Sentry that walked about to make sure that all was well. It was more to learn I know, but of what use for the future one would think, we were about to become fully mechanised.

I was used at times by our Commanding Officer, when I returned to my own Barracks. It seems that he wanted someone to take his horse back to his house which was in Cowes, this was about five or six miles from this Barracks. I was detailed to do this, no questions of volunteering, but at the same time it made a change from other duties. I would sit on his horse all the way. The horse took to me, but not before I introduced myself to him, this I do normally when riding a horse, I think he accepts you better that way. I would take him all the way which was mainly a hard road but at times there could be a soft verge, this I would guide him onto, better for his hooves and less tiring for his legs. When I arrived at the house his wife greeted me like a long lost son. I would then take the horse around to the stables, rub him down, take off his head harness, bit etc. and feed him if necessary. Then I would close the stable door and return to her house to be given a nice lunch, she would then take me down to the bus stop so that I could catch the bus back to the barracks, all a nice trip.

CHAPTER TEN

My First Manoeuvre

It was now the time for manoeuvres in earnest. This would be our first time, to take place up on Salisbury Plain, as it had been used for this for many years to train our troops, and still is today. First of all we had to march to Cowes and board one of the paddle steamers, which took us to Southampton, then a march to the Plains. We were heading for a place called 'Bustard Camp', so we marched up through the town of Southampton. Our first stop was up in the Avenue, in fact, we stopped outside a pub called The Cowards Inn, a well known pub on the left. The whole Battalion stopped here to eat their sandwiches. It just so happened that my Father turned up, how he knew that I was there, I do not know to this day, because we had made no arrangements to meet. How was I to know, to make arrangements like this would be out of the question? He was allowed to come over and speak to me, of course, I had my leg pulled over that, 'Did Daddy waddoms come to see his little soldier boy?' or 'Ah, how nice,' and many other remarks.

We continued on our march up to Romsey and on the road to the Plains. It was quite a march, there were always moans about marching, no one cared for it. Most ranks had to march except up to the rank of a Major, he usually rode a horse. On arrival at this Camp of Bustard we could see that there were bell tents rolled up on the ground ready for us to put them up. We had to put floor boards down first, in case it rained, so that we would not be sleeping in water. Once we had put the camping area in order we were allowed to relax and sort ourselves in our respective tents.

Come morning, I was the one that became detached from my Section, as I was earmarked now as a specialist, because of my training with horses at Bulford Camp a few months ago. I had to report to the Transport Officer where I was given a covered wagon with a seventeen hand, it was called the 'Officers Wagon' and only one driver needed. Why 'Officer's' I was not too sure at the time. What I had to do right then was to drive the wagon down to Shrewton to visit the bakery and pick up the bread for the battalion, about ten miles away, bring it back to the camp and distribute it to various companies. All went well on the way, but on my return journey, it had to start to rain and for some reason or other this horse did not like rain and, it became a bit stroppy. Coming up the hill out of Shrewton, he slipped, then there were problems. First of all he had slipped out of his harness, or part of it, he also fell down on his front legs, as a result, a lot of the bread came out of the wagon and landed in the road, so you can guess, there was a lot of wet bread. By the time I sorted him out, with his harness, and got him back on his feet, the bread was a mess. I had to hurry up and get it in the wagon. I thought, guess I'm in trouble about that when I get back, but as far as I could see it was of no fault of mine.

At the first Company where I stopped off to give them their ration of bread, I told the Cook Sergeant what had happened. He said, 'Never mind, laddie, put it down here. I'll soon dry this, I'll put it in this field oven and dry it off, they won't know the difference.' And that was what he did. I never heard of any complaints, just shows you, they eat anything as long as they have not seen what had happened to it before it got to their mouths.

When I had finished this job I had to report to the Transport Officer once again, he then said, 'Go pick up that big hairy eighteen hand, put it in the water carrier and go to a certain place, and pick up fresh water for the Battalion.' It probably held about two thousand gallons of water, this I did, with no mishaps this time.

For most of my training on up on these Plains, I was employed as such. I did do some field training, but nothing like as much as the others, they thought I was a blue eyed boy, being given these special jobs, which got me off a lot of

Bustard Camp, Salisbury Plain, 1934.
Author on the far right, aged eighteen years.

marching and running around the Plains playing soldiers. This went on for about three weeks and then we returned to Parkhurst Barracks, the same way as we came.

CHAPTER ELEVEN

Parkhurst Barracks

At these barracks, we of course, had to take our turns at the main gate on guard. We first of all had to go on parade and be inspected, there was always an additional man to mount with this guard, because he or some other would change places, if one of the Guards was smarter than he was, that man would be known as the 'Stick Man' for the day and would accompany the Duty Officer and the Duty Sergeant of the day on their rounds of inspection. This I managed to do at one time, still boasting I know, but these things did happen. When you obtained what we called 'best man of the day', you were dressed up in your best uniform, wore white tassel cord with brass ends to it, right across the chest, with a white pouch on the back. You also carried the Silver Cane tucked under your arm. They reckoned it was quite an honour to get that, it meant more ribbing from the troops, but I got used to that and just ignored their remarks, at least, it got me off that Guard.

But I did do that Guard Duty at times, not always the best man, that's just not allowed. I thought that this guard was a bore, when on duty, you had to stand out at the front of this building and march up and down with your rifle. You were under the eyes of all, including the R.S.M. If he found something wrong with your sentry go, he would bellow at you from a distance. Then there were the Officers who kept coming and going, up to the rank of a Captain. You had to slope your arms and give a butt salute. If it was a Major, you had to give him a present, and you bet your life the Orderly Officer and the Duty Sergeant would visit you as and when they felt like it. You would then have to turn out the whole of the Guard by shouting at the top of your voice 'Stand by the Guard, Guard turn out.' That would cause some confusion in the Guard Room, most of them were half asleep and equipment half off. You had to buckle yourself up, find your rifle, put on your hat and move in double time. If you were slack you had to do it again, getting told off all the time. The Sergeant of the Guard said to me one day when we were coming off Guard, 'How did you like that Guard?' I said to him, 'I did not, I thought it a waste of time really. What are we guarding? We are only stood here all the time, if we are supposed to guard the Battalion and the whole property, how can we just by stopping here. If the place needs guarding it would be more useful if it was a picket that patrolled around the grounds.' 'No doubt you are right,' he said. 'It's just a show piece really, a matter of red tape. But your point is taken, maybe they will do that some day, but they do not consider that necessary in England. You will find that they do that more when you do your service in India.' This I found to be correct when I got out there.

That year, 1934, came and there came out a draft list of men to be sent to India, much to my disappointment I was not on it. The list did include my buddy Curly Andrews, this I did not like and neither did he. I approached my Company Sergeant Major about this and he said, 'You know why you are not on it, don't you?' 'Yes, I think so, it's because I am on the Cross Country Running Team and they don't want to lose me,' I replied. He then stated, 'But if you put in for an interview with your Company Commander, and ask him to put you on, he might grant it.' This I did, but he said, 'It can't be done now, as we have our quota, maybe next time. Fall out and carry on.'

I was really concerned about my future in the army, mainly in respect of future promotion. If I concentrated too much of my time on sport I was not getting anywhere as regards promotion, that was how I was thinking. I wanted to be able to attend a few Cadre Courses to get a start as a Lance Corporal. I spoke about this to this Officer, and he said that I should not worry too much about that, someone was keeping an eye on me without a doubt. He then stated that he would consider putting me on the next draft.

About the end of 1934, we were all moved to Aldershot, this is a large training place with many troops. If you were interested in cross country running, you were competing with about three thousand runners. I managed to enter one of these races, unfortunately for us, we were given the wrong information as regards the running conditions. We were told that it was a soft run, and that running spikes would be okay to use, so this we did, but came upon some hard roads. This did not do our feet any good, in fact, it just about crippled us. My position was not so good on this run because of this and I came number thirty-sixth. Not bad considering, but not good enough, not my usual performance.

The rest of our duties were much about the same as Parkhurst, I did not think that I was anything outstanding. I did attend a Gymnastic Course during my stay there, I never did know the results, I just passed, that's all it said, it just gave me another kind of duty to do e.g. taking my platoon on physical exercises in the morning and later the company. This was much later, as a Sergeant. Little did I know that I was earmarked to be an N.C.O., I was only nineteen years old and had yet to gain experience to be able give orders.

During our stay here we were given an unusual task of loading up a ship with ammunition, this was down at Portsmouth Harbour. The ammunition was to be sent on to Addis Ababa, Ethiopia. There was trouble out there at the time, but to this day I do not know who it was for because it was the Italians who they were fighting. We were given this task, as the civilians who worked at the port refused to handle these explosives, so we were called upon to do it. We had no trouble with the ammunition, but we did have a casualty when some wood fell from a bundle being hoisted up on on a crane. A piece of this came loose and fell on a soldier's arm, the damage was so bad that he had to have his arm amputated, never did see him again. He was most likely discharged on medical grounds.

It was here that I paid a visit to my Aunt and Uncle's place in Southsea. I already had their address, so up I went to see them. I just walked into trouble. It so happened that my Uncle was there in his Officer's Uniform, as a Major. On first seeing me he said, 'Are you my young nephew, Douglas?' I said, 'Yes, that is correct'. 'Well man, what are you doing in that uniform?' he said to me. I was dressed as a Private Soldier. I looked at myself and said, 'What is wrong with my uniform, am I improperly dressed?' 'No, it's not that, but seeing as you had an education at College, you should and could have qualified for a Commission, so what has happened?' he replied to me. I then said to him, 'Well I received no guidance on what to do, I just went along to the Recruiting Officer, and joined this Regiment. Is that wrong?' He then said to me, as far as I can remember, 'No, there is nothing wrong with the Regiment. It's just that you could have thrown away an opportunity. So now, if you have a Commission in mind, you will have to work your way up from where you are, which will take much longer.' By the time that he had finished with me, you can guess that I felt about two inches high, and, was glad to get out of his way. We parted, never to see each other again. He never did anything to help me in that respect. He carried on his service, to become a General, me just a Quarter Master Sergeant, with just a few years service. He probably carried on until he completed forty years or more, he served in the Black Watch which was a famous Scottish Regiment.

Having finished our job at Portsmouth Docks, we returned to Aldershot to normal duties.

CHAPTER TWELVE

Draft to India

T hen what I had been waiting for happened. The word went around like lightning that a draft list had been put up on the Company Notice Board. I joined the queue to go and have a look, and lo and behold, I was on it. This of course pleased me as well as many others, we all wanted to get away from Aldershot, too much regimentation in this area. On this list were many men, it would take away nearly half of the regiment, a good three hundred or more. We were to join the First Battalion who were stationed in Rawlpindi, Pakistan, India.

The hubbub of preparations started. A few days afterwards, we were all assembled on the Barrack Square, and given a talking to about this move, by the Commanding Officer. On a certain date in March 1936, we were to set sail on the H.M.S. *Nevasa* from Southampton and the journey would take about six weeks. Our main task, he said, was to give a hand to squash the rebellion on the North West Frontier, fighting the Wazeristans and Pathans. It was no easy task, but with the training that we had had, he was hoping that we would all make a good job of it. The Commanding Officer then handed this parade over to the Second in Command, to give a further talk. One of the talks was in respect of the requirement of Junior N.C.O.s. He stated that as there were none on this list, they were giving this appointment to two of us on the parade. He said that when he called out the two names, he wanted the men to come forward so that everyone could see who they were. He said, 'You all remember this, these are N.C.O.s, and will be treated with the usual respect.' Now came the silence, we were all wondering who the blue eyed boys were going to be. We were all looking at one another. 'Right,' he said. 'Out here,

44

Private French and Private Clark.' I could not believe it, so out we marched to join him, then we were all gaped at, by all these men. 'Now you see who they are, these are now acting temporary Lance Corporals, for the duration of the journey to India,' he stated. He dismissed all the others, but kept us to give us a pep talk about the job we had now got to do, telling us too that, 'When you join the First Battalion this stripe will have to come down, as it is only temporary. But not to worry, it will not be long before you get it back and carry on and progress as N.C.O.s and Warrant Officers. Neither of you are experienced enough to take command of troops out there, you have yet to gain that knowledge of service in that country. You are also dealing with older soldiers, who need to respect good N.C.O.s, so good luck on your journey and for the future,' he said to us.

After that pep talk we two had to make our way to the Quarter Master's Stores, obtain our stripes and proceed to the Regimental Tailor's and have these stripes sewn on all our jackets and shirts. Including our Blue Patrol Uniform, which was if I remember a gold stripe. This all had to be done straight away so that the Troops could get used to us wearing this rank. As young soldiers, we felt quite proud of ourselves. It became a little difficult to start with as those who were our mates had to stand to attention which we found very embarrassing, and to address us as 'Corporal'. Discipline in those days I think, was harsher. We felt a bit out of place and it took some getting used to, but it came out all right in the end.

Our job on the ship would be to conduct reliefs on guards, attend to fatigue parties or anything else that the Sergeant or Officer wished us to do, except for training, we were not as yet qualified for that, that would come later after our courses. These stripes that they had given to us to wear were called 'salt water stripes', really they are draft stripes.

Off we went to the Port of Southampton in March 1936. I was just twenty years old then, so with all of us boarding this ship it was a complete new experience and you can guess that we were all looking forward to it. I personally had never been out of England and now we were about to gain that experience. This

45

ship they say, was a captured German ship from the First World War, that was not so long ago either. It was now converted into a troop ship, because in those days, that was how they used to get us around, no flying then, but then, these ships could carry large numbers of troops at one time.

I can remember my father being present at this farewell, I guess he felt proud of his young son, I don't know how he felt about me and my prospects. I think that it was a sad moment for him seeing me going off into the unknown, maybe for years. He was not the only parent there, of course, some had mothers to see them off, consequently there were a few tears, but not for me, I lost mine a long time ago. As the ship was preparing to leave the Regimental Band was playing a few tunes, the last one being 'Old Acquaintance', which must have brought tears to their eyes or a lump in their throats. There were of course a few colour streamers flying about and the hooting of ships' horns.

We glided away from the docks, being towed out by pilot ships for a few miles, then they let go and we were on our own. We sailed up Southampton Waters, out into the English Channel and into the Atlantic Ocean, through the Bay of Biscay and into the Mediterranean, passing Gibraltar on our left, but what scenery – blue waters and sky, high mountains and flying fish. They don't fly really, they glide, they come out of the water because other fish fancy them for a meal, so they do that to get out of their way. Sometimes they made mistakes in their direction and landed on the ship's deck, that's when the Indian Staff Cooks put in an appearance, they picked them up and cooked them for supper. The fish were not very big, about five inches long and very streamlined with pointed swept back wings, or fins, silver in colour.

The weather could not be better, the shirts and vests came off and the lads got into shorts, that was, when all duties and parades were finished. Don't worry, they were warned about sunburn but some did not heed and so paid for not doing as they were told.

Our first stop was at Malta, but we were not allowed ashore, we were only there for a short while, to drop off a few naval personnel and to pick some up who were going home as either their time in the service had expired, or they were going home on some leave, the long way round, but I don't suppose they minded that part of their leave.

On leaving Malta, we continued on our journey. We did stop at Port Said, we anchored just outside for a while, but it was not long before we were surrounded by Arab Merchants, selling their goods to us, or at least trying to. We did not have any money to spare on the items that they were trying to sell who wanted a tea service at our age? The only thing that they might have sold were some dirty postcards, and those were not allowed by rights. It was not permitted to buy them, and by rights, they were not allowed to sell them to us, but somehow they managed to get them into their hands. I saw some, but I did not think that they were so obscene, at least not the ones that I had a look at. To camouflage these pictures, they were printed on the normal playing cards, the pictures were on the other side. We, as junior N.C.O.s, did not think that it was worth charging these men for such a minor offence, we did not see any harm in that, so it was ignored and nothing was ever said. All we told them was to keep them out of sight, when someone of importance was about. We could not help but see the Arab stevedores who worked in the docks, the ones we were watching were heaving coal. They all looked so frail and half starved, but they must have been strong, nevertheless, to heave this about. They went around in a circle picking up the sacks of coal, dumping it on another ship, returning with the empty sack and picking up another They were working, as it seemed, without a break. They were already brown skinned, but the coal was making them black. I bet they had to work for a pittance as well.

Whilst we were watching these merchants, trying to sell their bits we noticed that one minute you would see them, the next minute they were gone. That was because the River Police were on their way, they got a signal from someone and they would vanish. I don't really know why, they had to get a living somehow.

47

The next excitement was sailing up the Suez Canal. This was just wide enough for two large ships to pass one another and was flat on either side. If you were on land and stood back from the Canal, it looked as if the ship was sailing across the desert, I did see that sight once. Cruising along this Canal was interesting, watching the Arabs walking along with their camels loaded up with goods, probably heading for the market. There were also some who were riding little donkeys with their wife and kids walking behind, yes, the men rode and the wife and kids had to walk. We did not think much of this, treating their ladies like this. Their houses along this Canal were very poor looking, just shacks really. We did not see the rich Arabs' houses, at least, not as yet. There were plenty of those about but not in this area.

The Suez Canal, as you know, was a joint contract built between the British and the French many years ago. I don't think the Arabs had much to do with it, except to get employment from it, probably the maintenance was carried out by them.

During our journey along the canal, of course, the ship was not allowed to go very fast. The wake had to be quiet and smooth so as not to damage the banks. At times, if you went to the bows you would see a few dolphins swimming and playing at the front, keeping up with the ship with ease. They would keep this up for miles, I don't know if the same ones were there all the time, they probably changed places at times. Another time, probably in the evening, if you looked down at the side of the ship, you would see the phosphorous which is coloured in the water. I'm not sure how and why this is formed, unless it's to do with the sun and chemicals in the sea water. It was all strange to us, we were learning all the time.

At the end of the canal, we ran into the Red Sea. They say that the sea water here is very salty, and when you are swimming in it it is not so easy to sink as it is so buoyant. I later found out that this was true, it was very salty. As the sea water dried on you it would leave a coating of salt on your skin, so one needed a shower to get it off. The sunsets were worth a second glance as well, as the sun went down, you could actually see it move, it seemed to disappear below the horizon quicker than back in England. The sky was so much brighter, maybe because we were nearer the Equator and it seemed also to be so silent as the end of the day drew near.

During our days on the ship, apart from various duties, we played deck hockey, this was interesting, you had to be pretty skilful not to let the soft ball go over the side, I think it was a pad of some sort and not a ball, but it was a good game. We also had boxing, someone suggested that all the boxers put their names in a hat and whoever we picked, no matter what weight, we would have to fight him. Rather a stupid idea, I think, but I went along with it and although I was not a heavy weight then I had to fight one. I was knocked out within seconds, in fact, I damaged my elbow when I hit the deck and had to have it in a sling for a while, not a break but badly bruised.

The evenings came along and we were allowed to do whatever we wanted, within reason, and eventually hang up our hammocks and get down to some sleep. It was nice sleeping in a hammock, it swung you to sleep and it moved with the ship's movement. You could just hear the distant throb of the engine which also helped to send you to sleep. Lights went out as per usual time, about 22.00 hours except for one light so that if anyone had to get up during the night they would not bump into anything.

Before I go too far, I forgot to mention that when we were back in the Mediterranean near Port Said, we were allowed to have a swim. As we were out in the deep, to save having to go down to the lower deck, we had to dive off the top deck, which was some 30 ft up. I'm not so good at diving. I and a few others, dived off and I seemed to go down so deep, I thought that I would never reach the surface. When I did I could hear the men on the ship shouting at us, as if it was some emergency. It sounded like, 'Get aboard, sharks!' Without too long a delay, we struck out for the ship at top speed, but the panic was all for nothing, they were having a bit of fun with us, all the same, I did not go in again, just in case there were some about.

I must say a little about one of our duties on the ship, I mean the two Lance Corporals. If we were on night duty, we had to make sure that all unnecessary lights were out, so that the men were able to sleep better.

We did make one or two stops in the Canal, just small places of no importance, probably to drop a few R.A.F. boys. We were always targets of interest to the local Arab boys and girls. They had a pastime, like I had back in England when I was a boy, that was diving into the sea and catching coins before they disappeared to the bottom of the sea, this was what these kids were doing, which kept some interested. These kids were called 'Chicos'.

Another sight was to see the ladies doing their washing. They used to knock hell out of it, by bashing it on a smooth rock, probably worn smooth by many years of washing on it. They would then lay it out on the ground to dry in the sun. I suppose that they used some sort of soap, but we could not see it from where we were. We had to remember that in this area of the Red Sea it was also rather dangerous to swim because of the more dangerous fish, such as shark and barracuda and also the stinging jelly fish, like the man-o'-war, the one with the long tentacles, we did not need to challenge that.

We proceeded down through the Red Sea, past Aden and into the Persian Gulf, as it was called then, it is now I think, the Arabian Sea. We were in for another long journey, with many more interesting places to see, like oil wells, passing Bahrain and Kuwait-Ibadan. We eventually pulled into Basra to drop off a few R.A.F. boys, round about fifty of them. It was here that we were allowed ashore, as there was no town for us to get mixed up with and get ourselves lost or into trouble. We had been on this ship for nearly a month now and really needed some good exercise. We all looked forward to this but it had to be under supervision as there was to be no running about and fooling. I was given the task of falling them into a parade. There was quite a large number of men for two Lance Corporals to handle, and you must remember that this was the first time that we had had to carry out this task, but we did it very well, no problems. We called them to attention and off we went for this march, they all seemed delighted to be out for a walk, if you could call it that and it was nice warm weather. We were just in our uniform with no other equipment, call it clean fatigue. They all marched along this road, very smart, so as to show the local natives how good they were. There was no trouble with anyone at all. We must have covered about five miles, and then we decided to turn around and go back, but not until we had had a break, a sit down or a look around nearby still admiring these fresh sights. We did not interfere with the locals and neither did they with us, all accepted us with smiles and a few waves of the hand.

On returning to the ship I was told that the R.A.F. had invited us to the camp and had given us permission to use their swimming pool and their canteen, both of which they regretted after a short while. What can you expect with about three hundred men, water everywhere in the pool area and we drank their canteen dry, all they gained was the profit from the beer. We were made to go back and clean up the swimming pool, but I did not give a hand there, I suppose it was Nobby Clarke who organised that.

That night we stayed there, as I believe that we had to wait and pick up some R.A.F. boys who were due some leave back home. Here, I made the stupid mistake of sleeping on the top deck, because it was so hot down below, in as much as when I woke up in the morning, I was covered in small bites from the sandfly. I don't suppose I was the only one, but I suffered for it many weeks after, by having sandfly fever. This gave me a temperature of 104 and it was far from pleasant, apart from the Military Hospital itself, which was most comfortable. It just so happened that I was the only one in this nice shiny polished ward, all beds were made up so nice and clean with mosquito nets on each one, just there waiting for customers and I was the only one for quite a while. Sandfly fever causes one to feel very tired all the time, something like a sleepy sickness, and left with no energy, but they soon had me in good order.

Back to Basra and our return down the Arabian Sea. As soon as we got going, we passed some of the Royal Navy lads on their

Patrol Boats. These were small boats but seemed to be well armed, to cover any emergency that they may have to deal with. We passed a few remarks to one another and got on our way. I suppose one could call these 'Gun Boats', there was no war on but I suppose the powers that be thought it was necessary to have these patrols, as there were a lot of military installations in that area.

We came to the end of the Gulf, and ran into the Indian Ocean, which covers many miles, we travelled many hours, out away from the coast, and carried on our usual duties until one day we started to run into an unusual smell. We soon found out that this was because we were approaching India, the smell was a mixture of burnt dung and camel urine, at least, that was what we young soldiers thought it might be and I don't think we were far wrong. We didn't mean to insult the Indian boys, there was also the smell of some tobacco mixed with it. It all comes from their way of life on this land, you got used to it as you lived there, it was not so unpleasant as time went on. As we approached the coastline we began to take a real interest. We pulled into the Port of Karachi, which was absolutely packed with people, mostly those who were about to lend a hand to unload this ship or clean it. They were aware that they were about to receive another lot of British troops, some were pleased about this and I guess some were not, the politically minded ones. We had to be aware of the types who liked to try and catch us green horns out, with their phoney dud coins. We were warned about that but it was hard not to be caught out, especially when they were dishing out some change. I was caught by receiving a dud one rupee piece, these were made of some soft metal, like lead, there were hundreds of these about, so after that I was more careful. I would stay with the merchant until I had checked the money, that meant ringing it out on the hard floor and I would make him wait there until I had made a check. They gave the change so fast that you had to be quick to notice it.

CHAPTER THIRTEEN

Now in India

'All ashore, who's going ashore.' All us young soldiers were on our toes and ready to go down the ship's ramp, leaving what had been our home all these weeks. All our gear was down in the ship's hold, it was not our job to unload it, but the Coolies, Indian workers, employed by the Dock Company that came along. It was then reloaded onto the train, a military train. We marched along to the station, all very smart, being watched by the local inhabitants. This train was to take us all the way up to Rawlpindi, which was about eight hundred miles north from here. The train itself was built specially for troop movement, it had wooden seats, no upholstery, the top bunk could be pulled down at night and used as a bed, the carriage, if I remember correctly held about eight soldiers and the mattress was in the form of a palliasse made up from straw, not exactly the Queen's bed, but good enough for us. The outside scenery once again was interesting with strange sights as we went along the track. The weather was warm as we expected but it was not their summer as yet. The ground was hard and very dusty and their form of transport was by bicycle or bullock carts, a bullock pulling a wooden cart which looked much too heavy to pull along, they all seemed to be doing something or other, going about their daily tasks, but so many of them. On the journey we passed through Hyderabad – Sukkur – Bahawalpur – Maltan – Lyallpur and many other smaller towns and finally, Rawlpindi. We admired the type of buildings, they were of course built by the British many years ago, like many other buildings built all around India. They were built to last and I guess are still in good use today.

Returning to Karachi for a while I will tell you of my first impression of the city. It looked large and very busy, there were thousands of people about. The architecture was so much different from ours, had to be I suppose because of their weather conditions, allowing for the heat. To us the majority of people looked ragged, we got that impression I suppose, because of their loose white clothing which seemed to be cheap muslin material, it looked good when new, but after a few washes it lost its whiteness. This showed up more I suppose amongst the poorer class of people and they were the majority. When one saw richer Indians, you could tell the difference by their dress. We also noticed that the poorer types did stand aside for the richer types, the rich treated them a bit like the under dog, which we realised to be true as time went on. I would think that at least eighty per cent were poor. There also seemed to be so many little boys and girls standing about holding out their little hands for Buckshees, with no clothes on at all, I suppose they were homeless and starving. No one seemed to care they were beggars and they all seemed to want a good wash, you felt like picking them up and dumping them in a bath of hot water. If you were on foot, they would make you their obvious target for a hand out, they would pester you to death. The whole atmosphere made you think it needed some organisation to put it all in order.

I dare say that to the older Indians, we all looked like fresh, pale young British Soldiers, just out from England and not as yet having exposed our limbs to the sun, as we were still white. The older soldiers called us 'White Leghorns'. So here began our education of India and didn't we have a lot to learn, it all depended how each one of us thought about it and what they wanted to learn about it. You could if you wanted try and learn their own language of Urdu, I started once but did not follow it up, which was another mistake. When you are young you sometimes need pushing.

The currency was rupees, the value at that time was I think about one shilling and nine pence to a rupee or sixteen annas, and the anna was again split up into pice that was, twelve pice to one anna. They had such a low standard of living that the pice was a necessity, some they say could live on a pice a day at those times.

We were mustered together at the station and marched off to the barracks where we were met by some duty Senior N.C.O. who took us to meet the First Battalion that we had heard so much about back in England. Meeting these seasoned troops was quite an experience, they looked well trained and confident of themselves. They were brown to start with and some of them, in fact, most of them, had the North West Frontier Medal up to show that they had that experience behind them, they had not long returned from there. I met my friend Curly Andrews then, he also had that medal on his chest and was proud of it, so he was one up on me. I think it was called the Momane Operation.

We arrived in the afternoon and we were all sorted out into various companies. I was sent to 'D' Company, Number 15 Platoon, I cannot recall the number of my section, but there was a Lance Corporal in charge of it and he was a bit concerned about me being in his Section because I also was a Lance Corporal. I said to him, 'I won't have this long, it's only for the journey, it will have to come down until such time as I can have it back properly, I have need of more experience yet, we were told about this back in England.' After a couple of days I was taken before the Company Commander and he said that I would now have to return to being a Private Soldier, and if I qualified for a promotion later on, then I could have it back. So I was back to Private again, which I did not like, but my prospects looked good.

We had a lot to do then to get settled into the company, drawing out our fresh bedding, and being issued with our equipment and weapons. We were given a meal, then the rest of the day was ours to make ourselves familiar with the surroundings, not forgetting the canteen. There was no NAAFI here, the canteen was run by an Indian called 'Shebodeen', not sure of the spelling of his name, but it sounded like that. He looked after us all as regards refreshments etc., in the men's canteen, the Corporals' Club, the Sergeants' Mess as well as the Officers'

Mess. He followed us even up to the Frontier, in fact if we received a medal, so did he for serving us, something like a Quarter Master's job, he was one that must have missed the British when they left India, as he lost his job.

We also had a barber called 'Nappy' in Hindu, a tailor's shop called 'Dursey' in Hindu. Outside each bungalow where we lived there was nearly always a char wallah, he used to sit out there on his haunches with a large tin trunk full of wads (cakes) and a large urn of tea. If you wanted him, you would only have to shout for him, and he would come to you. He would get used to your voice, so he knew who it was speaking. He would approach and say, 'Yes, Sahib what you like?' We would probably say (in Hindu) badly, 'Ack anna char and doe wad,' meaning, one anna of tea and two cakes. You would leave your money on your box and he would help himself, any change he would leave there, we knew he would never cheat us as he took a pride in his job and did not want to lose it, hence the reason for his honesty.

After looking around the barracks, most of us after that journey were feeling a bit tired, so it was not long before I got my head down, and did I have a good sleep!

CHAPTER FOURTEEN

Soldiering in India

The morning after our first night in this barracks we were up at about 06.00 hours, physical training to start with, wash and shave and then breakfast then back to our platoon to meet our Platoon Sergeant for the first time, he gave us a talking to about what he expected of us, so the training started. Because of the weather most of the training was to be done in the morning or at least, before 13.00 hours because that is when the sun is at its highest and it starts to get hot. There were at times, when we had to go out on what they called 'A Mobility March', this was as a platoon. We had to carry a full kit, probably about 60 lbs on our backs, as well as a weapon and ammunition. We had to double at times, with all this to carry. We would most likely double for quarter of a mile, then walk fast for about the same and we would have to keep this up for about twelve miles, so it was no place for any weakling. As far as I can remember I never did see anyone fall out, there was an unusual case once when a Sergeant who had just been discharged from hospital with malaria passed as fit, but obviously was not. He was sent out on the strenuous march, but it gave him a heart attack which proved to be fatal.

This exhausting training gave one quite a thirst, consequently when we got back to barracks and had a shower, we were inclined to go straight for a cool beer, and at times probably take too much. You could end up with colic, which would give you a severe pain in the stomach, we were warned about that, the beer by the way was called 'Eagle' beer and was brewed up in the hills of 'Muree', some fifty miles north, probably from the waters coming from Mount Everest. It was strong beer, so we had to be careful about that as if you got drunk and were found out, you were in trouble, but there it is, any rank could be caught out on that, it had happened at times.

We were soon approaching the summer heat, now about May or June, so parades had to finish about midday and in the afternoon we slept, or laid on our beds with a towel over our waist, we had the punkahs on which gave us some cool air but, if you did not cover up your stomach, you could get a touch of colic. Also on the doors of the bungalows we had what were called 'Cuss Cuss Tattees', this was fitted over the door space and was made of straw. The Beesty Wallah who worked for us had to splash this cuss cuss with water, so that the air that passed through would cool down before it passed into us, which was nice for us. We provided jobs for the Indian boys, who found it hard to find work. The Beesty Wallah, as they were called, were Indian labourers employed by the army to do these mundane jobs. We had to concentrate on soldiering and they were glad to have them.

Now for our laundry, this was a little different from that back in the U.K., here we used K.D. (Khaki Drill), this had to be smart at all times, there was the usual weekly wash sent in with your own laundry mark etc. but in between we used to send it to the Flying Dhobi, in other words, faster. You had to pay for that yourself, and it would come back starched. They called it 'Kungee', it was pressed smartly and stiff and you could stand your shorts up on the floor and step into them. These were prepared like this, especially if you were on a Special Guard, so as to look your smartest. It was everyone's ambition to try and obtain best man on guard, if you were chosen, you were then no longer on guard, you were Stick Orderly for the day, which meant you followed the Orderly Officer and the Orderly Sergeant around on inspections, an easy day of duty.

We also had at times one of these young Indian men as a batman for us, we would train them how to clean our boots and our webbing equipment, the scabbard that came with your side arm also had to be polished but not the bayonet itself, they were not allowed to touch the weapons at all. For this task we used to give them a few annas a week.

A few of my platoon. Taken at Barracks Rawlpindi, Pakistan, 1936. Mufti permitted after duty if required.

I must mention that after the afternoon rest, we were then detailed to take part in some sport or other for exercise. There were many things that I liked to do, so I took part in most things in the sport line, except football. My favourite sport was athletics. I think my best performance was on the track, for the two hundred yards, as it was then. I had the equivalent of the Olympic Record for that year of 1936, which was 22.5. In that year, these sports were held in Berlin with Hitler and his gang watching. In addition to track, I was still running cross country, but I had a bit of trouble at one time with my health. For some reason which I think must have been strain, I had a haemorrhage in my stomach. I reported this to the Sports Officer, and so to the Medical Officer and it was suggested that I stop cross country running, so I just kept to track running, hockey and boxing, that was enough in any case. But that was what we had to do after our afternoon's rest.

The punkahs by the way at that time were driven by motor, but some of the older soldiers told us that the punkah wallahs used to operate those by hand. They took up a position of ease near a wall and tied the rope to their ankle somehow and moved their leg up and down to make the punkahs swing. There were times, they said, that they used to fall asleep and they had to throw a boot at them to wake them up. Now those days were over, the machine did it for them, driven by electricity.

As I said earlier, I was now in No. 15 Platoon. To make a platoon in those days needed four sections. As I was now back to a Private Soldier I was given the job in this section as the machine gunner, I suppose mainly because I happened to be a marksman on this machine. It was the little gun, going by the name of V.B. (Vickers Berther) its weight was about 28 lbs, if I remember correctly, it was an extra weight to carry, much heavier than the rifle. There was also the ammunition to be carried, so to operate this weapon properly, we also needed a Number Two who also had to be as good a shot as oneself, he normally carried the additional ammunition and if required, need quite a bit of it. In addition, you had to be able to run fast with it, so that meant being very fit, which we were. Because we had this weapon, we did plenty of training on it so that when it was needed, we became very familiar with it.

I must tell you a story of embarrassment I let myself in for on about the first evening there, I wished to visit the toilets, so I asked one of the older soldiers where they were. He thought, this was an opportunity to have a bit of fun, he put his arm across my shoulder and pointed across the way and said, 'Well you see that bushy top tree over there, if you walk to that and go underneath it, you will see the toilets right in front of you. There should be a light on outside.' I did what he said and went under this bushy top tree and was welcomed by a thump on the shoulders when I arrived there. It was a hairy beast of a monkey which belonged to the soldier who had shown me the way, he knew that this monkey would drop on my shoulders. Unknown to me, he followed me over and was in time to say, 'Hey, don't put your hand up to it, he might bite.' It came as a surprise to me, but made a few of the others laugh. I suppose it was a bit funny, but I'm not so sure that I thought it was, they were taking advantage of a rookie to India.

Whilst on the subject of toilets, a word or two about these, always something to learn. We were warned once again, like many things, never sit on those seats, unless you give the seat a good bang, the reason, our little friends the scorpions seemed to like to hang about underneath the seats for what reason I'm really not sure. If there was one there and you sat in his area, he was going to sting your bottom and their sting is not very pleasant. I had the job at one time of taking a fellow soldier to the Medics at midnight once, because he forgot to bang the seat. He was alright, all he received was another injection for forgetting. You can have a guess where the sting was, not on the bottom this time! Again these toilets were the responsibility of the 'Beesty Wallah'. He would signal if you were sitting, that he was about to replace the bucket, oh yes, there was a system for nearly everything. This fellow that I had to take to the Medics, I had to take him on the bar of a duty bicycle. That was all the transport that the duty Lance Corporal had, so like it or not, it got him there fairly fast. I bet he never forgot to bang the toilet seat again. These scorpions were usually the yellow type which are not supposed to be as dangerous as the black ones, which were smaller but more lethal. As I am talking about these insects, I would like to mention a few other things, that we used to do to prevent being caught out by them. That was to bang our footwear on the floor to make sure that some of these insects had not taken up residence. I have known men put their bare feet in their shoe, and receive a nasty shock when they did this, so we would also take heed. All these things after a while, became instinctive. He that is wise does not forget!

CHAPTER FIFTEEN

The Division at Rawlpindi, Pakistan

In addition to our regiment, we also had three other regiments, usually the U.K. regiments, English, Irish, Scottish and Welsh. We hardly ever met all together except for when we had our manoeuvres, other than that, we met individual regiments at some sport or other. There were of course some Indian regiments attached like the Punjabi Lancers, Garwalies and the Gurkhas, a famous old Regiment, that has served so many years with the British Army, only little men, but good hard fighting soldiers. These natives of the frontier, had a tradition of serving with us, let's hope that they do not disappear.

The sports contests inter regiments were of great interest and were taken very seriously. The football teams caused a lot controversy, I was at a match one day when the spectators got at one another with rifle chains and service belts. It caused so much trouble that the Military Police had to be called in to get it under control, and I can assure you that a lot of men needed some medical attention. The boxing matches also caused some trouble, these fellows were all young men and competition was so great as well as keen, it caused arguments even days after the competitions. If you happened to bump into one of them when you were out on your leisure trips and having a peaceful drink at some bar, more than likely someone who had too much beer would feel like a fight. Army athletics are not quite like that, a little more civilised. Those were the days that I really enjoyed, track events, as well as field events. So much for sports, the army gave one great opportunity for that.

It started getting very hot around June until the end of August, when we had to move up into the hills, near Muree, the foot of the Himalayas. The heat down on the plains could reach

The Division at Rawlpindi, Pakistan

Us marching to Hill Station from Pindi to Murree Hills,
south of the Himalayas, 1936/37.

the region of 112° fahrenheit, or ever more, bearable yes, but not comfortable for long periods, so up to the hills we went. We had to march up there, the exact distance I'm not so sure, probably about sixty miles. On the way up, we stopped at three camp sites which were permanent. It was a steady climb all the way, when we arrived at these camps we had a certain amount of work to do before we could settle down for the night, like the beds, they were three tier and made of wood. During the time that they had been empty the bugs had got into the creases, we had to take them outside onto the concrete and bang them to extract them and there were quite a few that had to be brushed up and burnt. The water had to be turned on to get rid of the brown muck that had collected all the time it had not been used. After all these chores we were ready for bed after a day's march, but for some it was Guard Duty. I had to do this one night, this was a must with the military, we had items of military value to take care of, like weapons and ammunition. We would also have time to have a shower and a good meal, but this was prepared in advance of us, the cooks would go on ahead and prepare this.

Up fairly early, around 07.00 hours, we would be on the road again, stopping every hour for a ten minute break, putting our feet on something to help cool them down. You must remember, that we were marching in hot weather. The places that we stopped at overnight all had names but I can't remember them.

On our third day, or was it our fourth day, we ended up in a place called 'Bahrean Camp' situated under some trees. We were probably up to the height of seven thousand feet above sea level and we had a terrific view. Each morning we woke we would be looking at Mount Everest, which was most likely seventy miles away, not always clear, it used to have a mist around it. We settled down to live here which made a change, and we carried on with our usual training and Guard Duties.

During my duties here, I was selected to go on a Junior N.C.O. Course, which lasted eleven weeks. It covered weapon training of all types, field tactics, drill and semaphore, plus map reading and the use of a compass, all useful items to learn for when you became an N.C.O., which now seemed promising. You have to remember that in those days, I was young and rather ambitious, for reasons of more money and better privileges. I was not satisfied to remain as a Private and be pushed around, many others thought my way.

Just down below the hill that we were on, there was a Camp called 'Murree', you could say it was a bit of a holiday camp. In our turn, we could have a week's holiday there. There was not a lot to do, just a canteen, a cinema and a couple of bars, we would sit at a small table drinking Eagle Beer and giggling, it was a rest from normal duties, just doing nothing of importance.

I would like to tell you about the bear that visited us up at our main camp at Bahrean. We were told these bears were about but very rarely seen. There was an alarm situated in the camp like an iron triangle, with an iron rod. If there was a bear about the nearest person would have the job of beating this triangle as hard as possible to warn the camp. You needed to be warned about these bears because they are rather large and can be vicious if you were in their way. What we had to do if this alarm was sounded was to go in our hut, and lock the door, not show ourselves at the window, grab a rifle, and shove a round up the breech and if he attacked, shoot but not to kill just for the sake of killing. As they said, they were his woods and he should be allowed to wander around at will. The first large bear that I had ever seen waddled through the huts on his hind legs, with his upper arms high at the side of his head, looking rather menacing. He must have measured about seven feet tall, so we all kept quiet and watched him waddle on. He took not a bit of notice of us, and disappeared out of sight into the woods. As I said, he was a massive fellow and best left alone. I have been told by some of the older serving soldiers, that if one was upset he could tear the camp to pieces. If he did that, he would have to be shot, but they are a protected species. So much for our bear, I never did see one again, at least not out in the wild.

As I have said before, I did a lot of running for the battalion, so I kept up training during my stay up in these hills. At most times I used to have the company of someone else who was in training, to come with me, it was safer that way as well. For company, we used to carry a long stout pole with us, about five foot long, which had a long sharp nail fixed to the top to give us protection in case we happened to meet some stroppy wild animal, those animals were about. I'll tell you of two occasions when I met them, it would happen when I was running on my own. First I was well away from the camp out running and after a while I decided to have a rest on a rock near the roadside, I heard a rustle in the bushes and became alert, but what came out of this bush was a kitten, a black panther. I was not scared of him, but I knew full well that his mum could be about, so I did not hang about either. I took off at a hundred yards sprint, which lasted about a mile. Number two mishap, I was out again running and decided to take a short cut through the woods to the camp, consequently the track was not as wide to run on as the road. This time I ran into a school of baboons, so I had to make up my mind quickly, whether to carry on or go back, but as I was already half way through them I decided to go on, these baboons were up in the trees, not on the ground, but when they saw me, they decided to come on down after me. If they could have got hold of me, they would have torn me to pieces, they are powerful animals, and have rather large teeth that I did not fancy. I won the World Record for the hundred yards then, I should think, it was another lesson that I learnt the hard way. But, I did pass on this information for the others to take note, henceforth I was more cautious.

The time came for us to return to Rawlpindi, it meant a march back again to carry on our usual duties. I was notified that I was to go to school to study for my Second Class Certificate of Education, if I passed this, I would be able eventually, to reach the Rank of Warrant Officer, providing I had other qualifications, but that was way ahead as yet. I studied for this and to cut the story short, I passed.

So what's next? Yes well, I was shortly notified that I was to get my Lance Corporal's Stripe back permanently this time, as by now I had the qualifications.

I was told that I had to go before the Commanding Officer at a certain hour and on a certain day, dressed in my best uniform. I was rather surprised about this event really, with the palaver that I had to go through. I was marched in by the R.S.M. and stood in front of the C.O. I saluted with my best salute, and stood there a second or two looking at him and he looking at me, he seemed to be summing me up. 'Well, French,' he said, 'You have been recommend by your Company Commander to become one of my Junior Non-Commissioned Officers. Are you willing to take on the responsibilities of the Rank, and abide by the Rules laid down by 'Kings' Rules and Regulations', to honour and serve His Majesty's Army?'

What could I say but, 'Yes sir.'

'Then you are now appointed a Lance Corporal, which is a probation period until you are recommended for the full Rank of Corporal, if to the satisfaction of your Company Commander,' he said. When I left I had a feeling that it was rather official, for such a low rank. I was told to go back and report to my Company Commander and Sergeant Major. Off I went and did just that, I had to take nearly all my kit to the tailors and have this stripe sewn on my jackets, shirts, pullovers and including my overcoat. Having all this done, I returned to my company with a different feeling, which is hard to express, all the lads that knew me were having a bit of fun standing to attention and saluting, which I was not entitled to, only the attention bit. It took some getting used to at first, but as time went on it became instinctive. I was congratulated by many and was given a section of men and it all fitted in well, and we got on with our soldiering. I was of course given a few talks by my seniors, about not to take any back chat or any other nonsense from them, if you stay strict and be fair they will then know how to accept you. If you are easy going, you will find that will not work out for you and your job will become a bit of a misery.

So my life in the army changed for me in lots of ways, it is probably the worst rank that you can get, being a Junior Lance Corporal, you get pushed around by the Corporals, who try to push some of their responsibilities onto you so you have to stand up to them, and give as good as you get, you can be the lackey of all ranks above you if you are not careful. To start with, giving orders did not come easy at first, if you asked a Private to do something and he refused you warned him a few times and if he still refused you had to charge him with 'Disobeying an Order, given by an N.C.O.' Some took it and said nothing, but there was always the odd stroppy one who would give you some bad language to go with it. You then had to charge him with 'using obscene language to an N.C.O.' If this happened too often, you got annoyed with the job, but if you were on the ball they eventually knew that you were not going to take insubordination and there were less of these charges in the future.

It was not long before I had to make my first charge: In each Barrack Room there was always a full Corporal in charge. One late evening there was a disturbance in our room at about midnight, when a few men were playing cards well after lights out, which is usually about 10.30 hours. They were playing cards for money by candlelight. It would have been alright if they had kept quiet but they started to argue because one of them was cheating. A fight started, so this full Corporal shouted out to me, 'Shut that lot up, and if they don't shut up straight away, stick 'em all in the Guard House.' I got out of my bed, only in my gym shorts and approached this lot, saying, 'Come on now pack this in at once, and get to bed.' But they were already in a bad mood, and they told me where to go, in no polite manner. What do I do next? Before I could think about it this Corporal said, 'For Gods' sake, get four men out of their beds, and take them over to the Guard Room, put them under close arrest, for playing cards after lights out and, number two, using obscene language to an N.C.O. and fighting, which causes a disturbance to other soldiers who are asleep.' Well that did it, I dug out four men, who were all fast asleep, and they did not like that. They had to get dressed at that hour, and they were having a good cuss.

I got all this lot together, I had to get dressed myself, fall this lot in outside the bungalow and march them over at that hour. When I got to the Guard Room there was all hell let loose, with all this lot trying to get organised. I took them to the Guard Commander who was a Sergeant, he wanted to know what it was all about, so I told him. He opened a couple of cells and put them in for the rest of the night, he said to me, 'You will have to bring the charges in first thing in the morning.' So I marched the escort back to the Barrack Room and we all got into bed.

Come morning, I was up early to get advice as to what to do about this charge in writing to the Guard Commander, who had said he wanted it off me first thing in the morning. I was beginning to think,who wants this job as a Lance Corporal, it stinks. After having my breakfast I had to go to the Company Office, and get Charge Forms and fill them up, under the guidance of the full Corporal, I then took a copy over to the Guard Room. He scrutinised it and said, 'Well, I guess that will do. You had better get some more advice on this subject, you are a new N.C.O. aren't you?' I said, 'Yes, that's right.' 'Well, see your own Platoon Sergeant as soon as you can, and he will put it all in order,' he said. So that is what I did.

But the worst was to come, these men had to be marched over for Company Commanders' Orders at 10.00 hours that morning, and I had to appear as Charging N.C.O. I got in such a state, quoting these charges, that the Officer said to the Sergeant Major, 'I can't consider a verdict at this time, return this lot to the Guard Room for the day, we will hold Office again tomorrow morning.' So the lot were returned to the Guard Room. He told me to stay where I was, he wished to talk to me. When they had all gone he said to me, 'Now look here, Corporal, I know that this is your first charge, but you have to get your charge sorted out in your mind and spit it out without any problems. You have all day to go and sort yourself out, confide in your Platoon Sergeant and he will put it right.' That is what I did. I was put at ease by my Sergeant and by the next morning I had it all sorted out and it all went off smoothly, so I was once again at ease. We must remember that N.C.O.s are very rarely popular with the Private Soldier, yes, there are likes and dislikes, if one had to be an N.C.O., we all found that out, amongst all ranks. We all went about our tasks in a different way, we were all in this army as volunteers, whether we liked it or not, we had to obey orders, otherwise nothing would be done and no wars would be won either. In some ways the selection of N.C.O.s can be a gamble by the Senior N.C.O. or Warrant Officer and Officer who selected him to become one. I am not so sure that it is always left to one Officer to select, it must be the opinion of more than one, none of them are sure that he is going to make the grade. I know in some cases he did not, because you may have passed your exams and Cadre Courses, that still does not make you successful, the same with a Commissioned Rank.

CHAPTER SIXTEEN

Khyber Pass and North West Frontier

Visiting these two places always stand out in my memory. Let me first of all talk about the North West Frontier. It came to the time when we were all required to move back up to the Frontier, most of the battalion had already been up there, so were well aware what it was about, nothing new to them. To the ordinary soldier it was not so obvious, as in those days we were not kept so well informed, we just had to do what we were told and be quiet. I guess I was a little more interested with the word 'why'. What I gathered was that we were to go up there to fight the tribesmen known as Pathans and Waziers (if that is spelt correctly), and that their leader was called the 'Fakir of Ippi'. The British had been fighting these tribal wars, I should think, for three decades. He was now skirmishing with the Pakistani Army, which included us. The Fakir of Ippi was both an Islamic Religious Leader and a Warrior Chieftain. He believed he had come with a divine mission to bring an independent state along the border of Afghanistan, but the British had an objection to this, so I do not think that he ever obtained these new Tribal territories. He died much later in 1960 but it was his ambition. Those hills are very hard to penetrate, and we knew that many other nations had tried to overrun these tribes, but got nowhere, even the British with their modern weapons at that date.

Anyhow we made our journey by train as far as Bannu, from there it was on foot, many miles yet to march. This town was on the border line and the last town in these mountains. We stayed there for a few days only, and were allowed out to mix with the locals, who eyed us with suspicion, some of these people could be some of his men, seeing how we looked and what sort of weapons we had with us. With the bit of time that we had most of us gave their cinema a visit, probably an English or an American Film with sub-titles in English. The inside of this cinema was separated between us and the locals, we had the top floor, and they were all seated below, on the floor, consequently their clothing was subject to vandalism by our tough boys, it was really bad behaviour, when our lads had nearly finished with their cigarettes, they would nip them over the balcony and the butts would drop onto their clothing and smoulder away, thus causing a rumpus. Not good behaviour, for which they were later reprimanded. Evidently there must have been a complaint put forward by someone. Yes, these boys were a rough lot, but good at fighting, after all that's what we were wanted for, but a bit of good behaviour could be instilled into them, we tried.

After a short time we had orders to move on up to the Frontier and to proceed right into the heart of this hostile tribal country. They probably had some of their lookouts watching every move that we made. When we reached what they thought was the trouble spot we were told to spread out so as to make a more difficult target. Pretty soon after this we started to get shot at and for me, as well as some others, it was the first time that I had been shot at and it made your hair stand on end, I can tell you. In those days, they did not have such accurate rifles unless they could get hold of one of ours, that is why we had to make sure that we did not leave them hanging around unguarded. Even when we fired a shot, we were told to pick up the empty cartridge, because if they got hold of it they would refill it, so we had to pick them up and put them in our pocket. How they used to get their aim was a pre-zeroed mark on the ground, like a white stone and when one of us was about to pass this stone, they would fire their rifle and most likely hit you, not with an ordinary bullet, but with a Dum-Dum, which was a flat nosed bullet and when it hit made a nasty hole in you.

There must have been about three thousand of us troops, going up through this valley, I think it was called Surger Valley, in the area of Bitchy-cass-Ky. At this particular time, we were escorting the Manchester Regiment through. They were machine gun battalion, I think they were on their way to Nowshera. As we had to advance up this valley, we were of course exposed on either side to the mountain tops. So as to stop these tribesmen from sniping us, we also had to picket these hills and try and drive them off. Some task this was, these hills were some four thousand feet up and extremely rough walking.

We had many different tasks to perform here, in addition to picketing these hills we also helped to build a road. We were helping the Royal Engineers with this task by doing the manual work and we had to use explosives at times to shift the rocks that were in the way. The road that we finished, was sixty three miles long, it was not tarmacked, just boulders crushed up and laid out as flat as possible but we did have to dig a ditch on both sides to take away the water when it rained. When moving all these rocks we disturbed many scorpions, as well as spiders and quite often someone would spot one and shout, 'There is one, tread on it,' they could give you a nasty sting. The reason for building the road was mainly for trade I think, but the tribesmen did not want this. Many of these men lived in the villages nearby, and if we found out that they were the ones that were sniping at us, we told them that we would blow up the village and this happened quite a few times.

They said, that because that the terrain was so rough, walking on these sharp boulders would wear out a pair of army boots in three weeks and they were right about that. We were advancing up a hill at one time to chase these Pathans, when a bullet came pretty close to me, in fact, it hit the rock that was near me and a piece of rock hit me in the hip. Apart from a slight pain I did not take much notice of it, I did not know at the time that it cut my thigh a little, not until the time came for me to answer a call of nature. When I pulled my shorts down, my pants were stuck to my hip, so I did nothing more than wipe it off with some of my spit with a dirty handkerchief, such hygiene. The scar is still with me today, it just healed up on its own.

We had at one time been given orders to fix bayonets,

First Battalion 'The Royal Hampshire Regiment', North West Frontier, marching from Bannu to fight the Tribesmen. (I am there somewhere.)

probably about five to six hundred of us, we had to clear out some of these tribesmen, as they were causing a few problems. We were told to charge a hill in the usual manner, with a lot of shouting, giving them the impression that we meant business. I don't think that they fancied being mauled about with these bayonets, because when we arrived there few were seen. Before we started to advance up this hill, our Vickers Machine Guns opened up on them and that is pretty scary. I can hear those machine gun bullets now, going over our heads, they make quite a crack when passing by. There were one or two casualties, I remember one especially, a Major Williams was a special case. One of these tribesmen who was possibly a specialist appeared above a rock with his sword twirling around his finger and took his head off. For a while he stood there headless, until his body collapsed and rolled down the hill away. They were very smart with this sword action, but the tribesman that carried out this execution disappeared as quickly as he appeared. We have got to remember, that these men were born in this area and there was not much that we could tell them about hill fighting.

I dare say that we all looked like young boys up against them.

What made them look older, I suppose, was because nearly all of them had beards, there must have been a shortage of razors amongst them. I was about twenty years old then, some of these Pathans were also very tall men, on average, taller than us, and they were used to a hard life in the hills. They did not have our comforts in life, just tough and rough, one of the reasons why we did not get very far with them, a pure waste of time. In the long run, really what did we gain by being up there? Anyhow, we just did as we were told and returned to barracks.

Eventually the time came when we were ordered to get out of this area, all that needed to be done had been done. But they were not going to let us go in a peaceful manner, as we were preparing to move they decided to ambush us with a few thousand of their tribesmen. As we moved out we had very little cover, in fact none at all. We were all in the open so we were ordered to build sangars as quickly as possible (that is to place around each of us some boulders high enough to stop bullets hitting us). We gathered up boulders or rocks and made a kind of a wall in front of us, as time went on we would make some improvement to shield ourselves if we thought it was not good enough to cover us. We had to stay there all night in a small space, we were also ordered to fix our bayonets in case they decided to rush us and come to hand to hand fighting, but they obviously thought better of it and stayed away, but continued their sniping instead. We had to stand by for a long time, until someone said we could stand down, still leaving a few to keep watch and this was kept up all night.

Let us not forget that at night up in these mountains the temperature dropped down quite a lot, not to freezing but certainly very cold – about 45 degrees fahrenheit, this of course caused a problem. The Quarter Master Stores was not all that far away so the overcoats were sent for. They eventually arrived in the dark when it was not possible to find your own overcoat, so they were dished out spasmodically. If you were a Private, you could be wearing the Sergeant Major's coat, no one cared at that time, it was too cold to bother. It caused a bit of a problem during the night, when the Sergeant Major was going around to detail certain soldiers to go out on patrol. This was an unpleasant task, he would touch someone who had three Stripes on his coat and would notice that and say, 'Sorry Sergeant,' when in fact he was a Private, that caused a bit of a laugh at the time, he missed me, so that was a blessing. I did not fancy those patrols out in no man's land, it was very dangerous and pitch dark. I did not get away with it entirely, as I was detailed to go out on the very early morning one as I was at that time the number one on the light machine gun and they felt better with someone like me around with that gun, the tribesmen did not like it, it spat out so many bullets at once. Coming back from this patrol, after not meeting anyone at all, I managed to fall into the toilet trench that was dug earlier. Why me? I thought. I was dragged out and avoided for some while, I was treated like a skunk and they all went around me. The only way that I could get cleaned off was by rubbing sand into my boots and socks, I was a smelly object for a while. They would say, 'Who fell into the shit trench? Oh yes, Doug French. Avoid him.' But it wore off.

We passed the night with hardly any sleep, just an occasional nod, but being young and fit it did not do us much harm. Come early morning, about an hour before it got light, having just returned from patrol, we then had to stand to, just in case they made a rush at us, but all remained quiet. We had to get out of these great overcoats once again, get them rolled up and tied onto the camels and someone had to return them. We were glad to have had them, no need now as the sun was on its way up and it would soon get warm. We had to get out of this position fast, I believe that the machine guns opened up around the area where we thought the Pathans might be laying doggo, but we heard or saw nothing. We began to pack up and be prepared to move off in quick time. That was where I became involved once again. I was left behind to give covering fire with my machine gun, that is with my number two, who carried the ammunition. We had to keep a careful watch to make sure that they did not come out of their hiding and snipe hard at the rear of the main column of troops, if they did, I had to open up on them with this gun. We were to spray the area with bullets, if they showed themselves, but they were aware of the situation and they knew we were there with this gun. I had only to do it once when I saw movement and they did not show themselves again. We had to wait there until we were given the signal from the rear end of the column, by the waving of the green flag, which meant start running and catch up. This was some task, we had to be fit for that especially having all this weight to carry, but we made it in good time with no mishaps, we probably covered eight hundred yards by the time we caught them up, they said that there was no sign of them putting in an appearance, so they did not want to risk any injuries.

On we went, making our way back towards Bannu, I guess we did what we called a forced march, for twenty-eight miles to get ourselves clear of this hostile area. I reckon that we spent five months up on this frontier and it certainly kept us busy, we were even up there for Christmas but by then we had managed to build ourselves a fairly safe camp with a large rock wall all around us. In each corner we had the heavy machine gun which covered us all round and at night times we set hand grenades outside as well, in case they tried to sneak in the camp. We had to make good note where these grenades were, as well as not forgetting the number and where they were situated. We even had turkey and Christmas Pudding, not forgetting our normal bottles of beer, except the Sergeants and Officers, they had their spirits as extra, that was their privilege.

We returned to Pindi by train with the feeling that we were now rather more seasoned troops having seen some action with live ammunition. To prove this, they presented us with the North West Frontier Medal with clasp, being made of Indian Silver, it's the best campaign metal, that I have, because of its good quality and being my first medal, so I guess we felt proud of it.

I must mention that for a short while, during my stay up on the frontier, I had to go to hospital for part of the Christmas, because I had Sandfly Fever once again, that was the second time. Apart from having this, and I would rather not have had it, it made a good change to be able to get into a nice clean bed with sheets, plus the fact that I had a nice fresh looking English Nurse looking after me! I was in for just over a week, and the food was much better than what we were getting up at the frontier.

As soon as we got into our own barracks once again we straight away had to have a foot inspection, as we had all been hard on our feet and you can bet your life that there were a lot of bad feet. In those days, if you fell out, you could lose your efficiency pay, consequently, soldiers would put up with a lot of pain to stop losing that. The foot inspection was really necessary, if they were in a poor condition you were sent to the Medical Officer and his crew to put things in good order, this was then official and no pay was lost. For a few days we had very little to do apart from getting back into shape, having a bath, a haircut, a shower and clean clothes. Being up on the frontier for five months, I dare say we smelt like goats. Oh yes, we had baths up there, but most likely a rough one in a stream, it was all very primitive. After a while, we were back to our normal duties of Guards and Parades etc.

CHAPTER SEVENTEEN

Rumours of Moving
South of India – Kamptee

Once again the rumours started, never direct from the horse's mouth as they say, just rumours, someone usually let out a leak of information. But, after a few days, it became official and we were notified properly that we were to move down to Kamptee which was down in the Southern Provinces, so we started packing up once again.

The day came when we found ourselves on a long military train once again at Pindi Station and this was the last time we saw this station. We could see all the Indians watching us go, they were losing their wages because of us leaving and they did not know if we were to be replaced or not and we could not tell them. There were more than a thousand troops on this train. The journey was once again most interesting all the way down. I think it took us three days to get down there, stopping at various stations and watching the way the Indians behaved. There never seemed to be any organisation, when on their trains they were all over them just like ants, those that couldn't get a seat inside would sit on the roof or hang on the side of the carriage, no thought of safety. If one fell off and got crushed underneath the train, they did not stop, they just left him there. They made their life so cheap, no matter there were plenty more, if a person was of some importance maybe they would do something. We used to watch them when they made a stop, if there was a water tap on the station, they would all crowd around it, either washing their feet or having a drink or just splashing around the water like a sparrow. The men seem to be doing it all, but what about their women, didn't they want a wash and a drink? Guess they got it somewhere else, they pushed them aside. For our food we had haversack rations, the tea was made by the cooks, by taking their urn up to the engine and filling it up with the hot water, they poured in the tea and gave it a stir and that was a fine mug of tea, it went down well. We liked our tea made with condensed milk, thick enough to stand your spoon in it.

It was all very interesting for the Indians to watch us, I bet they thought that we were a mad lot, but were interested to see the way we went about things. The most unusual sight that we saw one early morning was their early morning ablutions. We pulled up near some station which was also on the edge of a village, it was probably about 06.00 hours when a large number of men came out of their shacks with their little brass pots of water, they made their way over to a large ditch which was their toilet. They did their business without a blush and took no notice of us staring at them, they washed themselves and then drifted back to the shacks. What also got us, when they approached this ditch, was the amount of flies that lifted off the ground, it was like a black cloud, when they all left, back they came again, no wonder there was so much sickness in their country with primitive sanitation like that. It was the first time that we had seen that, it was all brass pots and bare bottoms.

You can understand why we never did drink their water, all our water was purified before we drank it, and we always carried some purifying tablets in case we managed to get hold of some and were not sure of its purification. All beers and mineral waters were screwed tops as well, there was no draught beers in those days. I dare say we did drink some of their polluted drinks, unknown to us but what the eye don't see . . . !

For exercise at times when we stopped at a station we would all line up on the platform and perform some gymnastic movements which once again amused the locals.

We arrived at our destination of Kamptee. We were now down in the Central Provinces, I can't say that it was much different from up the North of India, maybe a little warmer. It was a little flatter country around here, and the barracks were situated near a jungle, so jungle training was forthcoming.

We all de-trained, fell in outside the station and smartly marched down to the barracks. Once again we were in bungalow type buildings but all in good order and just waiting for some more British Troops to move in and bring it back to life. There was also a large river in this area, so that came in useful also for training. It must have been a three mile and the gear on our backs was heavy, but I guess by now that we were used to this weight. Once again, we settled in and we continued with our training, there was no let up on this, and it was very important that we kept it up because we never knew when we might be called upon to have to fight for our country. Jungle warfare was certainly different, it was jungle and visibility was short because of the close undergrowth. There were insect menaces as well, like flies that really bite and the pest of the mosquito in this area, there were malaria types about so we needed to take precautions against this. We took a tablet called mepprican, a small yellow tablet, everyday, but if you took it regularly it saved you having malaria. If caught, it was a nasty disease and a job to get rid of it completely. Lucky for me I did not get this, only sandfly fever, this I have already mentioned. Then, if we camped in the jungle area we would be pestered with ants, black ones would bite you and white ants would eat your blanket overnight, not completely, but make a great hole in it. Too many crawly things about that we did not like and some spiders. We sat down once having a break, when we witnessed the bird eating spider in action, a small bird perched itself on a branch of a tree, when like a flash, a spider about as big as my hand swung around this branch and grabbed this bird and paralysed it with its sting, left it where it was for a while and then came back for it and took it away for his dinner. Such is life in the jungle, they devour each other I guess.

There were a few other buildings in the area, as well as the barracks. I will tell you another story about a Girls' High School nearby. There was a mixture of girls there, either Indian or British girls attended this school and there were boarders as well as day pupils. But here was where one of our soldiers wanted to make a visit without an invitation. He attempted to get in there one night, it was strictly out of bounds as you may well guess. He managed to get over the wall but one of the guard dogs heard him and set out the warning bark and he was caught by one of the Convent Staff who soon informed our Regimental Police and he was arrested and punished. I think he was given twenty-eight days detention for the attempt. I could never make out why these types want to get themselves into trouble like this, it's so foolish. Such are the things that some troops get up to, one can never tell what is going on in their minds. We get it with discipline, although all of us are volunteers, there are a few who because of their inability to progress become anti-discipline, so they then make it awkward for themselves by misbehaving. I had one not long after we came here, a smart soldier, always had been, but he had a personal objection to me being an N.C.O. as I was so much younger than he was. We had at times during the week to detail men for certain jobs in the Barrack Room so I detailed him to clean the ammunition, a bit of red tape I know, but those were the orders. A certain amount of this ammunition had to be polished. The cases were brass and it was put on show once a week on C.O.'s inspection. I told him to do this and he flatly refused with a bit of obscene language to go with it. I gave him three warnings but he would not do it, what made it worse for him, he was a time expired soldier, he had completed his seven years with the Colours and was soon to go home to England on his reserve. I could not make out his attitude in refusing to do this small task, because it was small, it would have taken him about ten minutes to do, so why? He carried out the refusal in front of another N.C.O. and he was a witness, so I had to say to him,' (his name) you are under arrest.' It would have been an open arrest, but as he refused with a threatening attitude and obscene language, he was now under close arrest. He of course flew into a rage about this, I had been fair enough to him, but he refused to accept my order. He was, I was told soon afterwards, due to go home in two weeks time. He was tried by the Company Commander first, but then had to appear in front of C.O., who gave him detention. He was sent away on this and I never did see him again. I know he had to wait many months after he had finished his punishment before he was put on a ship to go home, and all this went on his Discharge Character Report. What is the use of being like that? It is one of these unpleasant jobs of being an N.C.O., having to charge a soldier for lack of discipline, the thing is when we as N.C.O.s have to charge a man, we sometimes think it's our own fault for not putting it over right, in other words for not being able to control or explain things right.

We had another incident in another company, nothing to do with me, it just reached our ears one afternoon, that so and so had gone berserk in 'A' Company. He was Room Orderly, and consequently he had access to the arms and ammunition in his room. He grabbed hold of a .45 Pistol, loaded it and started shooting up the room, not the men that were in it, but just the room, knocking out the lights and the windows and things on top of their lockers. He was arrested of course for breach of discipline, he was not put in jail but sent to a Psycho Ward. They tried to get it out of him why he did it, I think the answer was 'Well I just felt like it.' These sort of things went on in the background but no one, very rarely anyhow, outside heard about them. I suppose it's best to keep quiet about it, because there is no explanation, is there?

We had another nice fellow who shot another soldier in his barrack room one afternoon whilst he was cleaning his rifle. He put one round that somehow he had got hold of in the breech of his rifle and shot the fellow opposite him who was sitting there reading a book. He shot right through the book and killed him for no reason at all. At least that was the verdict at the Enquiry, he could not supply a reason. So what goes on in our minds sometimes, one has to be a psychologist to find that out I guess.

Another incident involved not a shooting this time but a man who had no faith in doctors, so for all his complaints, he went out and bought his own medical supplies, herbs and such from an Indian Chemist. He had a bad cold at one time so bought something unknown to us to push up his nose and rub in his chest. What happened? He died. As far as I know he was a good soldier, clean and hardworking, no trouble whatsoever. The verdict on that I never did hear.

I'll tell you one more, which happened a little later on in Palestine. Two buddies, or mates, always went out together. There were no problems between them as far as we knew, but one had an Arab dagger and stuck the other one day and killed him. Another soldier with a good record, he was put in a mental home for a period of time, in fact, I had to do the guard on him with some of my platoon. I went into his hospital cell and spoke to him and he seemed as normal as anyone else. On the side of his wall he had drawn with perfect details a submarine, they must have given him the crayons in different colours to complete this sketch and he could tell me how the sub worked. This man by the way, had been a Junior N.C.O., but not anymore, I think he was discharged on medical grounds.

I could go on telling you I suppose of many incidents like this, after you have been in the army you just accept these things, that we are all different and all have different opinions about how things should be done or dealt with and how to go about things. There must be times when we do things ourselves and wonder, why did I do it that way? The next time I'll do it better.

Back at Kamptee it came out from England that the Infantry Field Drill was to alter much for the better, I thought so, as well as other Officers and N.C.O.s, it was called 'Battle Drill'. Instead of going across open country in long lines of soldiers, we moved about in a closer formation in sections with more powerful weapons. It made us into Companies, much smaller targets and much more controllable. Your N.C.O. was closer to his section for giving orders and stop the waving of arms. If the enemy spotted someone waving his arms he would automatically think, 'Ay, a leader, go get him.' So this Battle Drill came into force to stay. We also marched in threes instead of fours, all these movements made it easier to reach one's objective without being spotted so easily, most important for us as Infantry men. We kept this training up for about a year here.

We had to do a spell of duty at Fort Sitabaldi, not too far from here. It was some old Fort that we took possession of many years ago, the old smooth bore cannons were still there in place, these were just there as museum pieces, but nevertheless, were of interest, they even had the old type of round ball gun shot piled up neatly on the side as if waiting to be fired.

We managed to find somewhere to swim, there was no swimming pool, but about a mile away there was a natural spring which had over time, got some depth in it. There were alongside it, some rocks that we could dive off if required. We often used it, quite a few of us, but unknown to us, it was also a place that the local jungle animals used as a watering hole. I'll tell you now, I got a good scare one day. Two of us decided to use it one hot afternoon. The other chap said, 'I'll have to go now as I have a duty to perform.' So off he went and left me on my own. After a bit of a swim I decided to sunbathe on the rocks, at peace with the world and with not a care. I just happened to sit up to change position as the rock was a bit uncomfortable, as I sat up I could see about four hundred yards away a tiger strolling out of the jungle, his obvious destination was here for a drink. I wasted no time, all I managed to put on was my plimsolls, which was our dress in those days. I left the rest of my clothing and took off at a pretty fast speed, the hundred yard effort for about a mile. I gave an occasional glance backwards to see if this tiger was after me, but there was no sign of him, for which I was thankful, at least he did not have me for an afternoon snack. I of course reported this to the Authorities as a warning for others to watch out for. I was later told that this was the tiger that was wanted because it had turned out to be a man eater, or rather a baby eater. Reports had been coming in that the young Indian wives had been putting their babies down on the ground when they were tea picking and this tiger had been helping himself. So you can guess, that we kept that place out of bounds for the future. It eventually meant that a hunting party had to be organised by the C.O. to catch and get rid of this tiger. He was eventually caught, but it was not easy as he knew his way around the jungle.

He was found to be a rather sick and old animal, rather toothless and lame so babies were an easy target for him, but the local people were glad that he was caught. The skin is most likely still laid out in the C.O.'s lounge to be walked on. When you come to think of it, just by chance of changing my position on this rock, if I had not of done so, what would have been the consequences? Me facing a snarling tiger, and how I would have handled the situation if I had had to face it, I don't really know. He may have been old but was a tiger probably weighing about five hundred pounds, he was no pussy cat. When we arrived here we were not warned about such animals that could be wandering about. I can tell you, I was a lot more cautious in the future. I had to go back to this place and recover my clothing, I did not go alone or unarmed, but did not see any more tigers. We found his paw marks in the mud on the side of this pool, there was no sign of him disturbing the clothes that I left behind. Some said that they usually sniff around the humans clothes and at times even rip them to pieces, but I guess, he was old and just wanted a drink.

In a place like that there was very little to do as regards our own entertainment, except for the cinema with which someone in the Battalion seemed to lend a hand. I remember the type of films in those days, one was George Formby types, you know the song 'When I'm Cleaning Windows', or maybe it would be Gracie Fields, those were very popular in those days. These shows were better than seeing nothing at all, we would, at least most of us, buy a large bag of peanuts in the shell and sit there cracking and eating them, the shucks were probably knee deep by the time we left. We would wash the peanuts down, with a bottle of pop, the bottle in those days had a glass marble in the top and you had to push this down with a sharp blow using your thumb. You don't see that type of bottle any more, to keep them cool, they were placed in a bath tub full of blocks of ice, it did the job alright, but the action of using your thumb on this bottle did at times give you a bruised thumb.

One particular night we had a bit of trouble with the troops just because the film was a lot of rubbish, they started throwing bottles at the screen, so the Duty Corporal was sent for to try and get some order in the cinema. As he came in, someone threw a part eaten orange at him and unfortunately it did not miss him. It was a good shot, it hit him square on the face, which annoyed him very much, so everyone below his rank was ordered out and paraded outside and he tried to make the culprit own up. He received no reply and consequently said, 'All right, if no one owns up, you can all return to your barracks and no more films for you tonight.' I don't think he was very popular that night but they should not have thrown that orange, should they?

We did have other things to do, like sports, depending on what was your interest, mine was athletics. I spent many hours training as I was one of the Battalion Team members. I also took part in hockey and boxing, not particularly good at any of it, but good enough I guess to be selected for a team, I enjoyed it all the same.

During my stay at Sitabaldi Fort myself and my section had to take a turn at being on the Malaria Squad. This job consisted of visiting outside pools where female mosquitoes were breeding in their thousands, we had to collect some specimen mosquitoes for handing to the Medical Officer for analysing, to find out why they were carrying this disease and see what we could do to stop it from spreading. It was the cause of a lot of suffering amongst the population as well as our own servicemen. We were given some liquid to kill these pests, which gave us the authority to enter people's property if they possessed any still waters. We had to wear a special arm band to indicate what we were doing, we still did not barge in on people's property at will, I always asked permission if it was convenient to carry out this duty. It was some chemical spraying that we did, it certainly was a change from our normal duties, but not for long.

One morning when we were about to go out on this malaria business, as we walked out of the main entrance, we walked right into the middle of one of their religious meetings, held by Ghandi himself. It was the first time that I had seen him, there were most likely about a thousand of his followers at this meeting, but we nevertheless walked right through them, not on purpose to be awkward, but because he was in our normal area to walk about. They were aware of this, so they took no notice of us as regards our intrusion. To look at him, he did not have the appearance of a leader, he just looked a very small built man in his white loin cloth, wearing a pair of spectacles on the end of his nose, but nevertheless an educated man and I guess he knew what he was about. It was during this period that he was organising what we call 'A get out Britain', that they had had enough of us in their country, but he seemed to be doing it without any violence, up to then, anyhow. That did come later on, this was only 1937, as you are aware, we eventually got out in 1947, ten years later. They held many meetings up to that date. There were some who were not happy to see us go, we had as far as I know done a lot of good for the country, and to some of them, not so good. Even today, 1994, I have heard from people who have visited India, and spoken to some of the older ones and they have said they wished we were back there.

This reminds me of our char wallah back in Rawlpindi. This char wallah who got to know us well and even got to be fond us, one day, when he saw me come back from seeing the C.O. about my one stripe, said with a look of delight, 'I knew it Sahib, I knew it, you are now a Corporal Sahib and very pleased am I to see it. You remember my words, Sahib, one day you will be a General. No, you not laugh, because I think you will.' Well, I did not laugh, because I could see that he was quite serious, all I could say to him was, 'Thank you for those kind words, but I doubt it.' Well, we all know that was never so but one of my uncles made it, the one that told me off, when I was visiting him one day in Portsmouth, he was in the Black Watch. This char wallah went on talking to me and he said, 'It will be a very sad day when all you boys leave our country for good, we all know it is to happen one day, me, I shall have no work then. Oh yes Sahib, so very sad.' That is what brought my memory back to him and his few words. As time went on we all know that there were many political skirmishes between them about all this, it gave their Local Police a bit of a headache, as well as the serving British Troops who were still out there.

It was here that we had a bit of bother as regards hydrophobia, one of our lads went out and purchased a puppy mongrel but unknown to him, this puppy had this complaint, it had not really developed, but was at its early stages. Anyhow, this puppy in its playful mood bit him on the hand, he did not take much notice of it at first, but in about two or three days he became ill so to hospital the fellow went but in a few days, he was dead. As the dog had dropped a few smears around the barrack room it was most likely that we could have this on us, about fourteen of us had to report to the M.O. to have this anti-hydrophobia injection, which was a fairly long needle in the stomach and a very unpleasant injection. This had to be injected into us for at least four days, but there it is, it was better than having rabies and dying, we were still too young for that. In the early stages of this, one other soldier in the barrack room lost his marbles for a while, got hold of this puppy by the hind legs, threw him up against the wall and killed him. He then took him outside and threw it over the fort wall and it dropped down into the moat which was about forty feet below. This was not a good idea he was told by the M.O. He was told that he had better go down and get this dead dog and dig a deep hole and bury him and to put on some rubber gloves before doing so, he did this, and then joined us having this needle. I have not seen a man with this complaint, but they say that the human being goes through a lot of pain and distress, so I guess a good lesson was learnt from this. I know I did, anyhow I did not want any pets, my life was busy enough as it was.

I had to attend yet another Cadre Course, to improve my knowledge of all weapons and tactics. This lasted for about four weeks and the result of this course, as far as I can remember was good, but some did better than me, we can't win them all.

I should like to tell you about the baboons and the R.S.M.'s Parade on the Barrack Square, which was normally held on a Saturday morning, it was really the C.O.'s Parade, as all ranks had to attend. Our R.S.M. at that time was Billy Wells, who later

Our much needed char wallah, waiting for our custom. He sat on the barrack verandah for hours. There was tea in the urn and cakes in the tin box. This is at Rawlpindi, Pakistan, 1936.

on gained a commission and our C.O. was Lt Colonel Ramsden who later became a General. He played a good part in the Second World War out in the desert for a while. Let's now come to these baboons. These animals, seemed to know about this Parade, and they used to come over and watch us. There was a wall about four feet high running along the side of this Parade Ground and they would sit on it like spectators. It must have been the R.S.M.'s voice that attracted them over, but at times they distracted him when shouting commands, so he would order the Regimental Police to move them off and the Police would run along with their drill canes and knock them off, as they did this, they would jump up again, as if it was a game. It was just a waste of time, mind you if they could get hold of you their teeth would make a mess of you, they were tough animals. Anyhow when the parade was over and everyone had gone you would see them all disappear as one and go back into their jungle.

Our stay here was coming to an end. More rumours that we were once again on the move, where to now? I can assure you, that this was a secret move, we did not know where we were off to until we got there.

We had the task of clearing up and packing once again, not that we did such a lot as we were not the action groups, the Quarter Master's Staff were responsible for most of it. We had to make sure that we took all our weapons and ammunition, plus our own personal kit, most of this was packed in our kit bags, our bags also had our Number, Rank and Name on them. Once again we had to leave our wallahs behind, those little Indian men who did lots of small things to make our lives a little happier during our stay in this part of India.

CHAPTER EIGHTEEN

Palestine

Once more onto the train, all aboard in an orderly fashion into the unknown. The lads would say, 'Where do you reckon we are off to now Corp.' I'd say, 'Your guess is as good as mine, all I know is that we are headed for Bombay and we are to board a ship of some sort. They might tell us once we are on the ship.' So off we went again, on our journey further north, as I said, heading for Bombay, one of their largest cities, there seemed to be millions of people about and most of them in a poor condition. They all looked so thin. I suppose it was because of the poor food that they ate, not much goodness in it. Most of them were not in a good financial position to buy good food, the rich you could usually tell by the fact that they looked more robust and they were also not walking or pushing a bicycle with a flat tyre. They had so many strange customs to us that we didn't understand. I think you would have to live a long time with them and speak their language to get to understand them. They also had many religions and languages, so much so that some from the north did not understand them properly. We watched them as we journeyed along, I must say with interest, as I have said before, they did not appear to have much sense of organisation, there must have been some sort of system in their own way, but I could not follow it.

We were now in the Port of Bombay which again was all hustle and bustle, there were many ships and we were wondering which one of these would be ours. It just so happened that we were unlucky, and we had what we called a Banana Boat, as there was only room for a couple of hundred soldiers. Our sleeping accommodation was as usual hammocks, but as I have said before, these are quite comfortable when you get used to them. As we moved out of harbour we noticed that all port holes were covered and we had instructions to remain below top deck until we were out at sea, three miles away, such secrecy. We were not at war yet, but it was a military move, so we had to remain as inconspicuous as possible. We were moving westward, that's about all I knew, across the Indian Ocean. The weather was just fine, we were now way out so all port holes could be uncovered and opened if needed. The destination was still unknown, maybe the more senior ranks knew where we were heading for, but not us juniors.

After about three days, we woke up one early morning, to hear the anchor rumbling down the side of the ship. We got dressed pretty quickly and flew up on top deck to see where we were, all we could see was a large hill or mountain in front of us and some other British troops down on the dock side as well as some local inhabitants, who looked like Arabs. I shouted down, 'Hey mate, where are we and what is this place called?' I was told, 'This is Palestine, and that hill there is Mount Carmel.' So that's where we were. We had heard of this place and what our troops were doing here. We also noticed that there were a lot of Army 15 cwt trucks out on road, we all wondered what they were doing there.

We soon found out once we put ashore. The town nearby, was Haifa, which we got to see more of later on. We were called together and given a talk by a Sergeant, who said, 'Right, we are now in Palestine and this is Haifa and that is Mount Carmel. At the top of that Mount is where the Commander in Chief is billeted, most likely we will have to do a guard on him sometime.' That never came off, at least not for me. He then went on to say, 'We are here to try and keep the peace between the Arabs and the Jews, more or less a police job, you will soon find out what other jobs we are to perform. These trucks that you see in front of us, are now ours. We are now mechanised, each of these trucks takes a section of men. In the centre of this truck there is a Bren Gun mounted on a tripod, we will soon show you what these are for.' So we Corporals, were given one of these trucks to be in charge of. The drivers at the moment were local civilians, who were obviously trained and picked to drive these for us until we trained our own drivers, this did not take long. We were then told 'Get yourselves sorted out. The N.C.O. is to sit in the front and your men in the back.' The gun on the back that was mounted, able to swing around at a 360 degree angle, so no matter where and what side you might be attacked, you would be able to retaliate with ease. The whole object of having these trucks, was for patrolling, it enabled us to get to our destination in fairly quick time, despite the fact that these small trucks were governed down to 40 m.p.h., not fast, but I guess that they had a reason for that.

Our first place of patrolling was at Accre across the bay probably about sixteen miles from Haifa. There was also a railway station there, mainly for goods by the look of it, that was one place that we had to patrol, especially at night. At one time we had to do a search right through the town, inside people's houses as well. We were searching for terrorists as well as arms and ammunition, but we very rarely got much luck as regards to that. They were a little bit too smart at times for us to catch them or find anything like weapons. I can remember searching one house and interrupting a sad occasion, when some very old man was in bed ill with lots of people in there to see his last minutes on this earth. Being civilised people we left it without searching. I did report this and I was told that it could all have been a hoax, if it happened again, I was not to take any notice of it. Well, it was a bit hard on them if it happened to be true, women and children were there as well. It makes the job hard to operate properly, if they put up acts like that for us to fathom out, it's all a sad business, and makes you wonder what is it all about. Who started all this? Who is to blame? Is it our politicians? But we, as soldiers, were just there to do as we were told whether we thought it right or wrong.

In the short time that we were there we seemed to be moving all the time. It seemed odd to us in some places that the Arabs and Jews were living close together and seemed to be getting on with one another quite well, so we could not understand why all the trouble. It just so happened, that before the trouble started, that they were living close together then, and they just did not bother to move away. Most of the Jews, were now living in a Kibbutz, which was a large area surrounded by barbed wire and well guarded by their own troops. They felt much safer in these camps. While we were there we had to spend some time up in the hills picketing the area and watching out for terrorists. We were on top of a hill once called Nafdet, we were left up there for quite a long time and we built a high wall all round us, like we did when we were up in the mountains of Afghanistan. We put barbed wire all around us and set booby traps outside at night in the event that they would try and raid us, but we never did see any trouble, there was probably a platoon of us up there, eating and sleeping and patrolling, that's all we did.

Other times we were called out to either help the Jews or the Arabs, if they were being attacked by one or the other. It seemed to be mainly that we went to the aid of the Jews more than the Arabs, because I think, that the Arabs did more of the attacking. They used to do a lot of sneak raids on the Jews, and we would be called out sometimes late at night to go to their aid. We did not really do very much, probably fire a few rounds of ammunition over their heads but very rarely did they return the fire, then all would be quiet for hours. At one place we did stay the night, and the Jews looked after us very well as regards to food and wine, in the morning we all left early and had a good look around to make sure that no one was about to do them any more harm.

Another interesting guard that I did at one time with my section, was at a Government Stock Farm. It was for twenty-four hours, all of it spent outside the buildings because the farm was at times raided by these terrorists for the stock. We were situated in the middle of the grounds in the wooded part, once again shielded by filled sandbags, to keep an eye on the stock which was worth a lot of money. We would patrol for a while, and then settle down inside the sandbags for most of the night, keeping a sentry on guard all the time. I was woken up in the early hours by a sentry who whispered to me, 'Hey Corp, I think there is someone out there crawling about in the dark. Will you come and look?' I got up and did just that and I did see something crawling about in the dark at about one hundred yards away. I said to him, 'Let's have your rifle a minute.' He handed it to me, I shoved a round up the breech, set the sights at one hundred yards, took aim at the dark figure and fired. The result was a jackal, because I saw it fly into the air about five feet when I hit it, I also saw its eyes glisten in the dark. These animals' eyes did shine up in the dark, but you can bet your life he was dead. The sentry said, 'Shall I go out and see what the damage is?' I said, 'No, it will keep, we will look in the morning when it is light, if there are any more about, that shot would have scared them whether it be man or beast.' Come morning we did just that, on inspection we saw that I had caught him in the neck, which would have killed him at once, no suffering for him. Jackals go after chickens but this farm bred a good stock of horses, pigs and sheep as well as various types of fowl. I should think it had a good business in this area, spreading the stock around the country, that is why the military had to guard the place.

We must remember that in addition to soldiers, we had the Palestine Police doing a good job over there. Most of them were ex-military, so that type of duty did not come strange to them, we very often used to meet at certain incidents, needing them in attendance more on the civilian side of things. It was a job well sought after by ex-service men with the necessary qualifications, they did not just take anyone, they had to come up to their expectations.

From Accre, we then moved on to Nazareth for a spell, another well known place in the Bible, Mary's Well and the stable where Jesus was supposed to have worked at one time. We saw the well by the road side, it could have been genuine as it appeared very old, with an old piece of pipe jutting out of the bank, the water coming from a natural spring. The stable, we were not very convinced about that, it was an old building and it was overgrown with weeds and boarded up, we were not too sure about that. The town as far as we could see, was just about 100% Arab population, there were some modern buildings about, we had one for our use during our short stay there. We were there to sort out the good from the bad. Our duties once again were out on patrols around the area. Myself and my section were detailed to do a whole night patrol once, we had to waylay some Arabs who were suspected of being terrorists. We were told by our Arab informers that there was to be a meeting at a certain house out in the country between the terrorists themselves. It just so happened, that it turned out to be true, we saw these fellows coming in and heading towards the selected house, we waited until they had settled down and then went in with fixed bayonets, with a round of ammunition up the breech ready to fire if needed. I left some outside guarding in case some got away, but I went in with help and hustled them outside for a search and made them sit down on their haunches. After the search, I stayed outside with a few troops, and then sent others into the house to search for weapons. We did find just one old rifle and some ammunition but I was not happy about that, I was sure there was more than that about so I sent someone off to Company H.Q. to ask for our police to come out bringing with them a couple of policewomen, who I needed to search the women in this house, I was sure that they had weapons hidden under their skirts. When they were sat down you could see that there was a great deal of room under there which could hide a lot of weapons. Out they came, after a long wait, and lo and behold, I was right. As a result of this the men were taken to the Police Station back in Haifa, charged with terrorist action and sentenced, what they got, I did not hear.

This was the sort of thing that we were doing all the time, it certainly did some good, as things went very quiet for a while and we had very little trouble around here. There was a bit of a scare one time, when one of the terrorists threw a grenade over a wall where the Quarter Master's Store was situated, it did very little damage except that it injured one of the storemen in the foot, he was lucky, as there were other obstacles in the way of the grenade. Another was thrown at the building where myself and my section were billeted, but it did not explode, in fact it was lying there for a long time in the road side, then someone was detailed to clear that area and shoot it, causing it to explode. This was done successfully without anyone or anything being injured. Whoever it was that threw it in the first place, used an old car to drive through the town in a hurry and disappeared up the road. Someone set off after them, but it was too late they got away. It was not attempted again, they would know that we would be more on the alert next time. The incident made the Officer in Charge, turn out the whole area from their houses, men, women and children, we had them lined up in the road whilst a search went on. One Arab made a dash to get away as he was being approached, for that silly move he had the touch of the bayonet on his behind, and he did not care for that. No one told the soldier to do this, he just did the move automatically, he thought he was doing the right thing, but he was not reprimanded, he was just doing his job.

In this area, we were not too far from the Sea of Galilee, there was an old interesting fort there where we had to stay for a while, keeping watch. It gave us a good view over the area and we quite enjoyed it, it overlooked a village and I can't imagine why it was there. It was probably put there many years ago, when some other nation was attacking them, maybe the Turks. The whole of this area was very hostile towards us. I can't blame them I suppose, but I think that we were pretty good diplomats. The British soldier was not really a cruel soldier, if people behaved properly, we were inclined to help them and show mercy especially to the Arabs, we found them most hospitable, probably more so than the Jews, they could vary. I suppose it depended where they originated from, there were many Jews as you know, from all nations, some had a dislike of the British, maybe because of the stories that they had heard from their parents, something that may have happened years ago, but times change as the years go by.

It was not all duties for us, we had time off now and again to visit the town, the nearest to us was Haifa which was split up into two parts, part Jew and part Arab. We used to visit the Jewish side called German Town, parts of that were marked 'Out of Bounds'. To make sure that this was obeyed, the Royal

Military Police, did their patrols around, if they caught you in the Out of Bounds Section you could be charged, and in some cases put into a cell for a while. There was a curfew, I think you had to be out of the town by 22.30 hours, security was the reason for this. We also had to carry arms and some ammunition at times, to just protect ourselves because when we were out we never did go out by ourselves, there had to be two at least.

The cinema was a novelty to us, there was a sliding roof, when it was hot it would slide back quietly and then you would have a good view of the stars at night. You could also get a drink brought to you when asked for, you would push a small bell in front of you, your seat number would show up back in the bar some place, and they would come to you and take your order. There was enough room between the seats there for them to operate, all very advanced for those times.

Whilst in this area I should like to mention that we stayed in the large camp at the foot of Mount Carmel for quite a while. This was a well organised camp and had just about everything there that we wanted, a camp gymnasium, plus a canteen run by the NAAFI. It was very close to the sea, a place called Bach Delaine, a very nice sandy beach and a restful area for us, a break from the duty patrols and another chance to get ourselves cleaned up. This was also not too far from the Gaza Strip, which was a troubled area (still is today). There is a small British graveyard there where some of our lads are buried, the results of terrorist action, I hope it is still in good order. Also the Golan Heights, you often hear about that place today. Then there was the larger city of Tel Aviv, a nice modern town and a good job completed by the Jews once again and very attractive. We have to admit, that the Jews made terrific advancements in the country, it's a pity that the Arabs don't take this into consideration when trying to make peace, it would be nice if they could all live together, because they have many talents as well. Look at the cultivation of the land they have created, all those fine orchards growing that good fruit, right out of the sand, which must have taken some organisation.

Time for another little story, which happened one Sunday morning when most of us could relax from normal duties. It happened about 11.00 hrs during our stay at the camp at Carmel. About that time, we usually all drifted over to the NAAFI, either for a beer or a mug of tea, it depended how we were feeling. As we were about to move out of the Barrack Room, someone saw our Padre coming, looking all pleased with himself, but some of our boys saw him coming and gave the warning. 'Watch out trouble coming,' we heard a voice say. There was a dash for the door or an open window, but the Padre beat some of us to it, 'Right you lot of heathens, how about showing yourselves in my Church this morning. I haven't seen many of you in there lately. Any volunteers?' No answer was the stern reply. It's a funny thing when this happens everyone seems to have something else on at that time, it's not that we had anything against religion, but we also like to have some leisure time to ourselves at times and we did not feel like spending it in the Church. We felt that there was a time and place for most things, but not today, we wanted some other kind of pleasure, so I don't think that the Padre had many customers that morning. Yes, I was one of them, but we were young then and had different opinions of things at that time.

Another day I was a hero, so they say, no medals for it but nearly a box around the ears. We were on a nice sandy beach, but the sea was a bit rough. I was standing on the end of a jetty nearby just watching the swimmers, when I noticed a young girl about eleven years old struggling, she was caught in a current and seemed a bit distressed. I dived in and grabbed hold of her and brought her in to safety, as I was doing this, her parents, who were Jews, were watching and were a little concerned about her being in my grips. As soon as I got her on dry land, they came up and snatched her away from me, no thanks for saving her from drowning. The girl had a surprised look on her face as well, as if she objected to their ungrateful behaviour, which was true, the lads that were watching said the same. 'What a shower!' said someone. As they walked away along the beach this young girl kept looking back as if to say thank you but could not because of the parents' attitude. They disappeared out of sight, but about an hour later this girl came back and thanked me, just a shake of hands, and a smile. She made up her own mind about that but I did not see the parents any more, I suppose it was a difficult situation for them.

One evening Curly Andrews and myself were returning to camp on foot, as we had missed the returning truck to barracks. As we were strolling along the road towards Nazareth we were fired upon from behind us, so we immediately took cover in a ditch nearby and waited to see if they would have another go at us. I suppose they were not able to see us so I put my hat on top of my rifle, and waved it about whilst Curly and I kept a look out to see where the shots were coming from. The waving of the hat, gave them another chance to have a shot at us, we took notice where it came from and straight away returned some shots in that direction. Evidently they did not care for that as no more were returned, so we stood up and walked back to camp. It was a good thing that we had taken our rifles with us, just in case this sort of thing happened.

Another time, I was out with my Platoon Sergeant Rougie West, up in German Town some place having a quiet drink in some bar, when one of us just happened to look at the time and realised that it was nearly curfew time. We only had five minutes to get out town but we would never make it so we were prepared to have an answer to the Military Police if they caught us out, which they did. It just so happened that these two police were of the same rank as us, but the rule applied to all ranks. After a few smart alec words to one another they said, 'Sorry but we have to take your names.' So Sergeant West, became Sergeant Jones and Corporal French became Corporal Love, instead of us being billeted at Accre, we were down in Nazareth and instead of us being in 'Z' Company, we were in 'A' Company. Off we went, knowing full well that they would have a job to trace us when the time came to do so. In about three weeks time we suddenly had to have an identity parade but in the meantime Sergeant West had grown a moustache. I had not done anything to change my identity, I was to take the risk.

These two Military Police, were there to try and search us two out, the names they knew were false, it was the identity that they were after. Sergeant West stood in front with the duty roster in case it was needed. He had attended these parades more than once. They did not recognise him with whiskers, but when they came to me they asked the Sergeant what my name was and he gave it as correct, Corporal French. They wanted to know from the Sergeant where I was on this night, he looked at the roster and said, 'He was on duty picket that night.' They were not too sure about all those lies, but there was little that they could do about it, they just gave up and went on their way.

In this area we had what we called Flying Patrols, we had to take our turn on these. All patrols were sent out in different area, it broke up the monotony, in fact we all looked forward to them, whilst in the zone of Dalliet-el-Carmel, up over the hills, looking down on the coast line. It was out in the wilds a bit, situated near an Arab village, this was a patrol that we had to do on foot, a change from riding in the truck. In this instance we had to perform a helpful task, we came across some senior Arabs trying to get their car out of a ditch, it was obvious the driver had slipped into the ditch as it had been raining. There were four Arabs in the car, but they did not have the strength to heave it out, so I gave the signal to my lads to give a hand. There were eight of them, and in seconds their car was back on the track. This sure came as a surprise to them, it made them realise that we are not all bad fellows, they even came over and shook our hands. They got into the car and took off and we continued on our patrol. In about a couple of hours time, we returned to our billet and as I was going into where our guard was, the Corporal shouted out to me, 'Hey Doug, there is a parcel here from some Arabs addressed to you, not in name, but just to the Corporal of this afternoon's patrol who helped us get the car out of the ditch.' We looked at this parcel with some doubt as to whether there was a booby trap in it or if it was genuine. I looked around it and could see no wires so I decided to have a look inside, all was well, it was full of cigarettes, the flat type, that they smoked with an unusual aroma to them which was quite pleasant really. 'Good for them,' the lads said. More for them really, as I did not smoke very much. These Arab gentlemen, were the owners of a tobacco factory not too far away.

CHAPTER NINETEEN

A Reprimand as a Lance Corporal

We had yet another move in this country, this time to a very new barracks called after a famous cricket pitch back in England, Trafford Camp. It was certainly a great change for us to be all together again as a battalion, moving to a camp like this. Each room was fitted out with electric fans and the newest type of radios, really up to date washing facilities, a nice canteen and even a Corporals' Club, Sergeants' Mess and Officers' Mess. I'd seen nothing like it, since we left Rawlpindi, there was even a flag pole with our Regimental Flag flying. It did not suit some of them as it became too regimental especially with the flag flying, this had to be saluted if you passed by it, which I did not do at one time and got into trouble, more on that subject in a while.

Once again we started to carry out patrols, I had to go on an early morning one once, in fact a whole platoon of us. This meant four sections this time, no Sergeants or full Corporals, just one commander who was a Junior Officer. We turned up on time at 06.00 hours, all in our trucks waiting for him but he was late. This was something unusual for me, as I had never had to wait for an Officer before, so it was a problem as to what to do. It just so happened that I was the Senior N.C.O. on this patrol, so it was up to me to make a decision, should I go on and take the patrol, or wait? I thought I should ask someone a bit more senior, so I asked the Guard commander, who was a Sergeant, should I go on and take the Patrol? 'Yes, why not,' he said. We took off, I knew where to go, and I carried out this patrol with no problem. The problems started when I did return. I dismissed the men, and as I did so, I was arrested by the Duty Sergeant for taking out this patrol without the Officer. I was

103

feeling a bit down in the mouth, I just thought that I had done a good job of this patrol and yet I came back to being put on a charge. As I was walking back thinking about this I forgot to slope arms and salute the Regimental Flag that was now flying. Lo and behold, who was about to witness this but the R.S.M., it just so happened that his billet was nearby and he spotted me pass this flag. He bellowed at me from about one hundred yards away, 'Come here you, and at the double!' I perked myself up and doubled over to him. 'What's the big idea of not saluting your Regimental Flag? Slope your arms now and march up and down here until I say stop and make sure that you salute the flag each time that you pass it, and make it smart.' So that is what I did for about fifteen minutes until he stopped me and then gave me another lecture. It was not over yet, after I had my breakfast I was informed by my Sergeant Major that I had to appear before the Company Commander that morning at 11.00 hours, to face him on this charge of taking out a patrol. I thought to myself, who wants to be an N.C.O.? Anyhow, it looked as if I wouldn't be for much longer. The time came for me to get myself dressed in my best uniform and tell my story to the Company Commander, I had to make myself smart for this, or else I would be on another charge for being sloppy. I was not going to give them another chance, it was all happening to me this day. I was marched in front of the officer, the charge was read out, (i.e.) 'Taking out a Patrol without the consent of the Officer.' 'Now Corporal French, what have you to say in your Defence?' I was asked. 'Sir, it was detailed on the notice board, that I and my Section, as well as others, be at the Guard Room at 06.00 hours this morning ready to go out on patrol along with the other sections. The Officer in Charge of this Patrol, was not there at the time notified, I waited another five minutes, but he still did not turn up, so as I was the Senior N.C.O. present I thought I should do something about this and get the patrol out. I thought it best, first of all, to ask someone more senior if I should take it out or still wait, as the officer concerned had not turned up, I guessed he must be sick or something. The Sergeant of the Guard agreed with me that he thought it was best to get on and take out the patrol, so that is what I did. By the time we got out it must have been ten minutes after the allotted time. The patrol was carried out properly and I returned to barracks and dismissed them,' I replied. All this time the officer concerned, was stood near me listening to this and so it was his turn to have his say. He flatly denied all what I had said, so I said once again, 'The other N.C.O.s that were present on this patrol, will also confirm that he was late, also the Sergeant of the Guard, could they not come forward and confirm this and show that I am not making this up.' But I was refused this request. I also mentioned that I had not received any previous instruction as regards to the officer in Charge of the Patrol in the event that he did not turn up, I simply used my initiative and thought rightly so, that I should get on with it. I was then told that I should have waited for him no matter what, but what got me, was that he refused to listen to me and what I had to say, and the officer concerned would not tell the truth. I have not in the past been proved a liar. I was then told to be quiet. 'I, as your Company Commander, can punish you for this offence, if you refuse to accept this I can only refer you to the Commander's orders. So, what is it, yes or no?' Well, I knew what it would be if this was taken further, that I would not stand a chance against this officer's word, as I am only a Junior N.C.O., so I gave in and said, 'Yes Sir, I am willing to take your punishment.' He then said, 'Right, I reprimand you, and don't let this occur again.'

I returned to my Barrack Room feeling that this was a most unjust Charge and punishment, a real unjust decision, in fact it upset me so much, that I had to say something to somebody about it. So I spoke to my Platoon Sergeant about it and he could see how upset I was. He knew me well enough that I would not wish to tell a lie, but he did say, 'You were not right in taking out that patrol, if he was late then that's his fault, not yours, then you would not have got into this mess.' Well and good I thought. He must have spoken to the Sergeant Major about this, because he had a word about this with me, and put me at ease. He said, 'No doubt by now you have realised that you did wrong in taking out this patrol. The other part of the officer being late may have been true, but he doesn't like to be told by a Junior N.C.O. that he was late. I have spoken to the Company Commander about all this and he said to tell Corporal French not to worry too much about it as it will not appear on his Record for long, and to carry on with his duties as he has been doing.' So that was that, I felt better after that, and as he said it did not affect my future service, but was still not forgotten, we live and learn. My future went well, until I was wounded and discharged from the army much later.

We had one more part of Palestine to visit, at Sarafand, there was an R.A.F. Station there, as well, not too far from us. These Barracks had been there a long time, all fitted out as at Trafford Camp. The duties were much about the same there, we did have to do a guard at one time for the R.A.F. Station, I don't know why we had to do their guards but we did. I was given the job at one time to do a spell of duty there, off I went to take over this guard. I was to take it over from the R.A.F., the Guard Commander was a Corporal the same as myself. On taking over in accordance with army routine, I asked for the Guard Orders, he said, 'What's that?' I said, 'The list of duties that have to be carried out during our twenty-four hours whilst on duty here.' 'No such thing here mate,' he replied. I said, 'Well in that case, I cannot take over the Guard.' He suggested that we speak to a more Senior Officer on camp about this. I said, 'That's O.K. by me, you know the way it's done.' We always obey the last order given by a senior. He approached his Warrant Officer about this who came up and settled the problem, he said that I should take over the guard without orders so this I did. The Army are more inclined to have a little more red tape than the R.A.F.

But events were not yet over for me. It was usual for us when we were on guard at any place that we would get a visit from our own Duty Officer. This would happen to me, about 2 o'clock in the morning, the Duty Officer did visit us, but before coming to me he thought he would visit one or two of the sentries around the camp. He would of course, find one that was not all that alert, so he was charged later on. He made his way to me eventually, the first thing that happened was the sentry saw him coming and lo and behold it was the R.S.M. Billy Wells. The usual thing that the sentry has to do is to shout out so that all can hear him in the Guard Room, 'Stand by the Guard – Guard turn out.' As per usual, there was a big scramble to get dressed properly, putting on equipment, finding your rifle and getting outside and lining up, with me at the side of them and me to say to him, 'Guard present and correct, sir.' His remarks to me were not so pleasant, 'Yes, I can see that, but you took too long in coming out when the Sentry shouted for you to turn out, you can dismiss them and do it all over again.' So back to the Guard Room we all went and the sentry started shouting once again, this time of course it was much better because we were all dressed but what with the Sentry shouting, the R.S.M. shouting and me shouting there was quite a noise going on for two o'clock in the morning. We suddenly had an interruption from a voice not too far away, 'Do you bloody lot have to make so much noise at this time of the morning, we are trying to get some sleep?' The R.S.M. said to me, 'Whoever that is, go down and book him.' I said, 'I don't think that I can do that, sir.' 'Why not?' he said. 'Well he happens to be the Camp Warrant Officer, so that makes him my senior, right?' He said, 'I'll see to him.' He left us to carry on and he went down to see this Warrant Officer, what went on between those two is anyone's guess, I did not see the R.S.M. again that night, not until I returned to our own barracks and I had to tell him about there being no guard orders. I don't suppose that anything was done about that, as we were about to move off again. It was during my stay here that I chummed up with a soldier older than myself by the name of Shave, he was then a Corporal like me, but I had not seen him since my days at the depot. I was surprised that he was still a Corporal as I thought he was a good N.C.O. but he told me that he got himself in a bit of trouble with having too many Brown Ales, so the C.O. took his third stripe away. It was not long before he had it back again, you can't keep a good N.C.O. down too long. This is the sort of thing that happens in the services, with all ranks, we sometimes do silly things, I have done so myself. I don't mean I lost a rank but did something that I should not have done. Shave had the nickname of Chesty Shave because that was the way he walked, his chest seemed to stand out more than some of us, he was quite a lad and I enjoyed his company. I lost touch with him when I was sent home to England as an Instructor. I think he became an R.S.M. eventually, where is he now I wonder? I've not seen him since we were in the desert at El Darba.

CHAPTER TWENTY

The Desert

From Palestine we went to the Western Desert, a little place called El-Darba which was right on the coast of the Mediterranean Sea, all part of Egypt. We were in a very warm part now but were thankful to be so near the sea which was good for swimming. We used the sea also to wash in, as we were issued salt water soap which was a bit rough but it worked. There were no barracks here, we had to live in tents which was quite nice, but we had to put up with ants, spiders, scorpions and beetles. Living in the desert seemed so much quieter than back in barracks, I suppose, there was not really so much traffic about except our own army vehicles. The tyres had to be changed on these to balloon tyres which would grip the sand better than the hard ones which just sank into the sand and one could get bogged down. There was just this one main road that ran right across the desert for many miles.

As soon as we got there, we had to start training for desert warfare and that was tough, the toughest part was the walking in the sand, you would take a pace forward, but slide back half a pace and until we got used to it, it sure did make your legs ache. We had to learn not to drink water in large quantities, that again was a hard part of training, there was no water laid on here in taps, not even a well. It had to come up by a train wagon that was made of iron and with that hot sun on it for many hours the water, when we received it, was near to boiling. The only primitive method we had to cool it was to put it in an earthenware pot and place it under the sand fairly deep and so as to remember where it was you had to place a marker over it like a stick, or your bayonet. If it was left overnight when the desert cooled down a bit it would be cooler by morning, but never really cold. As you can imagine, water was precious, more so than a glass of whisky. That is why people like me who had that experience do not like to see water wasted. As I have said before, to bathe ourselves we had a salt water soap issued to us, this also helped our skin to get hardened to the desert sun, most of us were very brown after a few weeks, even the very light skinned men. The only persons that really suffered from the sun I think were the ginger haired men, some so badly that they had to be transferred away, some liked that and some did not. We at times had to march deep into the desert on this training, about eighty miles inland and back again with as little water as possible. You could not drink it on your own, you had to wait for permission, if you were caught drinking it you were in trouble.

There was an obvious reason why we were here as well, as the German Army were about to attack the world with their mighty Army and Air Force that they had been allowed to develop over the years since the First World War. What was our Intelligence doing to allow this to happen? With our out of date war equipment we had to take this lot on eventually. In the meantime, we had to carry on our training and try and make ourselves as strong an army as possible. We had the right type of man but not I fear the weapons to fight them off, they would walk over us.

In the meantime, some of the N.C.O.s had to attend yet another Cadre Course most especially on weapons, hand to hand fighting and bayonet training etc. From the result of this and many other courses I for one was promoted to a full Corporal.

During our stay here because of my swimming ability I was put in charge the Life Saving Squad, we did a bit of training for this as a team and found that we were quite good at it. This was brought into force because of the drowning of a young sergeant, who was a good swimmer, but he drowned because he had just a part set of false teeth that got jammed in his throat. This happened when a wave hit him in the mouth and dislodged them from his mouth. It was a very unfortunate accident, he was a good N.C.O. as well as a likeable man. As I say, that was the reason for a Life Saving Squad, it came in handy for all. During our duties on this we saved at least five men. The sea there could be very rough and at times there was an under current which could take one out too far. We never did see any hostile fish like sharks, but there were at times some nasty stinging jelly fish about. A few men were treated for that, it left a nasty looking rash on the skin and could even be the cause of drowning. Most of the swimming was done in the nude, there were no civilians about out in the desert so who cared. At one time they sent me and my section down the coast away to a little place called Hamon, all I had was nine men armed with a machine gun, a few cases of hand grenades along with our fifteen cwt truck. We had to guard about a fifty-mile front and keep a watch out that no enemy attempted to land any troops, either German or Italian. What we could do was anyone's guess, we were not very powerful, it was a death and glory affair, but nothing did happen to cause any alarm. We quite enjoyed it there, I used to send one man down in the village each morning to pick up some Arab bread, freshly baked. Oh yes we actually had a baker in that area, there were a few hundred Arabs living there so it was not all that in the wilds. We did a few weeks in this place until I was informed to return to the unit.

I felt that something was in the wind, like a move somewhere. It was soon put over on the radio that we had declared war on Germany once again because of their invasion against Poland, this being about the 9th September. It was not long after that that twenty of us Senior N.C.O.s were called before the C.O. and were told that we were being sent back to England as instructors to form other battalions for the Hampshire Regts, this of course came as a surprise to us, it was going to make this battalion seem weak. Of course, they had that in mind as they were sending out to us here the Regiment's reserves of ex-soldiers, which were mainly N.C.O.s. So we were off back home to train the men being called up to fight this coming war.

We got on a train to Alexander and as we were going along

we stopped at a little station for a while and lo and behold there the reserves were, on that train going to join the battalion, that was well timed. We all poured onto a ship and rushed across the Mediterranean escorted by a small warship from our Navy, unknown to us then we were heading for the Port of Marseille. It was October 1939, the French were informed that we were on the way and they welcomed us with one of their Army Bands, and they played our National Anthem, and one or two other songs like 'Hang out your washing on the Seigfried line', this was the first time that we had heard this song. From the port, we were put onto a railway station and we had the company of some French girls, who were selling refreshments on trays. We gave them a bit of hassle with our usual nonsense, they took it all in good part. The war atmosphere was beginning to show amongst the people.

CHAPTER TWENTY-ONE

At War Training

From Marseille to Cherbourg, here we were met again by the French who greeted us with pleasure. Again there were the girls on the platform trying to serve us, but I think we were a little better behaved this time. Now they put us all on one of our Cross Channel Paddle Boats of all things, but there were more of us N.C.O.s this time, many more were at this port, most likely about three hundred of us. What a capture for the Germans if they only knew, we were all instructors. This was some trial for this old Ferry Boat, they had it going flat out across the Channel and we also had an escort of two of our frigates as well as a submarine so we were told. Well, I guess you could say we were precious cargo. It was really a rush up the Southampton Waters, we landed at one of the docks there, they rushed us through the customs, no problem there. What next we thought? We twenty who had come from the desert (The Hampshire Regiment), were put on the Isle of Wight Ferry and landed at Cowes. We were then taken by truck to Parkhurst Barracks. Most of us had already seen these barracks, we got there in the late evening and as the war was on, all was in blackness, there were no lights on anywhere and we were falling into the ditches and other obstacles. We were not used to this blackout business, but we had to get used to it. We were ushered to a barrack room, where we were given a nice clean bed to sleep in, but were given a meal first. We probably visited our clubs and messes for a pint of English beer and so to bed and had a real good sleep.

Up in the morning, we had to parade and go and see the C.O. for further instructions. It was here that for the first time we saw Army girl soldiers on parade, being drilled by an Army woman

113

sergeant, and to hear her high pitched voice brought a grin to our faces. One of the sergeants in our lot could not prevent himself from mimicking her, this he should not have done as he realised afterwards. The lady Sergeant heard him, so she halted her squad of women soldiers, stood them at ease and walked over smartly to us. 'I know you are a lot of hard bitten soldiers with medals on your chests, but would the person responsible for that mimicking like to come forward and approach me and repeat that. If not I am likely to make a report about this to my Company Commander. I will accept an apology if he is man enough to do that.' The Sergeant responsible said, 'Oh yes darling, here I am, what shall we talk about?' She said,'I did not care for your remarks whilst I was drilling my Squad, unless you apologise I will report you to my C.C.' He made no immediate apologies to her right then, so she did what she threatened and he had to appear before her C.C. and was reprimanded for his misconduct and made to apologise to her in front of him. It was only right and proper that he should do so, I guess it taught him a lesson and he would not behave in such a bad way again.

In a few more days when they had sorted us out, we were once again on the move, down to the Port of Cowes and on another ferry heading for the town of Southampton. Then, on to Blighmont Barracks which was a Territorial Units H.Q. the boys that we used to call weekend soldiers, but this attitude towards them soon changed as we got to know them, they all played an excellent part for their country during the war. One of those soldiers who became a sergeant with me was a friend of mine for many years and still is today, 1994. I often see him and his darling wife Betty where they live down in Hythe, just outside Southampton. He got himself captured when we landed in North Africa, not his fault, but a mix up in higher orders, someone got it all wrong and he and a few others were rounded up by the German Troops. This barrack was where we first met, we were both full Corporals at that time and got on well together. I may mention him at times, his name is Norman Bryant, I have a photograph of him and I together. He thought he could run until he met me! We have some very pleasant memories of our service.

During our short stay here we managed to get hold of three boards each and lay them on a wooden trestle along with a palliasse, a kind of a mattress, filled with straw, not too bad to sleep on for a while.

We hung around for a while, waiting for the powers that be to sort us out as to where we were to be sent to train these new call up men so that we could then form another battalion. One morning we were told that we were to be put through our paces by an R.S.M. being posted to us from the Coldstream Guards, they used to do that in those days, because they thought that they were the cream of the British Army. His name I must mention, Tom, yes Tom Barnett, he had the nickname of Bismarck, named after that German Battleship. I suppose he got that name because of his bark and appearance, also we thought he looked like a German with his close shaven head, but his bark was not worse than his bite, once you got to know him. He was a disciplinarian and helped to mould this battalion into good shape, bless him. So Tom had us on parade, I guess to see what we were like on drill as well as us giving out our drill commands. We all thought that we did well, there was many a time that I had to take squads of men on drill, so I think I shone a bit in his eyes. I was also sent on a Drill Course to his Regiment in London under the Drill Instruction of a well known R.S.M. called Britain, he was a man about 6' 3" and pretty wide around the girth. When we were in the mess, two of us could get into his Sam Brown you can guess he was fairly wide. I hope to remember to talk about him later on in this story, but I'm trying to keep this in some order.

Back to Tom Barnett for a while, I can say a few things about him now that we are no longer in the army and I'm sure that they are harmless words, the fact is that as I have said before, he put this battalion into good shape. He would check nearly everyone if he could see a fault like walking about in a sloppy way, hands in your pockets, hat not on correctly, an improper salute, even a young Officer who failed to acknowledge a salute

Out into civilian life, about 1956.
Myself and Norman Bryant – friends for life.

from a lower rank. We were taught to salute the King's Commission not so much the man, and they should acknowledge that salute, why not? So they should. So much for Tom Barnett, he was still with the battalion when I left, because I became a casualty which led to my final discharge on medical grounds.

I had to grin one time when a private's wife saw him one day and said to him, 'How are you Mr Bismarck?' 'What did you say?' he said. 'Well I thought that was your name.' Nothing more was said on that subject.

Most of us were eventually sent off to a village or small town by the name of Shepton Mallet. I had never heard of it before, it must have been early in January 1940 when they sent us there, we got off at the station and marched down very smartly through the town so as to give the locals the impression that we knew our business, not that they would have noticed if they were non military. We halted outside the Bunch of Grapes pub at the lower end of the town, my company which then was B Company was situated opposite Frizbys Shoe Shop, little did I know that a little later on I was to marry one of the girl assistants in that shop. Her name was Audrey Richardson and she was only about fifteen years old then. She later on reckoned that I kidnapped her, I must have been just twenty-four then and a Corporal. I think I'll say a few words about Audrey and how I came to meet her.

Curly and I decided to have a bit of an evening out and one of the pubs that we visited was the Hare and Hounds. On the way out about 09.00 hrs, coming out of the main entrance, I bumped into someone because of the blackout and it happened to be a couple of young ladies. I made my apologies to her, I can't remember what her answer was to that, but I did get a bit of a look at her and then went on our way. Come Sunday morning I was standing on the corner by the Conservative Club and a couple of girls came along and it just so happened that we both recognised each other. She was with her girlfriend, Nancy Trippick, so I went over to them and had a few words with them. Before we knew what was we were all off for a walk together, for obvious reasons I latched onto Audrey. What was the reason? Normal reasons I suppose, I found her very attractive, a young healthy country girl and in no time at all I was obviously in love with her and she with me. From then on we saw one another quite a lot, I have to admit my first love affair. It was not long before I met her parents who lived down in Zion Hill in the smallest cottage that I have ever seen. I had not had much experience of country cottages, being born in the city of Southampton. Knowing her made my life much more interesting, I was a little older then her, a matter of eight years, but that is not much as one gets older, this was early 1940 so after a couple of years, in January 1942 we both decided to get

Sergeant Douglas French and Sergeant Norman Bryant.
Taken at Wateringbury, Nr. Maidstone, Kent, 1941.

married. She was eighteen years old and I twenty-six. She was now married to a Sergeant in the Hampshire Regiment, so I guess it changed her life a bit. I ended up billeted in their cottage for a while, as and when I could get away from my job as an instructor, but you can guess, I managed as much time as possible.

I must remember my friend and adviser Jock Barfoot, he came along with us, he was also my best man at our wedding. As I said he did advise me on a lot of things regarding soldiering as he was a little older and was in the army long before me, he was the one I met in Pindi in 1936. I was Battalion orderly

*Audrey and Douglas when courting. Taken at 36 Zion Hill,
Shepton Mallet, 1940. You could wear civilians at times.*

Corporal and he was just returning from his leave in England,
we more or less got to know one another from then onwards. I
was later his Lance Sergeant and he was my Platoon Sergeant.
Norman Bryant was sent here as well, Joe pinnegar, Rougee
West and Ted Payne, the Corporal in the signals. He also
married another girl from this town and is still here. I only wish
that I had kept a diary, then I would have better details of the
things that went on during the war. Some people did and got
away with it, but we were not supposed to do that, it was really
a matter of security.

I used to have a private who did look out for me, in respect of
seeing if my girlfriend was about, if so he would let me know,
he seemed very keen to help me in this respect. We were
billeted in the hall at the rear of the Conservative Club, the
room overlooked the road opposite the cinema. When parades
were finished I would be taking off my side arms and he would

notice that movement and he knew what was to be my next move. He would look out of the window towards the crossroads and see if she was there, if so he would let me know. I can't even remember his name, not so important in any case it was just one of these little things that occurred, although it was important to me.

The time came for us to get to the railway station and meet the call up men. Of course, they came from all walks of life, most of them were around my age, some a little younger, not many older but a few. All these were interviewed to find out their qualifications because there may have been some there with University Degrees and could therefore be applicable for the Commissioned Rank if they wanted. I only had one, after a short while he left and I never did see him again. It was a strange position to be in as an Instructor, I mean, to take on men who in most cases had no previous military service, although we may have known our weapons and drill it still had to be put over so that it all made sense. We at times used to get some senior Sergeants come around with an Officer to listen to us to see how we were coping. Whether they were qualified I don't know, but I should think so, they did not stay long. After a few weeks I was promoted to a Lance Sergeant and so had to move out of this room as I was then entitled to a room on my own or even a room in some hotel with the Platoon Officer, as we worked close together, we had an extra allowance to cover this. I did give them a pep talk about life in the Army, the rules and regulations that affected them in our every day life, who to salute and who to stand to attention to, the usual discipline that we had to enforce.

We did have a discussion about the war and why we were about to take part in it, they were aware as to why we were in this man's Army, there just seemed to be just two choices for us, either kill or destroy the Nazis whose intention was to dominate the world and to destroy some of the nations such as the Jews. If we took the other view the Government would lock us up for the duration of the war and probably be disliked for the rest of our life. There were special cases we know of people who would not kill, who at that time were not accepted by most, but the ordinary person of, say a high rank, was not qualified to say if they were genuine or not. It really needs a psychologist to analyse that person, we as just soldiers were not the people to decide as to who was genuine or not. I did have a young soldier at one time that I had a problem with, in the end I persuaded the Company Commander to transfer him to a Non-Combat Unit. I was pretty sure that it really hurt him to have to destroy anyone, no matter how bad that person was. It came about when I had to take him on extra bayonet fighting, he just would not, or could not even stick a bayonet into a sack of straw, he was in tears, and how can a man produce tears for nothing. It just hurt his feelings, I did ask him when he was called up for service if he made that point about not wanting to fight, he said,'No I did not think of it at that time, but since going through all this training to kill, it has been bothering me. It's not the noise of the battle that bothers me, but the actual killing.' I said, 'Right I'll see what I can do for you. I'll recommend that they send you to a Non-Combat Unit, like the Army Service Corp.' I dismissed him.

The next morning, I spoke to the Company Commander, he said he wanted to find out from me the results of my training him and talking to him. So that was what I gave him, that I was convinced that he was genuine and suggested that he would be more suitable to a Non-Combat Unit, so he said 'I'll bear your words in mind when I see him.' I did not see that man again, as he left us to join another unit. It's a subject that one can spend many hours talking about, the rights and the wrongs, I suppose it's a subject that is best left alone, everyone has their own opinion. They asked me many questions that I was not able to answer, like about the German Army, all I could say was, 'The proof of the pudding is in the eating. They are obtaining all their objectives with ease there was no one or nothing to stop them for the simple reason that they have been allowed to build up a powerful Army, Navy and Airforce, right under our noses, whilst we have been out sunbathing. They are going to take some defeating but we need the manpower as well as good weapons. At the moment our aircraft are tied up with bits of string, our weapons have not changed much since the First World War. So, someone has to get us all moving.' That was when our Mr Churchill came into power.

I must say a few words about myself at this time, as I have said I had just been promoted to a Lance Sergeant and to us as youngsters and full of ambition it was a good step forward. I had only been a full Corporal for about six months, only just about got paid for it. Being a member of the Sergeants Mess is something of a change, one had to learn mess ethics, like not walking into the mess with your hat on, or wearing side arms, or sitting down to a meal without your R.S.M. first, or if he was absent the next Senior Warrant Officer, mess dinners and the passing of the wine at the table and many other minor things. If you were not careful you could end up buying drinks all round, you were now a Junior Commander or as they say 'the back bone of the Regiment'. Some would have a different opinion now. There are a few others that were promoted at about the same time, like Curly Andrews, Norman Bryant and others who do not come to mind but, I should think nearly all those that came over with us. I must not forget Tank Mash, he was also made a Lance Sergeant. When I got married we were invited to stay at his Mother's house for our honeymoon down in Winton, Bournemouth, which was nice of them. We did not have much money in those days, so that was a help.

So much for promotions, let's get on with this training in my platoon, all new men, all thirty-three of them, to them the training was hard. We first of all had to get them fit, so that was marching, physical training, running, bayonet fighting and even boxing for some of us. Some of the marching was carried out with full fighting order including their weapons, this went on for quite a few months.

The first long march was from Shepton Mallet to Warminster, we had to go there to carry out further training on a mock up building of the Siegfried Line, it was supposed to have been an impregnable defence position in Germany, we carried out this in case we were sent out there to attack it but it never did come off. I think it was taken by the paratroops in the end, making it an easier task, so say us who did not take part.

At Warminster, I was lucky enough to be billeted in the Anchor Hotel, right in the middle of the town, just the comfort that I like. My platoon had a club room opposite, down a side road, they were comfortable enough. We continued our training here and after about two weeks we returned to Shepton Mallet to finish off. Not long after returning we all had to take another journey, this time by trucks to Tidworth to give them some firing practice, both on the rifle and the machine gun. I'm sure that they all enjoyed that, they had so much practice firing at nothing, but being taught the rules of aiming. When we left they were all full of their own skill, accuracy and the feel of the rifle. Some were looking forward to the next time on a range, so after a while at this place, we returned once again to Shepton Mallet.

Then came the sad news that we were about to leave this town and leave our wives behind, although I was not yet married, that came later when we moved to Doddington in Kent. We were now off to a place called Royston in Hertfordshire. I was sent on in advance as a Billeting officer, I had to be accompanied by a civilian policeman and had to find suitable accommodation for our troops. I found some huts for one company on some open ground, and then some stables and farm land very near the town. I had one of the small stables for my bunk, there were others for the remaining senior N.C.O.s. I found some pig sties there which had a good clean over, they were scrubbed out and whitewashed and made fit enough for soldiers to live in. The stable that I had, had at one time belonged to Gordon Miller the one time famous jockey. I think his horse that won the Derby that year was called Golden Miller, I hope I'm correct on that point. It was at this place that I was given a temporary job for a while as Company Sergeant Major, only acting, not promoted.

It was at about this time that General Montgomery had take over our Corp No. 10, I think, 46 Division and at this town he decided that on one day a week everyone from the Rank of

Major had to double everywhere that we went. I guess it caught a few out like the fat ones, they did not last long in the Infantry or Commandos. Some Senior Officers tried to get out of it, or were told to lose weight very quickly, some could not so were transferred. It certainly sorted out the unfit ones.

I can also remember the General had to sort out some R.A.F. as well in some respect, according to him they needed some drill and some strenuous exercise, not too far from us, but I don't think I will go into that, it might upset some R.A.F. boys. They were doing a good job at Bassingbourne Aerodrome, the Wellington Bomber Men.

From this town I was sent to Regents Park Barracks attached to the Coldstream Guards on a Drill Course under the then famous R.S.M. Britain, he was well known.

When we arrived there about forty of us, all senior N.C.O.s and Warrant Officers, we were given accommodation in the barrack rooms like the soldiers, as there were not sufficient bunks for us to sleep separately. In a way, we were treated just like we were recruits, each of us given jobs to do in the room, like a room orderly. This did not suit some of them, one Sergeant Major absolutely refused to accept this, he was reprimanded by the R.S.M. for refusing and so was returned to his unit without completing his course.

On the very first morning as we were all coming down the barrack steps that led to the barrack square, the R.S.M. shouted out, 'That Sergeant with the medals up, come over here at the double.' Well, there were more than one of us with a few medals up, so we were looking at one another trying to find out which one. It appeared that it was me he wanted, so I walked over to him smartly, did not double, that annoyed him straight away. When I got to him he said, 'Sergeant, when I say double I mean it so do it next time, do you hear?' I couldn't help but hear what he said, you could probably hear it a mile away. 'What I wanted from you Sergeant is this, those ribbons that you have on your chest, at your age are you entitled to them?' I nearly said, 'Well would I be wearing them if I was not entitled to them?' But thought better of it, I merely said, 'Yes sir, I was on the North West Frontier of India and the Campaign in Palestine.' 'Right,' he said, 'I'll check, fall out and join the others in quick time.' So off I went, they all wanted to know what all that was about, so I told them, 'Bloody cheek!' someone said. We carried on our course for a few days, when he called me over to him once again. 'Sergeant,' he said 'You must accept my apologies, you are entitled to those medals. The reason I checked was because I had a Senior N.C.O. at one time here who was not entitled.' I really did not care for being checked like this, as I would not wear false decoration but I had to let it pass.

The course continued, we had to visit the barracks next to the Palace called Wellington I think. We had to drill a special squad of men who were instructed to make errors during their drill and you had to spot them, or you were for it. Also, we had to take a turn at mounting the Guard at the Palace which was quite an experience also, St. James' Palace. This continued for about two weeks and once again back to Royston, we were there for about three months. In our spare time some of us were asked to help train the Home Guard as we really expected that we would be invaded by the Germany Army the way things were going. We did this in the early evenings, I quite enjoyed it really, some had already been in the army and were too old for war, but young enough to do this job in an emergency. They would have given a good account of themselves when needed.

CHAPTER TWENTY-TWO

Garden of England

We were then off to Kent, where we stayed for a much longer time. There was a good reason for this I guess, as we thought that this area was the most likely place for the German Army to land, the shortest route from the French coast. We were there to prepare the coast defences for their invasion which was very likely, the way their success was going. We were training more than ever here, as I have already said, this included the Home Guard because every man who was capable was needed. Little did they realise that they had to deal with our Air Force which was now being built in great haste, both in this country and America. For a while we were used to help protect Manston Aerodrome, this was a set off point for our Spitfires, which were kept very busy having dog fights with the German fighters. They may have been just as fast as ours, but ours seemed to have a better manoeuvrability and some special skills in bringing them down. I know that we lost a lot of good young men in that business, but they saved the situation for us. The Germans thought twice about sending over an invasion force. We were aware that they did try to make some effort, but the R.A.F. discovered some movement of their invasion barges and made a mess of them, so because of this they thought it was unwise to make another attempt. We witnessed quite a lot of dog fights over Kent and the English Channel, the Spitfires when they shot down an M.E.109 used to come in and do a victory roll, which was eventually stopped, as one pilot came in doing that one day and was too low. For his effort, he lost us a good pilot so that was put a stop to. These M.E.s flew over our camp a few times but they were too quick for our Bren Guard Sentry to give him time to recognise the aircraft. We lost another chance to shoot one down, not their fault really, because they flew in so low over the ground and disappeared too quickly for him to get an aim.

I remember that at Manston we had an unfortunate attack by their bombers one night. The girls, quite a number of our R.A.F. girls, were killed, somehow or other the German pilots heard about this and sent over an apology to the C.O. of the camp, they said it was foolish of them to have their girls sleeping so near the danger area. It could have made sense. These girls were not fighters, all they had to do was administration work, helpful work, no doubt. What they did about that I don't know. We continued doing many mock battles in and around this area for a long time, we always seemed to be moving a lot. Maybe it was to outwit the enemy as to our whereabouts. Our Company moved to a small place called Plucks Gutter, alongside a river. This we used for training, crossing over with nearly a full kit on our backs. You really had to be a strong swimmer, we nearly lost one of my platoon. He went down with all his kit on, but as the Brigadier was watching this crossing he smartly jumped in and pulled him into the bank, good for him. This type of exercise was never used by us during the war, but we knew how to do it if it was necessary. Then we had another place called Sarr Bridge, it was here that I was an acting Platoon Commander once again, my officers seem to disappear a lot. If I had only realised it when this happened. I am sure that I was on some sort of observation to see if I would make the grade of an officer, but, I seemed rather slow on the uptake. Where else? Yes, we were at St. Nicholas at Wade for Christmas 1942, we managed to have a good Mess Dinner at the Village Hall, I have a couple of photographs taken at this place.

Another posting was at Sittingbourne, also Margate where we had to dig up the front lawns and put in gun emplacements. This rather annoyed the Lord Mayor, making a mess of his seaside front lawns. A lot of invasion preparations were carried out in this area, as it was a good place for the enemy to land on a nice sandy beach and was flat as well. The people of Kent saw

Fifth Battalion Royal Hampshire Regiment, Village Hall, St. Nicholas Wade, Kent. Sergeants Mess Members, Christmas, 1940.

a lot of the Hampshire Regiment in those days, most likely a lot of our men married their girls, but they lost some of them which was unfortunate for them.

Then we were off again, this time to London, no riding in trucks as yet. We marched a very long way, to make us fitter. We got as far as Rainham before we were picked up by army vehicles, ending up at Leytonstone. The nearest pub was the Green Man, many people know of that place, we were billeted in a Girls Grammar School and were very comfortable there. I was lucky as I managed to get my wife up for a while, that was nice. We even managed to get to a Sergeant's Mess Dinner and Dance, I'm sure she enjoyed that. We used Epping Forest a lot for training and I was once again used in the evenings to help train the Home Guard, mainly this time, down at Dagenham Docks (Ford Company), they enjoyed it as well as ourselves.

There were also one or two villages that got us to train them around this area.

I must not forget the village of Doddington, it was here that I left for a while to marry Audrey. That was some occasion for us two, it happened on January the 7th 1942. My best man was my friend Jock Barfitt. We were in the same platoon together for a while after our wedding. As I have said before I was called back during our honeymoon, to get back to Doddington as soon as possible. I took my young wife with me and found some place to stay, with the help of Rita Plucknett (the wife of Jack Plucknett our Company Barber). When I reported to my Company Commander Major Darling, he said, 'I'm sorry to have sent for you, but we were for a while earmarked to carry out that raid in Dieppe. At the last moment it was cancelled.' A good job too because that was some hard task. Many good Canadians were lost on that raid. It was a bit of a flop they say, but something was learnt of the German defences, so not entirely a waste of time. He said to me, 'You can carry on and finish your honeymoon around here some place.' That is what we did. By the way I must say that Rita and Jack Plucknett after the war settled down in Newport, Isle of Wight and had their own hairdressing business, so they did well for themselves, they are now retired. I do see Jack sometimes at Southampton at our all Ranks Dinner Party.

Having left this village of Doddington, Kent and finished our tour of duty in the London area, they moved us down to Fleet in Hampshire. I could feel that we were getting near to the date of real action, this town was not far from Aldershot Station. Although we had not yet been told. I could only think that the nearest battle area now would be out in North Africa.

Here we were at Fleet, the people had to put up with us for a while. We also had some Canadians stationed there so the place was flooded with troops. We unfortunately had a bit of trouble with a few of them one evening. It just so happened that our boxing team had been away boxing another regiment and we were in a certain hotel having a celebration when one of the lads came in and reported that our boys were having a bit of a dust up with them. They had all been drinking and someone had started an argument about some subject or other, would we join in and clear them out? Well this was an awkward situation for us as we did not like to use our skills for this sort of thing, but some went in and more or less calmed the situation down a bit just by using their ranks. Unfortunately some of them did not want it that way and just wanted to fight and one of them took on one of our boxers and came worse off and was sent to hospital. The result of this was that the Canadians were confined to their camp for the period that we were there, which was not very long. We didn't wish to fight our own troops, it was just not right, but that was the sort of things that happened when you get fighting men together, they even fight each other so it was nothing fresh.

The time was now coming close for us to have to go into action, we all had that feeling, so where it was possible we all tried to get in a final weekend with our wives. I for one had not as yet been married one year and it was a terrible wrench to have to leave our loved ones, in our minds we might not ever see them again. I was off down to see Audrey, thinking it was the last time, but I did manage to get her to come up and see me once more. I really should not have sent for her, her trip was a bit hazardous coming up on the train with all those troops. It must have been quite an experience for her at that age. It was easier for her I guess because she was in uniform of the Fire Service. There was very little room on the train and she said that some soldier offered her his lap, which she took, so the soldier was lucky. All was well, she said, 'I told them that I was on my way to see my husband at Fleet.' They asked 'What Regiment was he in so she said 'The Hampshire Regiment'. 'Oh that's our Regiment as well. Do we know him?' they said. 'I dare say, it's Sergeant French.' 'Oh yes, we know him.' Maybe they took more care of her then, anyhow they helped her to find me on arrival. I was asleep in my billet when someone came in shouting for Sergeant French. 'That's me,' I said 'Who is that and what is the problem?' 'Well Sergeant the problem is that your wife is here and wants you,' I was told. I was up in no time and went to her and then with the help of a friend of mine, Sergeant Patten I think it was, he found me a room where he was already staying. I was in luck, or I should say we were in luck, it was here in Fleet that I spent a heavenly night with my young wife. Funny thing is John was born just nine months after, I wonder what happened?

Now to the date which stands out in my mind. It happened to be our Wedding Anniversary, just one year's marriage, we set off on this date. It was a rather noisy send off as well, about 2 o'clock in the morning. I can tell you I was even thinking of Audrey as we were packing up and getting my platoon moving to get on parade fully dressed ready to march to Aldershot Station. In a way it was a good job that I had a lot on my mind to take it off thinking of her, it was a terrible wrench. I was wondering at the time how she got on in the morning return to Shepton Mallet, I know I was not the only one who had this problem.

As I said, we set off early morning with much noise, someone even found a bugle to blow going along the road. The people in their houses were leaning out of their bedroom windows shouting at us 'Good luck boys, give 'em hell and come back safe!'

On arrival at the station, you can imagine the organisation there with the Military Police out in full force, keeping unwanted people away and taking charge of the movement of military vehicles. There seemed to be thousands of us there, young men going to war, hardly started living their lives yet and now about to lose it to fight for their country. I can imagine what was going through their minds, an experience never to be repeated again in our lives. To most we were off into the unknown, I've got to admit some made a good guess where they were bound for. It was pretty obvious I suppose if you had been following the war.

It did not seem long before we came to a stop at a station, it was Glasgow, so we were in Scotland, but where to next? The train continued on its way and we finally arrived in pitch darkness at Greenock, then onto a ship and we had to sort where we were to sleep. That was soon arranged, most ranks, corporals and below were swinging in hammocks, sergeants and officers were in bunks. Greenock was sheltered from any surprise attack, whoever though that out, it was good thinking. There was some armada in this bay I can tell you, not forgetting the Royal Navy escort, who would be with us all the way to wherever we were bound for.

We had one instance where one soldier decided he did not want to go, so despite the cold water in January, he jumped overboard and swam ashore which must have been a good half a mile. He was picked up by the Military Police and returned to our ship. I had to deal with him on instructions from my Company Commander, I must say it took some guts to swim in that cold water. He returned wrapped up in a blanket, but he had to be put under arrest, he was absolutely saturated and shivering. He was given warm clothes by the Quarter master and had a good rub down, given a meal and placed in a ship's cell. It was up to me to decide what to do with him, it was left in my hands. I left him in the cell for a while to give him time to think about himself and what he had just done. There was a sentry outside his cell, I told him that he wouldn't be there very long, I would be dealing with him. I did not care for the job but orders are orders. After leaving him a while to think things over I went down to see him.

I said to the sentry, 'Open the door and just stand outside whilst I talk to him.' To the soldier, 'You know that you have been the cause of a lot of trouble haven't you? What made you think that you could get away with this? An attempted desertion, you are lucky that it is left in my hands to deal with you. What you did was very stupid, you could have killed yourself in the attempt. What was your reason for this action?'

'I guess I had a lot on my mind, sarge, my main reason was that I did not want to leave my young wife. I've only been married a few weeks and I left her crying her eyes out, I could not stand the thought of leaving her and I wanted to get back to her,' he said.

'Look,' I said 'How old do you think I am? About the same age as you I dare say.'

Yes,' he said, 'I dare say you are, yes.' 'There are many more on these ships who are the same age, all young men leaving their young wives. None of us like the thought of leaving them behind but we have to, it's our job at the moment. I've only been married one year and I feel the same as you. What if we all attempted to do what you did? You know the answer to that question don't you? I am going to leave you here for a while to give you time to give me an answer to this – what is your intention for the future? Are you going to attempt this sort of action again? Like desert in front of the enemy. Your answer will decide what I am going to do for you, or to you. So think about it.'

I then left him for a while to do something else. After a couple of hours I returned to him once again to finalise this problem. I had it in mind to release him, after all we were all going into action and this was of very little importance now. He had probably had enough of it in any case, he would prefer to return to his mates and talk to them about it. So I said to him 'What are your thoughts on the matter now? Do you intend to make another attempt later on? Or, do you consider it unwise?' He was looking sorry for himself, I can tell you. 'Well, sarge,' he said, 'what are you going to do with me then?"

'I have already said, it all depends on what you say to me, have you dropped the idea of trying it again later on in some other place?' I said.

'I think so, sarge,' he said. 'Especially after your remarks about our young wives, leaving them behind and also that I am not the only one going through the same misery of leaving them behind.'

'Well if that's clear in your mind, I'm letting you return to your platoon and just hope that you do not repeat this action any more, as it will certainly get you into trouble, especially if you do it again during your duty in the line,' I said. He went back feeling a lot better after our talk and as far as I know, there was no more trouble from him. In fact, I lost trace of him after that, I reported to my Company commander as to what action I had taken, and he was in agreement so the matter was closed.

The journey was pretty rough, very high seas and the ship was rolling so badly that most of us were sea sick. But at least having rough seas would keep the German subs at a safe distance, not easy for them with a target that kept disappearing under the waves. Come breakfast time after a good night's sleep, I made my way down to the Sergeants' Mess for breakfast, out of about fifty of us as far as I can remember, there were two turned up. The other one was my faithful friend Curly Andrews, we had to have a joke about that. We were lucky enough not to get sea sickness (touch wood!), but I did a rotten thing to one of my other sergeant friends, Sergeant Joe Pinnegar, who was up in his bunk feeling a bit sick. He did not want any breakfast either, but I took him a nice smelling kipper, holding it by its tail and dangled it in front of his nose. If he had been well enough, he would have strangled me. A lot of the men below who were sleeping in hammocks had to be brought up into the fresh air to help get them over this sickness, Medical Officer's orders. On reaching the top deck, we asked one of the crew where we were and he said in the Atlantic and heading towards America, taking that route to try and fox the German U boats. I doubt if that was necessary because of the high seas.

Eventually we changed course and entered the Med leaving the Rock of Gibraltar on our left, and of all ships to break down, it had to be ours. There we were stranded in this open sea, a target for the enemy and left all by ourselves. That was the order then, if any of us broke down, we had to fend for ourselves, so I guess the engineers down below were hard at work to get it going once again. We must have been floundering around for a good hour, thinking that we might get a torpedo into our side, but, as I have said the sea was on our side this time. Suddenly we felt the engines throbbing and we were once again on our way. By now, we were aware that our destination was Africa, North of course, but all of us on this ship or nearly all, were not required for action as yet. We were mainly reserve troops, reasons why we were not wanted as yet I don't know. I knew the reason why I could not go into action yet was because I had my arm still in plaster as I broke it back in England, when practising for the high jump for Regimental Sports. I could consider myself lucky for a while, as far as I knew the rest of these troops would not have long before going into action.

CHAPTER TWENTY-THREE

Contact with German Soldiers

We were now at the port of Algiers, just about the busiest port out in this area, full of troops and war equipment. Whilst we were disembarking there was an air alert, so we had to get off very quickly. A few bombs were hitting the port, but not too close to us, they chose some other area a few hundred yards to our right. We had to fall in on the road carrying all our kit and march on the main road heading for a place called Fort de Lieu. The march must have been about twelve miles. This was a transit camp, already full of troops, so about 500 of us settled down in tents, which were already up and well organised. These were all under trees and very near the coast, so it was very convenient for a swim, which we had later on.

The rest of the division had been transferred to Navy vessels and were about to land at a place called Bone, I heard about this a little later on. They went into action there and they say that they did not meet much opposition, not until they moved in a bit then they met the German Army and it became a bit stiffer. Whilst they were at this, we were miles away at a safe distance.

There was an assortment of troops here, some fresh ready to go into action and some that had already been into action and had some minor wounds and some with other forms of sickness. During my stay here I was not idle, I had to take various troops on weapons instructions, like the P.I.A.T. weapon which meant Personal Infantry Anti Tank Weapon, it was new to us all. The Adjutant called me in his Office and gave me a manual on the weapon and said, 'Sarge, here is this new weapon, read and learn all about it and take some Junior Officers and Warrant Officers on it in the morning. Teach as many as you can in the week, don't worry, they don't know anything about it, only you will know.' I spent a few hours going through this book with a couple of other Sergeants and I think we learned a bit about it, enough to show them what it was all about and how it worked. Come morning, we got cracking and told them all we knew, we made a few blunders, but as I said it was a new weapon so we all learned as we went along and all went well. By the way, I had Joe Pinnegar with me at this camp, can't remember why he was here with me, unless it was his malaria trouble that I think he suffered with at times.

One morning we woke up to be informed that myself, Sergeant Pinnegar and some other sergeant from a different regiment with a captain were being sent way down to Morocco to train the Free French Troops in the use of our weapons. As you may know, they were pushed out of their own country by the German Army and they were scattered about quite a bit. This lot that we were going to train had joined up with their own French Foreign Legion. I know that they didn't like the idea of us having to train them, but the order came from their higher ups and they had no alternative, as they had lost all their weapons. Some were even in our uniforms, but most of them settled for the idea and we got on well together. Language was the problem with us, my part of it, I only learnt the basic French at school, like objects but very little conversation. The other sergeants were worse off than myself, they had no knowledge at all, I'm not sure what the captain had, hardly even saw him, so I guess he was busy with some of the French Officers.

Our accommodation was a small stone built hut, plenty of room for just us three, comfortable enough, good ablutions etc. We had to have a guard on us at night, this was carried out by regular French Troops. The reason behind this was because there was such a mixture of foreign men in the Foreign Legion that they were not to be trusted. They had political reasons some of them to try and kill us, yes this was true and we were warned about it and to keep alert as regards to our own security. We had two sentries on guard all through the night armed with machine guns. I can tell you they were a rough lot, kill their own grandmother for a pint of beer, some of them. This is a short list of some of them, English, Scots, Arabs, Germans, Greek, Italians, Polish, Welsh and Americans, they just about covered the world in races. They must have started out young, living a hard life, some had a taste of prison and some escaped prison. But, you put them into action against the Germans, well even the Germans feared them, very little mercy and took no prisoners. The discipline was hard to put over to them, they would obey the officers and sergeants in a slap happy way, they knew if they didn't they could be shot.

The first morning that we had them on parade we decided together that to introduce them to us nicely would be to have a bit of a tough mobility march, in what we called clean fatigue. That is no wearing of equipment or taking of weapons with us and carrying no water. The temperature out there in the Morocco Desert was about 120 degrees Fahrenheit at midday. I was delegated to get them on parade, bring them to attention and set them off at quick march, it sounded like this:

To bring them to attention – Garravold

To stand them at ease – Repoe

To set off at the double – Parr Gymnastic March.

The spelling must be wrong, but it sounded like that, it's some time ago. The march and doubling was for about ten miles. We of course had to do it with them, you can't tell them to do something like that and not do it yourself, you have to set an example. There did not seem to be any complaints, but I was getting a few hard looks from some of them. All this took place at 06.30 hrs before we even had breakfast, so it was straight in and under a shower, have their breakfast, which was a hearty one because their next and last meal of the day was at about 20.00 hrs and lasted about two hours, tell you more about that in a while.

The next parade was in my thoughts because of my lack of knowledge in French of the names of weapons in their language. I made an attempt at it but was not getting anywhere, it was lucky for me that a voice in the background stepped forward and said, 'Sarge, if you don't mind me saying so your knowledge of French stinks.' I said, 'Yes I agree.' He was an Englishman who was a Sergeant in their Legion. 'So would you come forward so that we can discuss this problem, it seems that you are just the man that I require during our short stay here with you. You can interpret as I go along,' I said to him. So that is how we managed, Joe and the other sergeant were demonstrators mainly, but as the days went by we managed to pick up a lot more French words in relation to the instructions.

The sergeants in this army used to eat in the Officers Mess, as they did not possess such a thing as a Sergeants Mess, but at times we were invited out to various other Mess Halls, as they seemed to eat in groups of races that they got along with. By the way the whole of this army here was called 'The Free French Army' and was attached to the 'French Foreign Legion', as tough a bunch of men as one could ever get.

In addition to us teaching them the use of our weapons, we also built with their help an assault course, the same as we had back in England. This was to make them even tougher, things like climbing up ropes, jumping and climbing over high wooden walls, crawling under barbed wire and firing live ammunition near them so that they could get used to the sound of bullets. We threw bakelite hand grenades at them, they did not hurt anyone, these were just demoralisers. They had a ramp to run up and at the end of it was a twelve foot jump to the ground. They had to do this in fighting order with their rifle bayonets fixed at the high port and jump to the ground with this, keeping it all together. One French man did this and broke his ankle, he was real mad about that. He got up most awkwardly and attempted to lunge at me with his bayonet as he was in a bit of a temper. For that attempt at sticking me, he was placed under arrest and I never did see him again. I don't know what happened to him, probably let loose when we returned to our Units, I don't think he liked me or us very much.

The time came for me to take off the plaster from my right arm, so you can imagine that this arm being covered up for so long was pretty white compared with my left arm. I had to get back some strength in it so that when I returned to the transit camp, I would be rejoining my battalion. But for now, I must tell you a bit more about our stay here.

As I was saying we at times were invited to one or the other's hut for an evening meal as well as entertainment. This particular evening as I was the guest, we sat down to this huge meal, one long table with about 40 men, the table packed with food. There was a whole goat, apart from being skinned it looked as if it was just lying down and it had an apple in its mouth, even the eyes were still in its head. It smelt alright, but I can tell you I did not eat any of it, the simple reason being, as a guest, I was offered the eyes first as a delicacy and a privilege. I was immediately a vegetarian, that surprised the man who made me the offer, so he just grinned and popped them into his mouth like a bullseye sweet. But I did not go hungry, there were plenty of vegetables as well as other things, also much too much wine. It was quite a spread, considering that there was a war on. Their system of obtaining food was by collecting money and going to the local market and buying it fresh, except the goats and sheep, they were taken from the stock on the camp. These people were very heavy drinkers, much more so than our army, maybe it was the heat of the desert. They got Joe pretty drunk, so much so that I had to give him a fireman's lift back to his room and he never did remember me doing that. I think the wine made him ill for a few days, so from thereon he was more careful. The entertainment during the evening was singing and some arm wrestling, not many soft games, like Blind Man's Bluff. It would go on to the early hours of the morning, but we did not stay on with them, it could get out of hand, we were English and supposed to be better behaved.

I was invited out one evening by one of the French Officers, he took me to his Mother's home in some nearby town, I stayed there for an evening and enjoyed their company, it made a change to be with some civilised people.

The time came for us to go back again and settle down to a few duties in this camp. We were out one day with some of the men here and during the time that we were out, our tents were raided by some local thieves which in this case, were young Arab boys in their teens. I suggested a plan to try and catch them, that I should lie in wait behind some kit bags and as soon as I saw anyone entering the tent, jump on them. It might be a long wait, but we could but have a go and put a stop to it. Next morning, when everyone had moved out of the camp, I sat behind some sort of cover, knowing that there was only one side of the tent that they could get in, fairly easy. I was not going to stay there very long, and I was pretty sure that the young thieves were watching us through the trees waiting for us to move out, and my patience was rewarded. I soon saw a boy trying to grab some article which was not too easy for him to reach, it meant that he had to get half of his body under the flies, that was when I jumped at him. He was as quick as I was, but in his haste to get out of my way he tripped over the tent's guide ropes, so by the time I got out of the tent he was not too far out of my reach. He was not aware that I could run so fast, so I had him in no time. He was a lad about seventeen years old, an Arab lad who now looked frightened to death. I was told if I caught anyone to bring him along to H.Q. and they would deal with him. I did hang about for a while to see what happened. All he did when he came out was to hand him over to the Regimental Police and then whilst the police held him, he put the boot into him, which to me was the wrong attitude, kicking them would only make them worse. He could see that I was not so pleased about that, but he said to me, 'That's the only language they understand.' After that they sent for the local Arab Police and they took him away, what they did to them I don't know, most likely just told them off and sent them home, telling them to be more careful. Anyhow, the thieving stopped from then onwards, so my idea was very much approved.

We did have a Sergeants' Mess but there was nothing in it in respect of drinks as per our weekly entitlement, no rum, whisky, gin. I tell you what had happened, they say that it was delivered alright but it all went to the wrong area. It was landed and stored at Bone further up the coast, where the battles were in progress, all neatly stored in a marquee. What happened? The Germans made an attack and drove us back a bit, but this tent, with all these rations in was captured by them, very much to their approval, thank you very much! So that was given to them with our compliments, we were without for a long time.

Something happened in this camp which got me into trouble. I met an R.S.M. who I knew from somewhere who had in his tent a crate of gin and he and two other sergeants made up a foursome to play cards one evening and he brought out this gin. I can truly say that I had never drunk gin in my life, we had it mixed with lemonade and it tasted very nice, little did I realise that I was getting drunker and drunker. We had no intention of getting drunk, I don't like being drunk, it's the after effects that I don't like. Anyhow, this gin did that to all of us, and when it came time for us to return to our own tents, I stood up, went outside his tent and I don't know what hit me, my head was swimming. The other two sergeants were on their hands and knees looking for white mice, as they were on the ground they were not conspicuous like me. Who did I run into on trying to find my own tent, two Duty Officers! What I am about to say, I really don't remember saying, but when I was charged, it all came out. The two Officers said to me, 'Come on sarge, let us take you to your tent, where is it?' I was supposed to have said, 'Do you think that I am so stupid that I can't find my own tent, do you see what I have on my sleeves, I am a Sergeant, so stand to attention and don't have so much to say,' or, words to that effect. One of them said to me, 'We must warn you sarge, that we are the Camp Duty Officers and you are drunk and should take heed what we are saying.' But, I would not shut up and made a complete fool of myself. I knew nothing of this until early morning when my Sergeant Major came to me and said, 'Doug, on your feet, you are on a charge for being drunk and insolent to two Duty Officers. So, what have you been up to.'

'Well,' I said,'I remember being in this tent playing cards with other Mess members.'

'Well who were they?' he asked. I thought to myself, be a pal and don't involve them, you are in trouble so why bring them into it as well, so I said, 'I don't know their names, complete strangers to me, just other Mess members.' I stuck to this story, I was caught so that was that, I should not have been standing up, I should have been looking for white mice as well!

I was under close arrest, and had to be escorted by another Sergeant, wearing side arms wherever I went. But commanding Officer's Orders were not until early evening, so I had to wait all day thinking about this charge. Normally being drunk whilst on active service is a court martial, so I visualised being a buck private once again, how that would please Audrey back home! I was for it.

But I still had a bunch of troops to take care of, so instead of having weapons instructions, I suggested a route march, we set off for a long walk, mainly for my benefit, to walk off my headache. I gave over the platoon to my full corporal to manage, it would give him some experience of handling troops. By the time I got back, I was truly sober and very sorry for myself, what an idiot to do such a thing.

Dressed up in a smart uniform, I had to form up with others who were on various charges. I had to wait until last, being a sergeant and a top one at that (or we say not top but a full Sergeant). This C.O. could charge me, but not if he remanded me for a court martial. In I was marched, and stood in front of the C.O. and gave him a salute. By his side were two young Officers about my age, who I did not recognise at all. The charge was read out, 'Sergeant, you are being charged for being under the influence of alcohol and causing some disturbance to two Duty Officers. What have you to say in your defence?' I said 'Well Sir, it does appear that this is true, but during the evening when we were playing cards for the want of something to do, I was with three other Mess members as well and out came some gin. Now this is true, that I have never drunk gin before and was not aware that it could be so strong. We drank it with lemonade and it tasted just nice and sweet, so I gave it no thought that it would make me drunk. It is obvious that I can't take such a drink and I can assure you that I will never touch the stuff again. When it was time to go, I was the only foolish Sergeant that stood up. I don't remember these two Officers at all, but it is obvious, that I said some insulting words to them, for which I apologise.' This I could see, brought a grin on their face, 'Well Sergeant, it is a fact that you are on active service and if we were to have to call on you with your platoon to go into action, you would not be of much use to us, so I have no alternative but to remand you for a court martial.' Well that did it, I was marched out in disgrace, so you can guess, that I was down in the dumps about this. He did ask me, I forgot to say, who were the other three that I was drinking with, but I gave the same answer, that I did not know their names and did not want them in trouble, as well as myself. Maybe he took that in mind to my favour, but I don't think so.

I stood outside with my escort for some while, he was getting fed up waiting to be dismissed. We were talking to each other when the R.S.M. came out all in a hurry and smiling to himself, he came up to me and said, 'Sergeant, you are to go back in again to see the C.O.' Looks good to me, so back in again. When I got up to his desk, I could see a Major there that used to be my Company Commander back in England. The C.O. said to me, 'It is very fortunate for you, that this officer that you can see behind me had heard about your problem and was very surprised to know that this could have happened to a person like yourself. Back in England you were his acting Company Sergeant Major.' He then said that, 'It has obviously been a big mistake on your part and he agrees that your explanation should be taken as serious and that we cannot afford to lose such a good Senior N.C.O. As he has come forward on your part and given you such a good reference I am considering offering you, if you would rather, to take my punishment. If you accept, it will all be well with you.' Well, this came as a surprise to me and I would be very foolish not to accept his punishment, so I said 'Yes, sir'. 'Right,' he said, 'You are severely reprimanded, take him away Sergeant Major.' So that was that, this escort sergeant of mine said, 'Well of all the lucky sergeants you are. If you fell into a bucket of horse manure, you would come out smelling of violets.' I was a good boy from then on. I did see these two Duty Officers shortly afterwards, in fact, I was instructing them one day with others on this new P.I.A.T. weapon and they said then that they were pleased that it all went well for me. As they said, they had no alternative but to charge me as I was so stroppy, and of course they did not know me well, otherwise things may have been different. There it is, they had to do their job.

CHAPTER TWENTY-FOUR

In Action (Look out here I come)

I was at last getting out of this camp and about to join my battalion, but unknown to me, it was not as I wanted. I arrived to join the Hampshire Regiment, no doubt about that, but when I got there I discovered that I was with the 2/4th Hamps. I was given the job of Platoon Sergeant, to a lot of fellows I did not know nor they me, it was bad for our morale. I approached the Company Commander about this and said that I would like to return to my own battalion that I helped to train. I told him that I was sent home from Egypt early in the war to train them so my heart was with them. I told him why I did not join them on arrival to North Africa and he said, 'I understand your problem, so we will arrange that you see the C.O.' This was done for me and he granted my posting. When I returned to this company, the news spread around that I was to return to the Fifth Battalion. Along came a few other lads who were also in the wrong battalion and they asked me if I could put in a word for them to go back, much to my surprise, this was granted as well, so I took them with me which pleased them no end. They said if they were to go into action at least they would go feeling contented, we were used to being with fellows that we knew and trained with.

Now, I wondered what the C.O. had in store for me, after being away for a few weeks, I very much doubted if I would be returned to my old Platoon. It was normal for Officers and Senior N.C.O.s usually to go before the C.O. for a short talk. I had to appear in front of him, his first words were, 'I hear that you made a bit of a fool of yourself back at the Transit Camp. I was informed by your old Company Commander, Major so and so.' I said, 'Yes, that was so, sir.' 'Well, let's not worry about that, we all do a silly thing some time in our lives and that was one of yours. I know full well that you do not make a habit of such affairs, so we will forget it. We have more important things to do right now. I want you to go over there to the 'Mortar Platoon 3" and take over as Platoon Commander and don't tell me that you know nothing about the 3" mortars, because you are not there to teach about the weapon, but to carry out administration work only. If you want to learn about them you can do so. When you get over there nominate one of the Senior Sergeants to carry out the duties of Platoon Sergeant. Off you go,' he said to me.

The C.O. by the way was Lt. Colonel Newham, whom I had known for quite a while, he was also in India when I was there, he was then a Major. I think he came up through the ranks, he therefore had been sergeant as well so there was not much that he did not know about the army.

Over I went to this Mortar Platoon and met these brave and seasoned troops. I got them together and told them that I was now their new Platoon Commander, not much response, they probably thought, 'Reckon we got a right one here.' I understood that Sergeant George Strugnell was the most Senior Sergeant in this group, so I told him that he was now Platoon Sergeant. After a few words with them, George Strugnell and I got together and had a private conversation. I told him, 'I have very little knowledge of this weapon and the C.O. was well aware of this, my job is to command. Nevertheless, I think it would be a good idea if I had some instruction from one of your good full Corporals on this weapon.' I think it was Cpl Perry who gave me these instructions and very well he did it. I did not agree that I should be a Commander of a Platoon, I had no knowledge of this weapon at all. If these lads got to know this I reckon it would lower their opinion of me, they had only known me as a Platoon Sergeant in a Rifle Company. Once I had received this extra knowledge, I could then get on with the other work of commanding.

The business of rounding up the beaten German Army was now coming to the end, the First Army, along with the Eighth

Army had them bottled up in the area of Cape Bonn. Their army was now in a state of confusion, it was most likely the first time that they had lost a battle since the war started. The result of this was the beginning of the end for them. It was to be a long struggle to defeat them as they still had a powerful fighting force to deal with, there were thousands of German and Italian prisoners, all wandering about. The Germans seemed to be dominating the Italian Solders, taking the transport off them and making them walk, they treated them as very inferior, more or less blaming them for their defeat, in other words, they were a poor ally to have in war. In our opinion we did not think that the Italians had their heart in this war, they should not have been mixed up in it, their leader used to be great to them but now that they were losing, he was no good. We know that the Italians gave up easily, they did not want to die for nothing.

I'll tell you a short story about that. I was out on a reconnaissance one day looking for a suitable place to position our mortars in readiness for an attack when we bumped into a platoon of Italian Solders in the command of one of their officers. I stood alone on the side of a slope in full battle order, tommy gun at the ready and pointing towards them when some of them saw me, they stood up and shot their arms into the air in submission. I beckoned them towards me, at the same time I signalled to some of my men to come forward and we took them all prisoners. We did not take their weapons off them, but made them unload them, we marched them to the nearest truck then took their weapons from them and escorted them to H.Q. for interrogation. They were only too pleased to be out of the war, as you will read a little later on, you will see that they gave in to us early in September '43 and gave us assistance.

After the North African War was over we all had to reinforce to get us up to strength once again, also to get ourselves cleaned up and start to train for another battle, no doubt across the Med, most likely Italy itself. We were now at a place called Boogee, it was here that we met the lads in the Eight Army, they had come a long way after many hard battles. They were as brown as berries, more so than us, because it took longer for us to get equipped with tropical kit, such as shorts. We were brown with the exception of our legs, although not white, nothing like the colour of theirs. We were called the White Leghorns, which in some cases started fights amongst our own troops, always wanting to fight someone. I thought we had had enough of that, but such is the way that our men behaved.

It was at this place that we all started to get the hang of beach landings using the L.C.I. (Landing Craft Infantry), a fast flat bottom boat that would take about a company of men. It would travel at about twenty-one knots, at the front of the boat were two ramps that shot out as soon as we landed near the shore line. There were times when the boat was not able to get in close enough, which meant that when we tried to get off we were nearly up to our neck in salt water, in some cases they would be out of their depth and had to be manhandled to prevent them from sinking. A special watch was kept up to see that this did not happen, it was not a very pleasant task to be wet through and have to stay in that condition for many hours, especially if it was cold weather. But once again we seemed to get over that without too many bad effects, I was under the impression that these boats were all American, but it was not so, it was a joint design, they were made both in England and America. For this landing we were called Twenty-one Beach Group, you can imagine that when the boat landed we had to get off very fast as we were sitting targets. To clear about a hundred and thirty men off the boat took about two minutes and then the boat withdrew quickly as it was vital to try and save it for another landing some other place, they must have cost a lot of money. On landing we had to dash inland as quickly as possible and take up a defensive position, or even attack at once, we never returned to the boat once we were ashore. The boat pulled out and moved out of sight, to get aboard again we met in a different place. These landing practices were numerous so as to get it as perfect as possible, speed was necessary.

It soon came the time for us to move off and get near the area where we were to board these ships, so we moved down to the

Port of Bizerta, which was already bustling with military movement. One could see in this area the remains of a battle that had taken place not so long ago, by the wrecks of old aircraft, German, as well as some vehicles. For a couple of days we kept out of sight under the trees, well concealed from any possible German aircraft, if they had any left. Whilst we were up under these trees, we were all preparing for the forthcoming action, like priming grenades and mines.

It was at this place that we had a dreadful accident, a disaster really. A few men were detailed to prime some mines ready for use, as they were finishing they were piling them in boxes, when the pile fell on some of the primed mines, which started a series of large explosions. The result was that about forty men were killed and many wounded. I heard all this, when I was about half a mile away as I and my Mortar Platoon had already moved down in the port area. We later asked what the noise of explosion was about and that was what we were told. I lost a good friend of mine there, a Sergeant Lipscombe, he came from Eastleigh, near Southampton, as well as many others. A terrible thing to happen after they had just finished our battles in North Africa, what a shock for their wives and mothers back home. I wonder if they ever did hear the correct story about their accident. This tragedy would of course upset the landing arrangements, as the company was now under strength and had to go into reserve.

The Americans were to take part in this operation with us, it was the first time that we had seen so many of them, it was our intention along with the Americans to defeat the Germans in Europe first and then to concentrate in the Japanese Zone. They of course, were looking forward to getting their revenge for the Pearl Harbour attack. It was in this area that I saw some American black soldiers across the field from us. Being me, I like to be friendly with anyone, I took a stroll over to them just to say, 'Hi there'. At first I did not seem to be welcomed, one of them shouted out, 'What the hell do you want, bub?' I said 'I just came over to have a chat with you that's all, after all we are allies and speak the same language, or near enough?' It gradually simmered down to be a little more sociable and I ended up having a mug of tea with them and left feeling that I had achieved a better relationship. Their concern was that as they did not get on with their own white troops, that I was to be the same, but I was not aware of this conflict between them, I thought that they were all buddies. In fact we were attached to them for this landing. Our Division 46th, were attached to their 5th American Army under their General Mark Clark but we never did see him.

It was the American Engineers that I understand cleared out the rubbish from this port which the Germans had put there to try and stop us from using it. But that did not work, it was now fully operational thanks to their efforts.

Going back for a while to our tragedy where all our men were killed, I often wondered what happened about their burial. We could not attend to anything like that as we were about to take off on this landing. I hoped that they were given a good send off by somebody, I never did hear any more about that, too busy with the war I guess. We had a lot to thank them for after all their action in North Africa.

During the time that I was waiting in the port area, someone had found a swimming pool and I decided that we would all go for a swim, we were all ready to take off as and when necessary. It was whilst I was there that I received a message to attend an Order Group with the Commanding Officer, no doubt about the landing. He must have known that I was in the pool with my platoon, because the message said, 'Come as you are, no need to change.' So along I went, all dripping wet, as I have said, it was for a briefing in respect of the landing but first of all, I was introduced to my new Platoon Commander, much to my surprise, I was not aware that I was to be replaced. He came from the Queens Regiment, no name comes to mind, but we shook hands and had a conversation about the platoon and the coming landing. He also told me that his wife had just presented them with a daughter and hoped that he would be able to see her some time. That never did come off, as he was killed on the landing.

I was given instructions to meet him when we landed at a certain farm in Italy that was marked on the map and then gather our platoon together and then be able to use our mortars against the Germans. This did not work out as planned. I was myself not happy about the arrangements, but that was how it was planned. Myself with all my Bren Gun carriers, which included the mortars and ammunition plus the drivers were put on a separate ship, driven by an American crew. The rest of the platoon with the new commander on another ship to act as infantry men, I guess this was arranged because of the previous accident with 'C' Company, the Battalion were short of the attacking fighting men. This just made us of no use to anyone, we had the mortars but no crew to use them, but I acted on my instructions and made my way to this farm as planned, got up there on my motor cycle. However, I am jumping ahead with my story. I am not there yet and much happened before we got there.

After leaving this meeting I returned to my platoon and gave them the instructions, I got myself dressed and we all returned to our area of disposal. We got everything ready and were prepared to move off at a moment's notice. During the night we were visited by a lot of German aircraft who took pot luck at dropping a few bombs in our area, he was on target. He managed to drop one amongst us, killing a few more troops and damaging some vehicles, all in the pitch darkness, we took cover in a nearby ditch and escaped any injuries.

In the early hours of the morning we moved off in the darkness. We were directed to our landing craft and got settled in and eventually moved off silently through the dark out into the mouth of the port passing the anchored warships, that would shortly be in action helping us out when we landed. There were both British and American ships also preparing for action against the enemy, little did they know what was heading their way, nor us in a way. Such are the joys of war, if one can call that joy, but as I have said before, we were all young in those days and by then used to war and what it involved.

By the time we had reached the open sea in the Med, it was daylight so we would be exposed to enemy air force, but so far not a sign of them. By now we understood that they were desperately short of aircraft, our two air forces had been busy shooting them down. The weapon situation for us was very much improved since the Americans came into the war with us, they took some persuading to do this, but since the Pearl Harbour attack on them, they soon made up their minds. Otherwise it would have been a long war if the Germans kept on winning battles.

We were now anchored off the coast of Italy opposite the beach of Salerno and could see the coastline not more than three miles from us. We had many craft waiting to land and get on with the attack, but now we had to be kept waiting until we had the word. It was a very fine sunny afternoon, you would hardly think that there was a war on. Suddenly we were put on the alert when the Navy behind us some way back started to shell the beach in front of us. We could hear the shells whistling over our heads and crashing onto the beach area, I would not like to be under that kind of fire. This went on for quite a while, softening up as they called it. Whilst this was going on a couple of German Fighter Bombers came over and dropped a few bombs and strafed a few of us. They managed to fire salvoes at us with a few cannon shells but it did very little damage, no one was hit. It was then that I grabbed a Bren Gun that was lying at my feet, actually it belonged to one of our men who was supposed to be watching out for aircraft, but he was a little slow on the uptake. I fired at this M.E. and up went the tracer bullets and armour piercing bullets and you could see them entering the bottom of the aircraft. I was not the only one shooting at this aircraft, a few others were doing the same as I was. We could see that we had hit it because it came down into the sea, way in the distance, so that one did not bother us any more.

What we did not like was the delay in attacking this beach, as it was no longer a surprise attack, we were giving them time to consolidate. We later heard that we gave them time to bring down to the beach area their Panzer Division, who were crack troops of heavy armour. For this delay we suffered badly, so who was at fault? I have a few ideas myself but the reasons I will never know, it's not easy to be a General I know, many things to think about. It was during the firing of the Bren Gun that I lost my steel helmet, therefore I felt a bit naked without one. The only person that I could ask would be the officer in charge of this landing craft, but they could not supply an American helmet, only the inner part of one. I landed with that on my head which would not have been any good if I was hit, but if felt better than nothing at all. It was not long after I landed that I found one of our own from one of our lads who had been a casualty. These American helmets at a quick glance could look something like the German helmet, so I soon lost that, one of our fellows had already shot an American Major because he mistook him for a German in the early morning mist many weeks previously.

The landing of Salerno began for us at about 05.30 on the morning of September 9th 1943. It started with a terrific bombardment by the Navy, another softening up, but despite this they still gave us a most unwelcome landing, the casualties were very heavy. Our ship had three tries at the beach landing, first there was a beach mine in the way and it had to withdraw and try again. The second time they dropped the ramp for the first truck to move off and the ship started to drift backwards and the truck toppled over the ramp and fell into the sea along with the driver and his mate. I guess they were lost, I never did see them again, amongst all the confusion of landing and being shot at. The third time we were lucky to move off the ship, then one of the carriers had a direct hit and the shell went right through the middle of it, must have been armour piercing, it did not explode, but just made a hole through the floor. I said leave it there for a while, we will send the R.E.M.E. down later on to recover it, as it still held a mortar and ammunition on it.

I then spotted a Flayer with revolving chains on it, that clears any mines that are in our way on the beach. I gathered them all behind me and we followed behind this machine until we were clear of the beach, it was very fortunate for us that he was working just in this area, this probably saved a few lives.

I advanced a few hundred yards inland and consolidated for a while, I left one of the senior N.C.O.s in charge whilst I tried to contact the new Platoon Commander. Off I went on my motor cycle to find him, but all I met was some of our troops still trying to capture this farm. It was still in the hands of the Germans and a battle was going on, I had to get off my motor bicycle and take cover as I was being fired at and the engine was still running. As I took cover in a nearby ditch I came face to face with a Corporal, who had his bayonet fixed, sticking through the hedge. He said, 'You better watch out, Sarge, we are about to make an attack on this farm and you could be in the way.' Without any delay I got on my motor and moved very fast out of the way, but I still had not found the Commander. I decided to return to my platoon as soon as possible as we were on fresh ground and they would be concerned as to what to do. On returning I found the area in a bit of confusion as some men from another regiment were mixed up with ours, I think it was the York and Lancs. Well, who wouldn't be mixed up with that battle going on, it took us some time to get sorted out, as I said before, we gave the enemy too much time to get organised, and we were not. They poured ammunition at us from all directions.

Then a strange event occurred. As we were advancing in this area, one of the lads pointed out to me that there was a small tent pitched just over there. I said, 'You give me covering fire and I'll go see if there is anyone in it or anything of value.' I approached it cautiously with my Tommy Gun at the ready, opened the flap of the tent and there was a body asleep, as if he was on a holiday. I poked him with my gun but it took some time before he sat up and paid attention. It was a German Officer, a young Lieutenant, it was obvious that he had had a hard night at drinking, because not only was he surprised but you could see that he had a hangover. He was holding his head. To think that he had slept all through that bombardment and it had not woken him up, nor was he woken up by any of his men, to me it was a mystery. I stripped him of any weapons,

155

searched through his kit, placed his dress dagger in my jacket, took him prisoner and kept him until I came in touch with my Company H.Q. They took him away to be interrogated, I did not see him any more, I bet he felt a fool, I wonder who he was with the night before?

Orders came around to move forward as one of our companies had reached the main objective so everyone could move forward. When I met my Company Commander Major Sawyer, he called me forward and said 'Sergeant French, you are back to Platoon Commander once again. Your new Commander has been killed.' I later heard that a whole bunch of them were mowed down by a machine gun.

CHAPTER TWENTY-FIVE

Salerno and White Cross Hill

So I was back to Mortar Platoon Commander, it seemed an unusual situation for me, with all this acting business, I had my own thoughts on it. If I was good enough to do the job for a number of months, why not give me the Field Commission and be done with it. It was obvious that I could do the job, otherwise why give it to me in the first place, it is quite a responsibility. When I look back to that time, I think I should have taken the job with more interest, but I kept having the feeling that it was only temporary so why take it too seriously. If I had done I'm sure I would have made a better job of it, maybe it was because I had got to my present rank too quickly and did not know my own abilities. Why did they keep my possibilities to themselves? Such was their way of thinking in those days, I don't think it gave a person a fair chance and that chance only comes once in a lifetime. Time goes by too quickly as you are aware. Talking about promotion possibilities, I think it depends who your superior is and how he may think about you and whether you give him a good impression and what kind of a personality you are yourself. We all have our faults and I was aware of one of my faults, I know I was too forward and what I thought about things and subjects I would speak out and it would, in some cases, hurt someone's feelings. But there again, some Senior Officers were impressed with a person that speaks his mind. I must have been under the one that does not like people speaking his mind. I know I let myself down at times in that respect.

For those who are not aware of ranks, in this case, I was then a Full Sergeant acting as Platoon Commander, which position should be held by a full Lieutenant. That was my acting rank, but I was not being paid for it. These circumstances happen in war, because of casualties these ranks cannot be replaced at once so one is appointed straight away as acting, as approved by one's Senior Officer, as in this case a Company Commander, Major Sawyer. In some cases when one reaches an acting higher rank, providing you can serve long enough you obtain it permanently, but in my case it was not to be so, as I became a casualty and was then out of my Unit for good and eventually Medically Discharged.

We had now been able to move inland quite a bit and we had to attack a range of mountains, some ten miles inland. We set off as a battalion in column, it was in the dark and we could not put on our headlights on any vehicle. I know I ended up going along a wide drain and did not realise until someone shouted down to me, 'Hey Sarge, what you doing down there, the road is up here?' To tell you the truth I was feeling very tired and I was not paying attention to where I was going. I had been very busy just before we left this area. I managed to get my small bivouac up and slide in to try and get some sleep but it seemed that I had just gone off into a deep sleep, when a runner was shouting out for the Mortar Platoon Commander. I heard someone say, 'That's his tent there, he has just got in there to try and have a sleep, he will kill you.'

'Can't help that,' he said. 'C.O. Order Group.' He woke me up with an apology, saying, 'Sorry, Sarge. The C.O. wants all Commanders for an Order Group.' So I got up feeling pretty sleepy, put on my equipment and found my Tommy Gun and went to this meeting. I didn't hear a word, I fell asleep in the chair. When the meeting was over I was given the Orders for tomorrow's attack by some other Lieutenant. I said, 'What did the C.O. say about me being asleep?' He said, 'Nothing at all, you were not the only one.' Going along this wide ditch was all right, it eventually wound itself back onto the road and I rejoined the column. On the way it was not a peaceful ride, we were welcomed with an occasional big shell that was trying to find us. We wound our way up the side of a mountain and eventually I took up position behind a church, got the mortar section to dig in their gun positions and sent up my Platoon Sergeant on observation, which was a bit higher up than where we were. Each gun had their own full N.C.O. to take care of things, and we settled down hoping that we would have as little trouble as possible from the German Army. It was all fairly quiet until about 03.00 hrs, when they decided to attack the hill, a few bullets and mortar bombs were giving us some trouble. I got on the field telephone to my Platoon Sergeant who was as I said up the hill which we called White Cross. He was there as an observer to give us the targets that needed to be wiped out. All I could hear on the end of this line was some shouting and machine gun firing but no George, he must have had to clear out as they were attacking this hill with the intention of driving us out of it. So, what was I to do? Without any information as regards who was up there holding this hill, had the Germans taken it and were our fellows still up there fighting? If I started to mortar them up there I would most likely be hitting our own troops so I had nothing to go on. I knew that machine gun bullets were coming my way, we were short of any information and I did not want our guns and crew captured. I gave the orders to pack up all guns positioned with the exception of two, they were to stand by ready to fire on this hill as soon as I heard that our own troops had left this position. Then the Company Commander turned up and was not aware of the present situation. A few hasty words were said between us which had no justification, it came to a pushing contest between us two. I said, 'What else could I have done in such a situation where we were not informed of the situation up on this hill?' He was not aware that as far as I was concerned I had the situation under control. What annoyed me was that he was accusing me of cowardice in front of the enemy, that really got my temper up. He said, 'You will hear from me later on about this affair.' If I remember rightly George had set up a mortar on the path where we were pushing one another, I had already told him that there were two mortars set up just a few yards away, but in all the confusion he did not grasp what I said. If I had known that this hill was clear of our troops, I would have poured mortar bombs on it, which we did, but nevertheless withdrawn from this position as the Germans had managed to take it for a while. I was right in that preparation in any case. We moved down a few hundred yards but the next day we took this lost position back off them again. We gave them a good hiding with our mortars and did so much damage to them that they never did come back again. They took off during the next night, I think they had quite a few reasons for this withdrawal in our opinion. Firstly despite the power of their Panzers Division they could not find them of much use for fighting up in the high hills, it just meant Infantry fighting to help clear the way, it was very difficult terrain to fight in.

I'll talk about a few things in relation to this Salerno attack, how I saw it, as a Junior Commander. Salerno was a good place to attack providing it was successful, which it eventually was, but to start with we thought it was going to be another Dunkirk. The powers that be did not make the attack as a surprise, I know I have said this before, but giving them time to get up extra troops was a disadvantage for us. We were so short of troops that even some of the Navy boys had to lend a hand, so I understood. Also some R.E.s had to be used and they were not trained as Infantry men. It was for a while touch and go. I think some of the ships had been given instruction to hang about in case there was this necessary, but we won the day. It took I think, about four or five days before we could convince the Germans that we had a good grip on the situation.

On about the fourth or fifth night, about 03.30 hrs when all was silent on the front line, we gathered that the Germans were withdrawing because it all went quiet. What we were waiting to hear was that the British Eighth Army had caught up with us, they were advancing up from the south. This was confirmed at this hour because we suddenly heard in the distance the mass bagpipes playing and it sent a most weird sound across the mountains, enough to frighten the dead. It made all the hairs stand up on one's body, the Germans probably heard it as well, which I guess was the object in view. They must have taken off at the gallop because we had peace for a while.

I must tell you another true story about myself and my mortars. First when we were situated behind this local church, I am sure that the local priest was most nervous as I had all my guns dug in and was using his church as a cover. We fired our guns many times, but did not get much retaliation from the Germans, up to that point they had not been able to find us. They were not quite sure where we were, but one odd bomb did penetrate his church by the altar, lucky for him that it did not explode, one of their dud ones, which by the way, very often happened with some of their shells, must be some kind of sabotage sneaking into their factories. Nevertheless, he still was very worried about it, he complained about it but I just said, 'There is a war on you know.' Luckily it was not completely destroyed, he would have to claim off his government I should think when the war was over.

Another thing that surprised us was that on a Sunday morning we saw a whole party of them all dressed in white making their way to a religious meeting and not taking a bit of notice that the war was going on. I suppose they relied on the protection of their God to keep them safe, which it seemed to have done.

I had another unusual experience later on in a different area. We were in a position near a farm and were busy firing our mortars and I noticed that one or two of their shells coming back at us were unusually close to where I was taking cover, which was in a disused well about four feet deep. It gave me excellent cover, but it seemed to me that there must be someone right close to me and observing me. Anyhow, I did not like this place so I picked up my field telephone and moved around the back of the farm. Whilst I was there, the same thing began to happen, these shells were following me but they could not hit me as it was too well protected with hard cover. I was foolish because I should have sent a few well armed men around the building to see if anyone had been left behind as observers. I thought about this later on when I was speaking to someone about it, but too late I had moved on, it never occurred again.

One more little story about White Cross Hill, during the time that the Germans were attacking us. I was touched on the shoulder in the dark by a young private soldier who was on the verge of tears. He was asking me where he could get his wound seen to, he was in a bit of a state about this and seemed very frightened. I said to him, 'How come you are here like you are? Where is your equipment and weapon?'

'I left it on top of the hill when the Germans attacked,' he said. I said, 'Well you should not do that.' He did not answer so I could see that I was getting nowhere with him in this state. I directed him to the First Aid Post and got rid of him for someone else to sort out, I often wondered what happened to him.

Another time I was approached again in the darkness, someone was shouting for Sergeant French. I said, 'Over here, what is the problem?' 'Well, I've come about four miles looking for you, Sergeant, as I have had an order from Sergeant Pinnegar to find you and give you a message as you were a buddy of his. I left him further down the coastline, he has died of wounds, but he managed to give me a message to pass on to you and he said to me, will you find him and give it to him. The message is "To wish you the best of luck, keep your head down and hope you get back home safely. Tell him that I've had it".' I know I was very busy at that time, but I thanked him for the effort of coming up and finding me. I told him, 'You had better get back in case they think you have deserted your Company. If you do get into any trouble, tell them I will confirm to them that you were up here delivering this message which you thought was only right to do so. I thank you as well.' So that was the passing of Joe Pinnegar who I had known for some time as well as many others in the First Battalion. He came from Portsmouth I'm sure.

There was another time when I was given an incorrect message from a certain Captain. He said to me over my 28 set, radio operated communication, that I and my mortars were to report to the Commanding Officer at field H.Q. which was a good way up this hill at 01.00 hrs. I repeated the message, 'Are you sure he said the 3 inch mortars.' He said 'Sergeant, when I say 3 inch I mean 3 inch. Yes, to the C.O. that is correct.'

You know carrying these mortars is no joke especially up those hills, they were very heavy but these lads carried them up the hill (not all of them, just one Section) but I was to accompany them. You can bet your life that there was plenty of moaning about this. We eventually got up, but when the C.O. saw me he said, 'What are you doing up here with a 3 inch mortar?' I said, 'Captain so and so gave me this message to report to you at once as you need mortar assistance.' But he said that he told him that he asked for 2 inch mortar assistance not 3 inch, he said that we must accept his apologies on his behalf. You can imagine what the men said who had been struggling up this high hill carrying this lot for the love of it, as well as myself. Never did get any apologies from him, how do they get away with it?

What did we think about the casualties that were going on all around us all day long? Well none of us wanted to be killed or wounded, but you never thought it would happen to you. Yet we knew full well that if we did not receive any form of injury, we would be very lucky to miss out, especially in the Infantry or Commandos. In the short time that I was a Platoon Sergeant in the fighting department, I probably had about three platoon strength replacements, that is probably about eighty men. The casualties were tremendous, more wounded than killed which was a good thing if one has to have casualties. I often get asked that question from the younger Privates, 'What's it like Sarge if one is killed or wounded.' Well, I have yet to find that out myself, because so far I have been lucky, except for a slight wound when I was in India on the North West Frontier and that was really minor. I'll let the readers know about that later on in the story, but really we did not dwell on the subject, we just got on with the job.

All this that I am mentioning, is what went on behind the lines, besides the fighting parts. About trying to protect ourselves during a battle, whether in defence or on the attack. A lot of that had been learned back in England, field craft or tactics, but there were times when we had to dig in. For this we were all issued with an entrenching tool, like a small spade, and when they said dig in it meant just that, you had to get on with it to save your life. During our stay at the church at the bottom of White Cross Hill, we were there for many hours and we sure had to dig in there and fast. Myself as well as a couple of others dug a good deep trench for us three and if anyone else made use of it instead of using their own, they were in trouble. All ranks had to use elbow grease to dig their own, but that is what happened. We sent over a good mortar barrage to the Germans and it was not long before they retaliated which meant a first class dive into the slit trench. I did a big jump into mine and landed on someone's shoulders, he let out a shout of pain. I said, 'Whoever that is, it serves you right, you should dive into your own trench, clear out.' Well, it just so happened to be the same Captain that gave us the wrong message about sending the mortars up the hill. He merely said, 'I think, Sergeant; that you have said enough.' But nevertheless he got out and found his own, which by the way he did not dig himself. His batman plus driver dug that for him, in doing so he was killed by a mortar bomb. Yes, there are many tragic tales to tell when one is in action, that very few hear about except the lower form of fighters. But this Captain never did say any more about that instance, he just got out of my trench without any further words.

No doubt the Germans were going through the same sort of things over the hills. Never under estimate the German soldier, he was a good fighter. I'm talking about the true German not the Nazi, their point of view in relation to the war was different to the true German soldier. I know I met many of them, they were feeling the same as us and were wishing that the war would hurry up and finish, especially as they were now aware that they were going to lose and have no home to go back to. We were destroying their cities like they had been trying to do, here we were all young men just killing each other, but for what? Who wins wars in the long run?

After the 50th Division had welcomed the Germans with

their bagpipes, the Germans must have moved back some thirty miles. We eventually got in the area of the River Garigliano also the Volturno River, very hard places to take because it had started to rain and we were beginning to get bogged down up to our axles in mud. This slowed us all up, it was a hard struggle pushing forward. I cannot possibly mention all the little places that we had to attack to clear out the Germans, there were so many, but none of them gave up very easily. I can only mention the main ones.

CHAPTER TWENTY-SIX

Cassino and Campo Village

To get to Cassino we had the very difficult task of crossing the Garigliano, it was all on the flat land and we could be observed by the Germans for many miles. They were occupying the hills and mountains up in front of us and to save lives, we could only tackle it at night, so you can imagine the difficulty. What with the dark, rain and the river flowing at about fifteen miles an hour, it was also about sixty yards or more across and out of our depth. We had to use capoc bridging to get over, these things were not very stable, they had to be linked up to reach the other side. Someone, usually a good strong swimmer had to go over in advance, trailing a rope the other end of which was part of this capoc bridging. He had to get to the other side and secure the rope to something stable, either a tree or an iron peg knocked into the ground, it just had to be firm because there was going to be a lot of weight behind all this. Not forgetting the water current was pulling away at a fair old pace and when the troops start to cross over these capocs, they were very unstable. You can imagine it took a lot of practice to control this movement and more than one would fall in the water with all their heavy equipment on. If they did, it was an immediate rescue, we couldn't afford to lose good soldiers. During the crossing they were being shot at, so you can guess it was no mean task. If you were wet through there was nowhere to change your clothing, which meant staying in wet clothes probably all night. Some might be lucky and find some place where they could get dry but I doubt it. In addition to that you would have to dig yourself another slit trench which would most likely fill up with water, it had been raining for a long time and we were on the flat and right by the river. We would all suffer for it later on in life I dare say, with aching bones or what is called rheumatism. Such are the joys of soldiering.

The local Italians said that this had been the wettest summer for twenty-eight years and that we were the cause of it with all this bombing, they could be right there.

As I said before, nearly all vehicles were bogged down and could not be moved, this of course affected both sides and that was one of the reasons why we were fighting too long in this Cassino area, we were getting nowhere.

It was in this area that I was at last relieved of my job as Mortar Commander. A Scottish Lieutenant from the Argyles came to me to take over. It was a task that he said he did not relish, because he knew that I had been Commander now for seventeen weeks and was full of vast experience. He had better knowledge of the mortars than I did, because he had been trained with them back home but it was his first time in action and as he said, he still had a lot to learn but we got on well together. During a break when we were situated in the village of Campo a fair way back from this fighting area we had to go before the Commanding Officer. He told me the situation about the hand over and he said to the new Commander that I had to stay with him for three weeks whilst in action and that he was to pay attention to the tasks that I had to perform to enable to keep this Mortar Platoon going. This we did and he performed one hundred per cent, I said that he had no worries, if I may say so, he was made for the job. We shook hands, wished each other luck and I don't think I saw much of him after that.

When I left him I was then promoted to Colour Sergeant or C.Q.M.S. (Company Quarter Master Sergeant) of 'S' Company, the same Company that I was in before. So I started another job which was completely different from all previous jobs, it entailed feeding, clothing and supplies for the whole company. I came under the wing of the Battalion Quarter Master Captain. It was a busy job and one also had to keep control of some bookwork, keeping records etc. It entailed a great variety of tasks to keep the company going but I enjoyed it and got stuck into it.

I also had at my disposal a jeep with trailer, a 15 cwt truck as well as a 30 cwt truck all for carrying goods. I had a couple of drivers to help out with all my tasks, although I learnt to drive most of these in case of emergency, unofficially! When delivering food to the troops, I sometimes had a couple of cooks.

In this area we were only able to use the jeep as there were no roads, only tracks. These jeeps could only go so far, the rest of the way it had to be manhandled, then it depended upon the distance, if it was too far away, they had to look after themselves with the issue of Compo Rations, boxes of mixed foods, enough in a box if I can remember for about twelve men. Those were graded, some contained different items that appealed to some men, like Grade A and Grade B, Grade A appealed to them, but these were fairly distributed so that one did not get all A boxes. Another piece of equipment was the individual tommy cooker, a small cooker for each man with a small supply of methylated tablets which burned long enough to warm up something to eat or drink. These are also smokeless which is a great help and again, if you happen to be in a small space when it is very cold outside, it gives out quite a bit of heat.

I'll give you an instance when I had a typical journey in taking up the Company's supply of food, which they were looking forward to having. They were fighting in a small town called Monte Squodo, or something like that. It was quite a major battle, when I got to the outside of this town at about 19.30 hrs I got stuck at a crossroads, where the Military Police were on duty and they held us up for a while. It was a German D.F. task, in other words they were dropping a few heavy shells around that area, consequently, we were unable to get through until there came a break in the shelling. This break came and they gave us the signal to proceed, but the Germans fooled us, as I was making my way an odd shell came down very close to us. It made the driver swing to the left and we went into a ditch and the whole of our food contents were destroyed. This meant that we had to return to our base, some six miles back and cook another lot. Of course our company was not aware of the reason for the delay, but it put us back about three hours before we managed to get up to them again. We were welcomed, but not without a lot of moans until I explained to the Officer in Charge why we were late, this was unavoidable, so all was forgiven. It was a typical journey, we never did know when we would reach our destination. There were times when we had to spend hours getting there and back, so you can guess that sometimes we were very tired indeed but the cooks had to get on and prepare the next meal. This was not always so, as I have said, there were times when they had to look after themselves which was quite often in areas when we could not get at them. This did not mean that I was excused from trying to reach them, we had to get other things to them no matter how difficult it was like ammunition and mail. This was a morale lift up, a letter from home could do wonders for them.

After a few months in this area we had the opportunity to be out of the line for Christmas. This must have been the end of 1943, this is where we were again in the village of Campo. On the way there, on foot for most of them, we came across a van that happened to be the ladies who ran the Salvation Army Mobile Canteen. They somehow knew we were on our way and had prepared a large amount of hot tea and buns. These ladies were Angels from Heaven for us, nothing was too much trouble for them to give us some pleasure like this and a dirtier lot I have never seen. We had not shaved for three weeks, so you can guess what we looked like, as well as smelt like and do you know, that one hundred per cent of us fell asleep because we were so tired and for a good three hours they watched guard over us. We were lying all over the place, just dropped where we were, hanging onto whatever weapons we were carrying, can you beat that? I bet they said, 'Poor boys, just look at them all tired out.' Anyhow, we take our hats off to them, they were always around some place when you needed them.

From the Salvation Army we made our way up to a village. As we got near we were ushered to the side of the road and into a wood where something was going on. A large van had been converted into a playhouse with a few balloons up and it was the entertainers, called E.N.S.A. (Entertainers Navy Soldiers and Airmen). These were special men dragged out of various regiments who had some sort of talent to entertain the troops when necessary and they must have thought that this was one time that we needed some. Well, in some ways yes, but on the other hand, most of us wanted a good bath, a change of clothing, a good feed and most of all some sleep. Nevertheless, we did enjoy their entertainment, they really made us laugh and that was a good thing that we needed, little did we realise it at the time, after a few weeks doing a serious job.

We then made our way just a few hundred yards to the centre of the village, were directed to our billets and got down to our tasks of cleaning up. Me, I had to organise a kitchen and get the staff to prepare a good meal, which they did.

After a hot shower and a change of clothing most of us got down to about twenty-four hours sleep. Someone had to keep guard, we were still on active service, you never knew when the enemy might sneak up on you, if you were not alert. We doubted that as we were too far back now, although you could hear the big guns in the distance. Myself and a few of my 'Q' staff were billeted in part of a private house and I can remember that I had a bit of sewing to do, sewing my Crowns on my sleeve and above my stripes. I had not as yet found time to put them on properly and I had been told that they must be sewn on properly, so I had better do it, when I found some decent time and that was now. As I started, the lady of the house spotted me doing this and took it off me saying that I looked silly trying to do a woman's job, so she finished the job for me. When she finished the job, she jokingly gave me a salute and said in bad English 'God Save the King'.

After this long sleep we were told to prepare something for our Christmas, so someone organised a collection for the men below the rank of sergeant to collect some money and go back to the nearest town which I think, was Naples and buy what they could in the form of drinks. They had their usual allowance of beer but as it was for a special occasion, they needed more. This was also arranged for the sergeants and officers, a small convoy went back and bought all this and brought it back and had it all laid out on their tables a few days afterwards. We could not waste time as we had only a few days rest and then we had to get back to the line of action. The main thing was that we let them enjoy themselves and let their hair down, if they got drunk they were helped to recover quickly. When the time came in the morning, they were still out in the village square riding about on poor little old donkeys, wearing some funny Italian hats, because some of the older men got invited into this binge. There were no young men, they were in the army and most likely prisoners of war, the girls, you can bet your life that mother had them locked up and away from these mad men.

I have not for a while mentioned my friend Curly Andrews, I must say a few words about him now. Going back to the landing at Salerno, he was a casualty, in fact someone told me that it was serious and he was left as dead, but I could not believe that. Well, it so happened that he turned up in this village just before we Sergeants sat down for our Christmas Dinner. I happened to be looking out of my window and I saw a lonely figure coming up the road and as he got nearer I could see that it was Curly. What had happened was that he was supposed to be in hospital, he had a nasty wound on the back of his head, but as he said, he was getting fed up staying in this place and was off to see his old buddy Doug French. He found me, goodness knows how he did that, but he did. His only thoughts were for me, so he said. As I said to him I was glad to see him, but should he be here in that condition. 'Ah shut up,' he said. 'I want you to have a word with the C.O. to see if he will take me back into this battalion.'

I said 'What chance do you think you will have even if he says yes? The Medical Officer will turn you down at once. You are not fit enough and you know it.' He was not either, you could see by looking at him that he had been through it for a while, he was nearly in tears. Oh yes, tough men can shed a tear at times. The only thing that I could do was to go see the

Adjutant and talk about it, but it was as I said, not on. He went to the Medical Officer and he said, 'I'm sorry, but you are not fit enough. Also, you discharged yourself from hospital and that is not the right move to take. I am sending you back on a truck after you have had your Christmas Dinner with your Buddy 'Q' French and from there it is in their hands.' So, that was what happened, he went but with reluctance. We were very pleased to see each other but we had to part. I did see him once again, it was during the time that I had to go to hospital.

After our little break in this village we once again had to return to the Casino area and get on with the war. The place itself hardly existed, even the trees were stripped of all their branches for it had been bombed and shelled now for about three months. As regards the people's houses those were all just rubble, anyone that stayed there were living in the rubble under the houses like rats. You dare not show yourself during the day, the whole place smelt of the dead, because no one could get at them to bury them, there were some terrible sights, I would not like to mention them.

I carried on with my job as usual. One particular morning I set off little knowing that I would not be returning to my billet any more because of what was in store for me. With the usual stocks of food, mail etc. I travelled by jeep and one 15 cwt truck. We had to stop and unload on a track as the rest of the way was on foot, a matter of about three to four miles, nearly all up hill. I was met by a sergeant and a party of men who were the porters to carry all this stuff, mainly Indian labour soldiers. They carried no weapons as they were not trained infantry men, but had their use as porters, at least that was what I thought until some problems with them a little later on. Probably about forty of these, there were some British soldiers with them, to give them some encouragement to face the shelling on the way up. We set off at a reasonable pace, it being a nice day for a change. Going up this mountain, which was called Orneto, we had to stick to a goat track so you can guess it was not an easy walk, plenty of rocks in the way. All was going well until we came in range of the German guns, and down came a nice welcome for us. Providing these shells were not too close, most of us took very little notice of them, we were used to them by now. But some of these little Indian men didn't seem to like them, so in panic they dropped the load that they were asked to carry and bolted for fear of their lives, not one but a lot of them. Some were carrying heavy boxes of ammunition which were vital to the fighting men up on the front, so the Sergeant in Charge had a problem to sort out. The only thing they could do was to pile them up near the track and go back for them, but it meant a double journey for some of them. So the little Indian men were not in favour. Whatever happened to them later on is anyone's guess, but it was not my problem, it was the Sergeant's. I guess he sorted that out later on but I can tell you because of these porters and the way they acted, it sure made a few of us angry, they were called a few bad names.

It was a long drag up this hill but I could see that we were getting near our objective. On arrival I had the feeling that I did not like this place, I could see that we were overlooked by the Germans, they were even higher up than us, so had a beautiful view of all that was going on below. I had to open my mouth and say to one of the Junior Officers, 'Whoever chose this position wants his head read. You are overlooked.' But my unkind words were heard by the officer who had chosen this spot, he said, 'Maybe you are right 'Q', but it is not for you to comment.' I understood that there was not much choice, as this had been taken over at night and because of the darkness the hills above were not spotted. Anyhow, I did not want to waste much time hanging about there, so I called in the Platoon Sergeant and his team of helpers to come and pick up their goods. Whilst this was going on Gerry was watching every movement so decided to give us a welcome with his 88 m.m., not a very friendly move on his part. I made for the deck at once as there was no cover at hand, I missed the first salvos but whilst I was on the ground, I spotted some better cover about twenty yards away and was about to sprint to it, so as to miss the next salvo that was sure to follow. But as I was in the sprinting position down came the second salvo and it helped me on my way to the cover that I was aiming for, I landed on my knees on hard rock and cut them. I attempted to rise from this position but something prevented me from doing so, I was hit in the back. I just lay there for a while, I did not seem to be in too much pain, I suppose because it happened so quickly. I know I shouted for some help which did not take long, the first person that turned up was my old friend Sergeant Major Tommy Race. He came over and tried to make me feel better with a few friendly words like, 'You're still in trouble as usual, Doug, let's have a look at you.' He took off my equipment, pulled up my jacket to have a look at the damage and said, 'Oh that's O.K. Doug, just a scratch. They will soon put that right for you.' But I could see a few tears in his eyes which gave me an indication that he was hiding his true feelings. He shouted for some stretcher bearers who were on the spot in no time, they asked me if I could get up. I said, 'No. It seems to be something in my back that is preventing me from doing so.' They also had a look at me and bandaged me up around the back, laid me on the stretcher on my stomach and looked around for some of my kit. They found a pack near me, thinking it was my kit, they forgot that I was a Quarter Master Sergeant and that I did not usually carry kit. We should do really, we get wounded as well as others. The pack by the way was full of cigarettes, which should have gone to the troops that were here, but in the confusion a mistake was made and this was not found out until I was in hospital some time after.

So the journey started to get me down this mountain. Every mile there was a First Aid Post, where I was looked at and given a pain killing tablet and sent on my way. The two stretcher bearers were two tall Sikhs, from the Indian Army Service Corp and I must say that they did a good job of carrying me down considering the state of the ground, full of rough boulders. They had to contend with the shelling as well but they took great care that I did not get hit again, I salute them.

On the way down I was wondering who would be selected to carry out my job, as it called for someone with quite some experience. Well I thought, what did I know before I started?

Not a lot. So whoever it was he would have to learn as well as I did, the taking of supplies into the line had to be carried out at least twice a day which was quite a task of getting through the lines and dodging the shells that came down as one moved along, never knowing when that would happen.

About the 88 m.m. shell that caused my injury, in a way I was lucky not to have been blown to pieces, as it was very close. What saved me from further injury was the fact that the shell landed in soft soil, it was in fact right where a dead German soldier had been recently buried. The shell managed to penetrate deep enough and explode below and just throw up a lot of debris, but the noise was deafening. I was very deaf for a time even after I was operated on, but the M.O. said not to worry as I was young and it would return, which it did later on but it never did return completely.

We at last reached the bottom of this hill and I was then lifted onto a jeep fitted up with stretchers so we could then get moving. It had been a few hours now since I was hit and I was beginning to think about my condition, was I going to make it? We stopped at another First Aid Post and here I was given a shot of morphine, this sent me off into a nice doze, but not for long as I was woken up a bit when they lifted me off a jeep and onto the large Military Ambulance, which of course carried more injured. It was here that I met another of our battalion, a Sergeant Sharp, I think his home was at Woolston, Near Southampton. He had been wounded on the ear lobe, although only minor, it was in a position where it bled badly. It took a piece of flesh out of the lobe in the shape of a 'V' and it bled so much that it looked worse than it was. I met him many months afterwards and he told me more about it. He said, 'All they did at the hospital was put a couple of stitches in it and pack me off back to the battalion. So, I was luckier than yourself, I used to wonder how you got on as yours was more serious.'

We had a problem when continuing on the journey, we ran into one of our very large R.E.M.E breakdown trucks and I could hear them having words outside who was to give way. It ended up by someone saying, 'Who should give way? We had better ask whoever is the senior around here.' It seemed to be me, despite of me being a casualty. I of course said, 'As we are casualties it is obvious who has to give way.' They had not yet made this track a one way, so that was the problem. So I said, 'You will have to ditch yourself, you are able to winch yourselves out no problem, but please get on with it'. The next thing I heard was this vehicle tipping over and we were once again on our way.

Altogether on this ambulance there were about eleven of us, most of them wounded by the same salvo as myself, I was the only one on a stretcher. We at last arrived at the Base Hospital, it had taken them about eight hours to get there so it proved how difficult it was to get us down, no wonder some did not make it. We were not blessed with helicopters in those days.

It was here for a while that I started to think of my wife Audrey back home, wondering if I would ever see her again. Also, I had a son back there that I had not yet had the pleasure of seeing, at least he was a part of me back there. For a few minutes I was left on the steps of this building for some reason and I began to feel very tired. I suppose it was because of the loss of blood, plus the journey down. They came down and took me up and did not waste too much time in attending to me. I noticed that there were many other casualties waiting to be attended to, mainly minor cases, they were all over the place. They took me off the stretcher and sat me on a table of some sort and for the first time they had to sit me up. I noticed that this room was surrounded by a lot of high mirrors and I could see the back of me in one of these. To all appearances it looked as if half of my back was missing, but actually the blood had congealed in a large area and gave it this appearance. I heard one of the casualties waiting say, 'Cor bloody hell, he's lost half of his back, what a mess!' It was at about this time that I was very sick, what made it worse was that they had a cold X-Ray plate on my stomach and back to try and locate the shrapnel that had entered my back. I was in a very poor way, soon after that a nurse came along and was giving me a blood transfusion at the same time as I was being wheeled along a corridor towards the Operating Theatre and so onto that operating table. I met the Surgeon who said, 'Don't worry Quarter Master, we will soon have you in order. Start counting.' I think I got to one and was away into a deep sleep.

CHAPTER TWENTY-SEVEN

Hospital

About two or three weeks afterwards, so they say, I was once again amongst the living. My first recollection of this was of lying in a bed, my eyes opening slightly and seeing something white going backwards and forwards which I could not really make out. I probably thought I was in Heaven, if I deserved that place, I must have gone back to sleep again. All this I was informed about when I could sit up and take notice. The time came for me to wake up and take more interest in what was going on and what they had done for me to try and put me in good order. The very first thing that they did was to give me a drink of hot tea, the orderly said to me, 'Can you hear me?' I know he said that because I asked him later on, also, I could see his mouth shape as to the words formed. I know I said, 'No.' My first thoughts were, I am deaf, which was true, for a while I was. He showed signs of drinking something, I nodded with a yes, so along came the drink, I was glad to have one as I was feeling thirsty. He sat and watched me drink this with some interest, the reason for this I found out for myself, I'm pretty sure that I was correct in my presumption, as long as the one that was drinking this hot drink kept it down he was going to live or at least improve, so I was one of them. I tested this some time afterwards, I watched one or two others who were badly wounded, they gave some others this test and those that could not keep it down did not live, what a place to be in!

I soon found out that I was in the D.I. Ward (Dangerously Ill Ward). It was not a very happy ward to be in, but there it is, it was here to do its best for you. There were so many of us, we even had a little Italian boy with us, because he had set off a Tella mine, one of the German versions that when you put your foot into it, it sets it off and jumps up to about waist high full of small steel ball bearings, so it could give a nasty wound if it hit you. This little boy was just an innocent victim, walking along to get to his home and he happened to wander off the path and his foot came into contact with this mine (trip mine I think we called them).

I had the same experience one day when out on a Reconnaissance Patrol. I was searching for a good place to sight my mortars, with a few others who were doing the same. The person in front of me set it off and I like an idiot stood there watching it rise into the air and come down again, lucky for me it was a dud one as it had probably been out in the wet too long. I saw it smoke and fizzle out, but I did not hang about in case it was a delayed one, I was glad to get out of that area, another name for this was 'S' mine. Many were taken up by hand but you had to be careful as some of them were booby trapped underneath. All these things were about, like the small mines that were placed in a bunch of grapes or even oranges or apples. Oh yes, he was crafty with his mines, you just had to be alert.

So, back to the ward again. I realized that I was sitting up in bed and that they had placed a donkey under my legs and strapped me down somehow, so that I could not slide down in the bed. After I had drunk the tea I could see that the orderly gave a gentle smile of content.

Next to me was an empty bed, but not for long, they brought in another young soldier who was in plaster from the top of his legs to his neck, he must have been held together with this. He was probably blown up and it was only a matter of time for him, he came round fairly quickly from his operation. He was lying on his back as they put him, no pillow just flat. He leaned over to me thinking that I could help him, but that was out of the question, he was asking for a cigarette which I had plenty of so I signalled over to the orderly. He came over to see what I wanted and I said, 'He is asking for a smoke. Can he have one do you think?' There was no denying him, so I told him to take one out of my stock in my locker. This he gave him, lit it for him and walked away, but I was keeping an eye on him. He probably smoked about an inch of this and I saw his arm drop down to his side with the cigarette still smouldering between his fingers. I signalled to the orderly once again, he came over and tested to see his condition, he was dead. He was not at all surprised about this, he was so used to it and was aware it was to happen. He was, I should think about nineteen years old, he signalled another orderly who came over with a stretcher and flung him on it just like a piece of beef, just another for the burial service. It sounds callous, but there was no time for sentiment in a place like this, there was a war on and many to see to.

On my right side was another sergeant, he was from the Royal Engineers, he had a bad wound on his side. He was taking up German mines when he had an accident, a shell came down too close to him and he rolled on one of those that he had taken up, but managed to scrabble away a bit so as not to take the full force otherwise he would not have been here. It is surprising the amount of miracles that do happen whilst doing our dangerous jobs, we seem to find a way to dodge them. I was pleased to see that he was getting over his problem before I left this hospital.

Again, opposite me, was yet another sergeant, he was from the Welsh Guards. To be sure, he was from the regiment that relieved us up at Orneto Casino. The Germans knew very well that they took over from us so they gave them another welcome as we left, so I was told later on. This welcome was what we call a good stonking, or shelling us to Kingdom Come. This sergeant was hit badly in his right leg, so much so that it had to be amputated. He had come from the same area as I did and it took a long time to get him down so that he got gangrene in his leg, the reason for amputation. It also seemed to have reached his brain and he was screaming in pain, despite the giving of many painkillers. We could not put up with the noise so I for one asked if he could be put in some other ward, they said, 'Yes, we do have that in mind that he is disturbing other patients in this ward.' So they put him upstairs some place. We heard that the poor fellow died overnight.

Another patient was unable to sleep in a bed because of the bed vibrations. He had a bullet lodged in his throat, a vital place that any vibrations could make it go the wrong way and that would kill him, so he had to sit bolt upright as well. It all depended on which way it made up its mind to go. I never did know the result as I was moved onto another hospital soon. Having had this experience of living in this ward of D.I. Soldiers was something never to be forgotten.

I must tell you about one more young soldier from our own Regiment who received about twelve bullets through his stomach and lived. It just so happened that not one of these bullets hit a vital spot to cause his death. He told us that he was on a particular attack when he turned a corner and ran straight into a burst of machine gun fire from about fifty yards away. It practically destroyed the whole of his section in one long burst, it was a miracle on his part to be alive. There were many really bad cases that these men I know would never get over and be able to return home to see their loved ones.

So ended my stay in this base hospital, I had to move on to make way for others. I was carried out and put on an ambulance for a journey to Fogier, not too long a drive down on the Adriatic Coast, which today is a holiday resort. Once again, it was full of wounded soldiers, we as well as Germans were in here. I was put in a room on my own here as proper to my rank, if you wanted you could protest and move in with others but I did not bother about that I was quite content to stay quiet for a while, not feeling too good. It was not long before I had a knock on the door and to my surprise it was a German Soldier, he spoke good English and introduced himself as a sergeant. He gave his name, but I don't recall that now. He said, 'I would like to have a talk with you about one or two things,' if I felt like it, so I said 'Well what is the problem?' He said that he had a complaint to make, so I said, 'Then why don't you make it to the Hospital Staff?' He said that he had tried that, but it did not seem to work, would I try to help so I said, 'O.K. what is it?' He seemed to be well aware of the Geneva Conventions about the treatment of war wounded soldiers and the taking care of them.

He said that they were having difficulties in getting proper care in the ward, like changing their bandages, asking for the pots etc. so as they could relieve themselves, they seemed to want to keep them waiting and could not care less. There were many other small things that annoyed them, the way they dumped the food onto them, it seemed that they had a grudge against them for no reason. I said, 'It is probably because the way your people are treating our prisoners of war that we hear about on the news.'

'Maybe,' he said 'But that is not us, we are not Nazis, just ordinary soldiers and we were not in favour of this Nazi movement in any case.'

'So why did you not all do something about it years ago and let them get into power?' I said to him.

'Well, what could us few do about it? Anyhow, do you think you can help?'

'I'll try,' I said to him, 'But I'm only a Sergeant and I am not powerful enough to throw my weight about. I will speak to the doctor when I see him again.' He shook my hand before he left, he seemed very much in earnest and a likeable man. When the doctor came in, I mentioned the conversation that he had with me and he said that he was not aware of such treatment but he would look into it. Obviously he did do something about it, because the German sergeant came in to see me again and thanked me and shook hands again with me. He stayed for a while and we had a talk about many things regarding the war. I did not see him again, as I was not to be long at this hospital either. I enjoyed my stay there as most of them were on the mend.

I was then taken away again on the ambulance down to the docks and put on a ship. This got us talking, were we being sent home? We could not get a direct answer to that question, maybe some of us were, but not me, I was taken off at the Port of Barie a few miles down the coast. I started to get some trouble inside me around the stomach area, it developed into an acute pain, so they whipped me quickly into the nearest hospital, which happened to be an American one. In no time I was on the X-Ray table. They were having a look at me to find out what was causing this pain, they found out that a clot of blood was jammed in my left groin, the result of my operation on my right side, the kidney operation. It was stopping the flow of blood getting into my left leg and starting to swell up and giving me a lot of pain, I was on morphine twice a day.

During my very short stay here with the Americans they had a visit from one of their Senior Officers who was dishing out Purple Hearts, a Medal that they gave to all their wounded, not us, all we got was a small brass stripe called a Gold Stripe, which was sewn on your left sleeve to show that you had received a wound. As this officer was approaching me, he said, 'As you are British I guess that you are unlucky.' I think I passed a remark like, 'Surely you could spare one, I am at least attached to the 5th American Army.'

'Sorry,' he said.

The Sergeant next to me said, 'Hey bub, you watch this move in a minute. You see that guy in the corner.'

I said, 'Yes.'

'Well,' he said. 'He will get one as well, but he was not wounded, he fell off the back of a truck and cut his knee badly. It is considered a wound during his active service. Not exactly a good and honest reward is it? There it is, who is to know when he gets home, if he gets home.' I was only with them a few days and our people came and picked me up and took me to the 84th British General in Barletta not far from there, but I liked the welcome that the Red Cross Nurses gave us at the docks when we came off the ship a few days before. They smothered us in chocolates, smokes and tobacco including a hot drink, plus a kiss and a cuddle, they just could not do enough for us. I only wish that I had been in a more receptive mood, but my condition would not allow this.

When I got to the British Hospital, I was in no time put to bed and given yet another examination. They found the trouble just as the Americans did, so in no time my leg was raised up from the bed at about the angle of 45 degrees, at the same time wrapped up in cotton wool, before they put this on they painted it with some soothing oil. This they did a couple of times a day, even that was painful as my leg was so swollen, I thought it was going to burst. They kept this leg up for quite a few days, to ease the pain I was given morphine, no more than two injections a day, when that wore off they gave me a large white tablet which worked, but not so powerfully as the morphine. The morphine one could get accustomed to, because it sent you off into a nice sleepy state, I used to look forward to that in the late evenings, it would help you to sleep for the rest of the night.

The day came when the doctor came around and said, 'We are going to let your leg down and get it into use once again, but we can only do it just a little each day until it reaches the bed top.' I can tell you, that was no joke either, when the blood started to circulate around the leg that sure was painful. Then, one day, I had more than one doctor come around me, discussing something about my leg, then they moved away talking about it, so that their speech was out of my hearing, they were looking at me, then my leg, I was thinking maybe they were going to take it off. When they all went away and my own doctor came back to my bed I said, 'What is the problem with me and this leg, are you thinking about taking it off?' He replied, 'As a matter of fact, that was the subject, but we decided against it, as you are a young man, you could get over some of the problems that concern this leg of yours. How did you guess?' By this time I had got some of my hearing back mainly in my left ear and it continued like this for quite a number of years.

I was in a ward this time at my request with the lower ranks and as I came in the ward all dressed for bed, they did not know what rank I was. I mention this because rank came into conversation a lot of times.

There were probably about forty men in this ward, from all sorts of regiments with all sorts of wounds, lucky for most not many seemed to have been hit in the face. I put this down to the way they were trained to take cover face down, steel helmet on the head, properly to cover the face and back of the head and neck, so it left open the chest and legs as well as middle body, mainly to bullets, as those used to come at you like wasps and in the thousands.

There was one thing that was not liked in the service, if you were an Officer or a Senior N.C.O. or Warrant Officer and you got wounded and you were not substantive you lost your rank and this hurt because you had already earned this rank with hard graft and study. In other words, you should not have got yourself wounded. No, we did not like that, it also put you back and it took time to recover it again. The Americans could not understand this order, why I am mentioning this, was because it happened to me once, not long after I came out of hospital, I was back to a sergeant, I didn't like it.

Back to the hospital once again, after a while one got used to these places, at least we were away from that hell let loose up the front line, I can see it now, all us allies shooting up the Germans and vice versa. Does it make sense? No, not when you are out of it for a while, you don't wonder at some of them deserting.

That reminds me of another event. I was out for a rest for a while and enjoying a nice peaceful sleep when I heard a voice in the distance shouting my name, it must have been about 2 o'clock in the morning. I tried to close my ears but eventually was shaken up by someone pushing my toes. 'Excuse me, but is that Sergeant French?'

I gave a grunt and said, 'Yes, who the hell is that shouting for me this time of the morning?'

'Sorry, Sarge, but the Adjutant wants you at once.'

'Right,' I said. 'I'll be along.' I had to get out of this nice warm bed and report to him. The Adjutant said, 'Well I'm sorry about this, but I have a job that is only suitable for you to do and in a hurry.' I could never find the reason for the hurry business. He went on to say, 'Well, here it is, we have two deserters here and they have both got to be returned to Battalion H.Q. and handed over to the R.S.M. I have a jeep and driver laid on to take you all as far as it can get, then it's a matter of a long walk.' The Regimental Police went off and fetched them from detention, two strapping men who did not look like deserters. The officer gave them a talking to first, telling them, 'If you do not co-operate with this Sergeant, he has our permission to shoot you both. He does not want any attempts from you to try and run away on your journey to the front.' With that, he handed me a captured German Luger .9 m.m., so I strapped this onto my side, no other equipment or arms. He said, 'Well here you are, Sarge, all yours.' I introduced myself to them, but it was not needed because they both knew of me and my capabilities. I also warned them that I didn't want to have to shoot them, for them to be wise and just do as I said and all would be well. They were issued with a rifle and equipment, but no ammunition as yet, they would receive some of that when they reached their destination.

Off we went, got into the jeep and set off in the dark, it was not long before it was light and by that time we had got as far as we could on the jeep. I told the driver to sit and wait for me, I should be gone about three hours, out we got and I made them walk in front at a reasonable space. We soon came within the range of the German shelling, one or two came down not too far from us and they started to drop for cover seeming very frightened. I stopped them for a while and said, 'Sit down on those rocks for a while, I'll have a talk to you about a few things, also try and find out for my own interest, why you deserted, you have most likely had all this talk on previous occasions. First of all, when these few shells came down just now at that distance, why does that make you nervous? Those are not going to hurt you, you two do not look the nervous type.' They said 'Well we are and we just can't help it. They scare us to death and we don't want to die.'

'Well none of us do if it comes to that, just think of all the rest of the men that you soldier with, how do you think they feel about it? You must try and control yourselves and ignore them, when you can smell the cordite from these shells then is the time to worry a little more. Is that the real reason why you deserted?'

'I guess so, Sarge,' says one of them.

'Let's continue on our journey and see how you cope with yourself if any more come down, which as you know is most likely,' I said.

So we continued on our way. I was supposed to know the way, but I began to realise that I was not so sure. I had not been up to this place before as they had advanced quite a bit since I was up here last. I came across a sign soon, saying 'Signals H.Q.' so I thought it best to go in and make some enquiries, this turned out to be an interrogation. They had been warned that there were some Germans dressed up as British, who had infiltrated into our lines but we were not aware of this. We were challenged as such and we thought to ourselves, this is a set up. I had to prove who we were, show identification, which we did, our own A.B. 64 with all our details on it, the name of the regiment which they had already asked, who and where we were off to now. I gave them the R.S.M., the Commanding Officer's name where I had just come from and why, it took some time to get us clear. It was some young lieutenant who was after promotion I should think, so once we were cleared it became a bit of a joke between us. Still, better to be that way than to be slack when they had been warned. They then directed us to where our H.Q. was and we set off once again, arriving safely with no bother from them. Their trouble started as soon as they were handed over to the R.S.M., he gave them such a dressing down that they would never forget, in fact, I should think that the German Army must have heard him shouting at them.

I left them and made my way back, all this had taken longer than I thought, mainly because of our interrogation, the driver of the jeep was getting concerned that something had happened to us or me. Anyhow, when I got back to the camp where I was staying for a while the Adjutant called for me again, just to tell me that those two men that I handed over to the R.S.M. had gone again, I reckon it was because of the dressing down that he gave them.

Back to this hospital once more. They were lowering my leg a little each day, until it reached the bed top, so they let me alone for a few days, then it had to start again. 'It's no good,' the Doctor said. 'It's got to come down to the ground yet and I'm afraid it's going to be a painful task. So it's up and down a few inches every day until you touch the floor.' This went on for about a week, I must have aged a couple of years going through this procedure. They kept saying, 'Right that's enough for today, some more tomorrow.' Then I had to put my weight on it, another murderous task, I went around the ward hanging onto the beds with a few laughs from other patients. From the start, it must have taken just over two weeks to get going again, but it was going to be a long time before I could walk properly, which it was, I was on sticks for a long time.

Then they decided to make me an up-patient, that meant me wearing my jacket which showed my rank (sorry to keep mentioning about my Rank, it's not because I am boasting, because it's not a very high Rank, but it is something that needs to be said as it is a military story and all are conscious of the fact that we are their bosses. Being too familiar with them, because of discipline is just not on, it's all part of Kings Regulations) I should not have been in this ward with them, so having to put on my jacket was yet another rule. It came as a complete surprise to a young private who was next to me all this time, to see that I was a Quarter Master Sergeant. As soon as he saw me he said, 'Bloody hell 'Q', we did not know.' He said, 'Our 'Q' is an old man up against you, he must be at least forty-five years old, you are only about twenty-four.'

'Nearly correct,' I said. 'I'm twenty-six years.' Because of the showing of rank, I had to move out into a single room, but I was in touch with them all day, helping out with things that they wanted or needed. I used to help the nurses as well, it was for the want of something to do and to get this leg moving. It came to the time when it was possible for me to go to the town of Barletta, there was a cinema set up by the British which we could attend if you could get there. I thought I would have a go at getting down there but it turned out that I was a bit too ambitious. The walk was too far and too soon for me, I ended up in some lady's house as I came over faint and had to have assistance. This lady came out with someone else and took me in to rest, but I could not stay there, I had to get back to hospital. In my best Italian, I told them to find the Military Police and get them to take me back. It was hard to make them understand, but it came about, they turned up and I thanked them for their care and I was taken back, with a reprimand not to do that again, at least not for a while. I did visit the cinema, but not by walking, I went down by a liberty truck.

All this began up in the Casino area as I have said, the time and date 12.30 hrs, 4th March 1944. I will never forget that date. Today, fifty years after I still suffer with the effects of it, one cannot forget. I had also lost part of my kidney and from that, I developed thrombosis in my left leg and it also affected my right leg, as it became a crutch to support my left leg.

Time went on and they thought that I had improved enough to return to my unit, so I was up for a medical. I had my doubts, but no doubt that I could persuade them. It just so happened that the army were getting rather short of Senior N.C.O.s of experience. There was a Captain from our own regiment looking for some possible available Senior N.C.O.s, he spotted me with my jacket around my shoulders and he approached me and asked me what did I think that my chances were of getting back to my unit. I myself could not be sure, it was of course up to the Medical Officer. I eventually got in front of him, he had a good look at me and said, 'Well, they knocked you about' and then asked me how I felt in myself. I said, 'Apart from this left leg not so bad. I'm sure I could be of some use to my battalion as a Quarter Master Sergeant.'

'Well,' he said 'I am going to risk it, no doubt your own Medical Officer will see you when you get to him, and he will be the one to decide.' So that was that, he gave me some marks.

After a few days, I was on my way back to join my Regiment, which by now was out of Italy and over to Palestine for a rest and to receive some reinforcements. I was about to go when the whole of the hospital staff as well as the patients were confined to the hospital compound, as there was a suspected flu epidemic in this area and so as not to spread it, we were all confined to this area until it was cleared up, this held us up for a while.

Eventually I was heading towards my unit. They were somewhere in the area of Damascus and Beirut, so I gathered my documents and was taken to the docks at Naples. There was a lot of confusion going on here as it was packed with Jewish people who were obviously making their way to Palestine, they must have had some clearance from the British Government as I think we still had some hold on the affairs in that area. As I approached the gang plank leading up to this ship, I met an officer who seemed to have some authority over all these goings on. I said, 'I hope I have separate quarters from this lot.' They all looked as if they wanted a good bath and a change of clothing, it was obvious that in the past they had had a rough time of it. He said, 'Not to worry, Sarge, your quarters are reserved, you have a bunk to yourself. All this lot is going to take some sorting out when we land over there. When you arrive at Haifa Port you will have a truck waiting for you to take you to the Barracks concerned for those in transit.'

On this ship, I soon learned that most of these Jewish people had come from Germany as well as Russia. They must have been held up some place for a long time, it was pitiful to see the state of them, one could see that they had all been suffering. It was only a short journey across the Med, not much worry as regards to having a visit from a German submarine or from any aircraft, we had practically chased from the skies. It seemed very strange coming back here once again, I was here back in 1939, nothing seemed to have changed. I was in the same barracks for a while, Carmel, at the foot of Mount Carmel. As I said, my stay here was short, I had to pick up some more papers and find out exactly where my unit was stationed. It was out in the desert or no man's land, not far from Damascus.

As soon as I arrived, I had to report to the Adjutant, who straight away said, 'You will have to have a medical by our own doctor.' I knew the results straight away without him telling me, as my left leg was swollen very badly. His answer was, 'Sorry can't accept you as you are.' So, after a good meal in the

Sergeants' Mess and a good bath, change of clothing, uniform and a good night's sleep, I was taken to a railway station. I caught a train to Damascus, and was met there by one of the staff from the Sergeants' Mess, who drove me to what I considered the smallest Sergeants' Mess on earth. It only held about six members, but it was very comfortable, all the orderlies were Arab and dressed up in white with red sash and fez. I had a very good couple of nights there, good food and treated like a lord, but my papers were made up to continue to the British General Hospital, Beirut.

An ambulance called for me on the second morning and took me right there, it was situated on top of a hill, overlooking the city of Beirut. It was then a beautiful city, full of white buildings and poplar trees (today that is all gone). I was given a nice room on my own with a good view, given good treatment and once again a good examination. They said, as all others, that I now had thrombosis in my leg and that I would need to rest it for quite a while. Well, this I did. I would rate this place as first class, all was spic and span, at times I sat outside the ward on a wicker basket chair with pull out leg rests and I was there sunbathing. I even had a cool beer brought to me when I wanted one, not too often I can assure you, that was not permitted.

What did I do to pass the day away? Well, mainly reading, but I was also encouraged to have occupational therapy, such as making leather toys for the Red Cross, even embroidery. It was surprising what these ladies would ask you to take on, anyhow no one was watching to take the mickey out of me. I did send one or two back home for our son John who I had not yet seen, one was a camel and one an elephant. I sent them home and they were received in no time, considering that there was a war on. I was here for about one month and I can tell you I was sorry to leave the place, those that managed to stay here were lucky. I had notice to move on, passed fit enough for return to my unit. My own feelings were different, I would return, but was sure that I wouldn't be there long, I could feel that my service as a soldier was going to be short lived. I was coming up for twenty-seven years old and I could have stayed in for many more years if I had been fit enough. Anyhow, I was soon to start to catch up with my unit again, by this time, they had moved back again to Italy, so that was going to take many weeks.

CHAPTER TWENTY-EIGHT

Back to Italy to Rejoin my Unit in Action

I was discharged from this hospital and proceeded down into Beirut to a form of barracks. They used to be occupied by French Troops, I had to hang around here for a while waiting for my orders to move. During my short stay I met another Hampshire Regiment Sergeant, by the name of Smith. He had just been discharged from hospital as well, but his problem was not of wounds but malaria of all things, so we chummed up for a while, not sure if he was going to return to his battalion or not. He was not with us, the 5th Battalion, his was the 1st Fourth Hamps. I am bringing him into this story because he had a tragic accident. We had organised a swimming party for an afternoon and we were all going to go down together, we had with us a life saving party as well, mainly because most of these men had been wounded and were not sure of themselves, so they were there to give assistance if needed. The parade was to go down by truck and we were to meet at a certain spot, but he decided not to go with us, he for some reason went down to another part of the beach on his own. I also decided not to go as I did not feel all that good, so I just strolled about quietly and gradually made my way down to the beach. As I was going out of the main gate a young Arab boy came running up to me all flustered and hot and babbling away in fast French. He could see that I was not grasping the situation properly, so he took my hand and dragged me down to the beach where, from a distance, I could see a body on the edge of the sea. Evidently, this boy had dragged him out on his own somehow, I went to see who it was and lo and behold it was Sergeant Smith. I can only guess that because of his illness he had a heart attack and so drowned, he was blue. I tried artificial respiration, but he was too far gone for any help. Just a few hundred yards from here there was a French Barracks, I asked to see the doctor so he could have a look at him and confirm that he had died, this he did, but was not too happy about doing it. I had to return to my own barracks and report it and they organised a party to go pick him up. He was buried locally in a Military Cemetery, I wondered how his wife felt about that, or was he confirmed as killed in action? I often wonder about these things.

So much for the story, I have mentioned many as it is all part of the soldiering, it's not all fighting. If you have been wounded you feel a bit of a loner, you seem to be moving about from place to place trying to catch up with yourself. My return journey was by the way I came, I called from one transit camp to another, the first one was at Toranto down in the heel of Italy that was packed out with troops, who didn't know if they were coming or going.

Then, it was on to some more army trucks and move off again somewhere northwards. It was just not plain sailing, we stopped at two or three transit camps on the way back to the line fire, most of us could not grasp just what was going on in these camps. There seemed to be a lot of men standing about doing nothing, there were many who were doing their best not to get put on the list as reserves for the front line. It was something that was very difficult to control, there were so many of them, some from the front line who had had slight wounds but bad enough to be an in-patient for a while. They then were sent to these camps, there were good and bad amongst them. At this particular camp I got involved in checking some men who were going round in a circle to draw a second lot of pay, what they had learnt to do was when some of the soldiers were killed they would actually take their A.B. Pt. 2 Army Pay Book Record, Number, Rank, Name, amount and record of credit carried by Service Men all the time, from their pockets and keep it for that use. They could not care less what they were doing to the government, who in the long run were paying for all this swindling. It was my job to try and catch

194

some of them at it, which I did and I had to charge them. Some of them did not care for my action, so they ended up with many more charges than they bargained for, their fault not mine, they asked for it.

The best story that I can tell you is the private who actually took the uniform from a dead captain, then deserted and kept up this pose for many weeks, calling at R.A.S.C. Depots and collecting petrol for his so called company or battalion and then selling it to the locals. He had deserters to help him with this racket, so he was in for some big trouble, whatever happened to him I don't know. Some of these lads were also selling some of their clothing to the local Italians, we caught them at it in a wood nearby, all no good men. Luckily there were not many of them, but the few that were doing this was enough. Many of us just could not understand why they wanted to do such harmful tasks. It's a wonder that we ever won the war with such persons about, who could think of nothing else but to cheat the Government. I was very pleased when I moved out of this camp, because I could not stand this kind of corruption, I never could. I was just not brought up that way or ever thought that way.

After a few more transit camps, I arrived back with my own battalion, but like everything else, we saw changes in those few months that I had been away. I had to report to my Commanding Officer, the usual things, 'Well how are you French? Just hope that you are fit once again. You may say yes, but it is up to our Medical Officer, so go along and see him first then report back to me, then we will see what we can do for you. I doubt if you will get your old Company back.' Off I went to see the M.O. 'Pleased to see you again,' he said. 'Let's have a look at you.' When he had finished his inspection of my body, he had a doubtful look about him. 'Well, I am going to give you a trial at it once again, but I doubt if you will last long, I'll risk it. If things get bad you know the answer, come and see me. I'll let the C.O. know about you, so you had better go and see him again as he said.' So back to him again. 'I see that he has passed you as a doubtful fitness,' he said, 'I'll give you "C" Company as their Quarter Master. You will know the Company Commander as you were sergeants together at one time.'

Over I went to this company, and saw the Company Commander. He said that he was glad to see me, that he heard that I was back and he asked if he could have me with him. So here we were back together again. I had to take the place of Wally Paddocks who was being sent back to Divisional H.Q., not sure of the reason, maybe he had reached the age of forty years, which is the time that the Infantry move you on, as they seem to consider that is the age to go. I did see him before he went and he seemed rather keen to get out of it anyhow, how he got on after that I do not know.

We were now fighting up in the Gothic Line, another defensive German position, where they were well dug in and hard to move on. Their tanks were well dug in, only part of them could be seen, they were so well dug in, but as usual we had them out by some heavy shelling by the Royal Artillery as well as other tanks. Myself and the Company Commander got on well together and I was quite happy to serve under him. He also asked me how I felt, so I told him the truth. I said, 'At the moment, not so bad, but I worry about my left leg, it swells up if I do too much walking on it. Anyhow, we will see how it goes.' So, I just got on with the job once again, in some ways glad to be occupied once again, back into active service. I must say that I did not feel so brave as before, I suppose it was the fear of being hit once again and next time not being so lucky, if one can call it that.

We were in action in the area of Florence around the river Po and one night taking up food and ammunition we had to cross a small but vital bridge that ran over a part of this river. Suddenly down came a very large shell and broke up this bridge and everything that was on it went into this river. That included myself and all my stock, all this material that I had to help feed the troops that were up in the hills desperately requiring it. Now it was lost until I or somebody could replace it. Because of the hills we were using mules to carry all this material, most of the mules went into the river with it, some of them cast their loads off somehow and were swimming free. One of these I grabbed for myself and hung onto his tail, he was a strong and powerful animal, so he got me onto the banks of this river. Of course, I was wet through and not feeling so good about all this. I thought to myself, Doug, you are a bit of an idiot coming back to this, surely you have had enough. You can imagine the state that I was in, what with losing all this equipment and mules disappearing down the river some place, most never to be seen again, all probably picked up by the local Italians at some place or other. The troops that were with me helping also went different ways, they just had to look after themselves and use their own initiative and find their own way back to Company H.Q. Can you imagine it all? Everyone wet through and cold, it was quite some time before I noticed that I had been hit again, not severely on my right thigh. It was not hurting too much I suppose it was because my leg was wet and cold. I had kept hold of this mule that pulled me out of the river, got on its back and rode it back to Battalion H.Q., along with a few other stragglers. I reported to the M.O. once again, but not until I had been back to my company and changed all my clothing and saw to many others that all needed a change. It was a right mess to put in good order, to reorganise another lot of food, find more mules to get it up to the troops and find someone else to take it up, another sergeant.

I was instructed then to go see the M.O. who gave me a lecture once again 'What again?' he said. 'I told you that you can't take much more of this.' He bandaged my leg, but was unable to operate, as the piece of metal was too deep for him to extract. 'I'm afraid it's hospital again for you 'Q' and just look at your left leg, see how that is swollen? No, that's it for you, you have had enough. You are off to get that seen to and don't make any efforts to get back here. By the way, since you came back I forgot to tell you that your friend Sergeant Major Tommy Race was killed a few weeks ago. You can see that there are not many left of the original so don't press your luck, stay away or it will be your lot next time.' Once again, all this soldiering was coming to an end. I was then packed off to hospital back into nice clean white sheets.

I spent a few more weeks in hospital, nicely fed and taken care of but what was to happen to me now? I was examined a few times here and down graded as no longer fit for active service, so my days of soldiering were over. I joined the ranks of sick, lame and lazy as we called ourselves, sitting back here doing nothing whilst they carry on with the battle without us. I guess we could say we had done our bit, so didn't feel so guilty about it.

There came a time, when I was called up to the C.O. to say they had given me a staff job as Camp Quarter Master Sergeant at a P.O.W. No. 368 Camp in Toranto, Southern Italy. Most likely the Germans that we took prisoners in the past were down in this camp, or some of them. I journeyed down to a nice quiet area, amongst the farming land. This was well away from the war, quite a different way of life, they hardly were aware that there was a war on.

The camp consisted mainly of Germans, Italians and some Mongolians and Russians, by the look of it a well organised and happy camp. It was really a transit camp, from the front line a lot of them came here for some kind of interrogation, a change of worn out clothing, to be deloused, washed and then most of them were transported over to North Africa.

The different nationalities were not mixed as that would not work, the Germans were more organised than the Italians and that's a certainty, they would not rub along together. The Russians and Mongolians also had a different way of life, for instance they had a habit of cutting up the flies of the tent and turning them into a pair of short trousers, they did not seem to like socks on their feet so those were turned into gloves. Their games for the want of something to do, were of the knock out types and if someone was knocked out they would find that very funny – strange! The Germans made themselves useful, with coloured stones, they would build the different cap badges of the British Army and prepare a bank of earth along and outside of the Army huts all in a neat row, they really looked nice. But our Camp Lager Sergeants, those who looked after the prisoners got themselves drunk one night and were stupid enough to run up and down them and destroy this good work. A very ignorant low down thing to do, it really lets our race down when they do these stupid things, I know everyone was disgusted with them. Most of them were charged with being drunk and disorderly and given some sort of punishment but being Sergeants, they could only give them reprimands. However this charge just so happened to have caught one of them out, it was revealed that one of them was not a sergeant but had been posing as one. He had dressed himself up as one from the front line, including identity A.B. 64 he had taken from a dead sergeant and had been taken as a sergeant for many months. This charge had shown him up to be a fraud, he was never seen again, so I guess he was in prison for some time.

At the camp, I had a rather large store with a lot of kit so I needed help in more ways than one. First of all I had a young German PTE of Intelligence helping me out and he was really glad to have something to do. He had lots of little rewards for doing so, he was a kind of a batman for me, he even laid out my water in the morning for my wash and shave, he cleaned and pressed my clothes and made up my bed, he cleaned up the store and tidied it up when it was needed. I found him very useful and we got on well together, he was a most pleasant man to work with. I have his photograph, his name was Heinz Tauber and he came from Berlin, that is all I know about him. He was just an ordinary soldier, I do not remember his regiment, probably Herman Goering's regiment. I wonder what he thought of his home town when his time came to return home, if he had one. I have often thought about him and how he got on when he returned home and what he did for a living after the war. I suppose I could have found him if I asked the Red Cross people.

Inside the camp where the prisoners were, it was built on rocks, that made it hard for them to try and dig themselves out but some of these rocks were large enough on the surface for some talented men to carve out the faces of the war leaders like

*Heinz Tauber, my storeman cum batman at
368 P.O.W. Camp, Toranto, Italy, 1944/5.*

Stalin, Churchill and Hitler. They were very well done, not sure whether it was a German or an Italian, it may have been a joint effort, the Italians were good at that sort of thing.

Concerning the Italians and what they thought of the war that they had become involved in, it was not the fault of the people but of their leaders, they just had to fight for their country whether they liked it or not. To us, they just did not have their heart in this war and they wanted out of it, especially from the beginning in the Western Desert when we first opened up on them. We just walked over them despite the fact they outnumbered us by five to one, they underestimated us, all troops that we had out there at the time were professionals but we could not proceed any further either because we also were not prepared for war. As the fighting progressed later on after the desert, there were times when we came up against them and they just gave up. Don't let us underestimate them as soldiers, they could fight if the occasion arose and if they thought it was worth getting killed for, they were rather annoyed with the way the German Army were treating them as second class soldiers. They eventually gave up as you know, in September 1944 when they saw us coming into their country, we and the Americans were running over them. Eventually they helped us, not so much in the fighting part but jobs like traffic duties on crossroads, general fatigues, we found a use for them. It was better than putting them all in P.O.W. Camps where we would have to find the staff to take care of them and have to feed them for doing nothing. They appeared to be harmless enough as helpers, glad to be out of it, we know full well that some deserted and got back to their homes.

Back to this P.O.W. Camp again. I must say that when I arrived my knowledge of the Italian language was very little but the Sergeant that I took over from had become quite fluent, as he said, it would come to me. We had to deal with many Italians as we were on an Italian farm and we employed some Italians. Within a few months I was speaking it quite well, in nine months, I found that I had no problem, not fluent, but enough for a general conversation, Southern Italian of course. The Northerners were aware where I had picked it up, the farm people said to me one day when I was talking to an American Soldier who come to visit us, they said in Italian, 'You Sergeant must be very intelligent because you can speak American, English and Italian.' So I said, 'That is not quite so, because Americans speak English as well.' Well, they just could not believe it, because of their drawl. These were simple country folks and they were not aware about languages of the world, until I pointed it out to them.

My job here was interrupted at times when I had to attend hospital for treatment on my wound, it took a long time to heal up and I had one or two other problems as well. My main job was to feed these prisoners and change their clothing as and when required. Most of the staff as I have mentioned before were ex-wounded or had some medical problem. We did have some time off to visit the town. There was a Sergeants' Mess, also a cinema which was run by the army, sometimes we went to the beach and had a bit of a swim and some sunbathing so, leisure wise, we were not too badly off.

We built a very small Sergeants' Mess in the camp and made a bar. The drinks consisted of our own supply, the rest was their vino of various types, so we did not do so badly. Food wise we did well, our own supply and the farm would supply me with plenty of eggs, to pay for them I would give them some old clothing or repairable boots, they were pleased to receive these items as I have said, they had nothing in their shops in those days.

There came a time when they said that the war was over and we could go home for some leave, but according to them, only for a short while. We would be coming back to help close down the camp, but as it happened this did not come about. I packed up most of my kit, but had to leave my wartime souvenirs to take home later, it was all packed up in a nice locked box with my name printed on it. We were to be flown home in an American Liberator, they had emptied out the gun positions and made room to take us troops to take back home. We made our way to Barie airport. There were quite a few others coming home on leave as well as us from this camp, but we had to wait for some good flying weather. This caused a problem for me, it just so happened, that a piece of metal made up its mind to come to the surface of my thigh and was turning septic. I had to show this to the M.O. who was not very happy about sending me off like that, the flight had already been cancelled twice and he said if it was cancelled the next day then he was afraid that he would have to send me to hospital again. He gave me something to calm it down a bit, I had a sleepless night. Next day was good flying weather, so we took off. I sat next to the navigator so I had more room to spread my leg out, although it was my first flight ever, I can't say that I enjoyed it because of this leg problem but I was pleased that I was on the plane as I did not want to lose this opportunity to get home to see Audrey, I had already written to her telling her that I would be on my way soon.

The weather held up for us, but it was a bit bumpy at times. As we were approaching Britain the navigator was talking on the radio to someone somewhere, and he said to me, 'I have just been talking to Diss Airport where we are landing to have an ambulance standing by to take you to hospital, so you will soon be made more comfortable'. So, that is what happened, the R.A.F. Ambulance took me straight to their hospital and in no time I was on the operating table having this leg seen to. I was off into another deep sleep, not so long this time, when I woke up I was situated in a nice warm, clean bed again and the M.O. said, 'All's well. We got the foreign body out and it should not take too long to heal up.' But after I had been there ten days and still no sign of sending me home to my wife, I was beginning to get concerned, so I had to think up something to get me home to Audrey. I said to the M.O. when he came around to me again, 'What if I told you that my wife back home is a qualified Nurse and that she could take care of this.'

'Is she?' he says. 'Well, in that case we will bandage you up nice and tight and send you off.' He was probably glad to see the back of me in any case. I got my kit together and away I went to the nearest station which I guess, was Diss. This took me to London's Kings Cross I think, this is where the problem started, as the bandage was on my thigh and the thigh wobbles when you walk, the bandage would not stay put, it kept coming down. At one time, it was hanging below my trousers as I walked along, I remember some men shouting, 'Eh Sarge, your petticoat is showing.' I was everlastingly visiting the toilets attending to this bandage but, of course, what was happening, was the serge from these trousers was rubbing into this open wound and it was not doing it much good, as well as making a stain on the thigh part. Not long after getting home I was back in hospital again, this time at St. Martins in Bath City. In the meantime, let's go and meet Audrey.

I arrived at Shepton Mallet Station and got off the train, but much to my disappointment, no one was there, not even a Union Jack Flag, so I started to limp down towards home. I had not got more than a couple of hundred yards, when I saw her coming along the road by herself. At last, I had my arms around her, after being away since January 6th 1943, until now, which was about November 1945. I had made it, at one time I had doubts. So, you don't need any imagination as to how we felt to be together once again.

CHAPTER TWENTY-NINE

Home on Leave to Audrey

We went down to 36 Zion Hill to the cottage where Audrey and her parents lived, not forgetting, meeting son John, for the first time. He was now about two years nine months, what can I say about a little lad like that seeing his father for the first time? You can't expect to see much enthusiasm, he is too young, I could be anyone who stepped off the street, but I dare say he felt a difference in his little way of life. I know that I upset him once, when I took him to his Aunt Winn's Shop. As always, I understood that she gave him a few sweets, so he reached up to get them and had a look at them and straight away he said, 'I don't want them, I don't like them.' So kindly Aunt Winn said 'Oh don't you, I'll change them for you.' But, I stepped in here, I said 'Now look here young fellow, when you are given something as a gift, you should show your appreciation by saying thank you and accept them gracefully. Be thankful, there is nothing wrong with those sweets, I bet another time you would eat them, so you take them and say thank you.' To Aunt Winn I said, 'Thank you for the offer but I don't think it is right to spoil him by changing them.' She agreed that her suggestion was not so wise, so it was left at that. I dare say he had some inner feeling about all that, but it was soon forgotten when I stuffed one of these sweets in his mouth. As I said just now, I was only home for about two days before I was back in Hospital, St. Martins of Bath, this was then a Military Hospital. I can remember John coming up there with his Mother to see me, but he was more interested in sliding on the nice shiny floor, as the Nurse said 'He seems pretty active.' I was on penicillin once again as my leg was very sick. It took about another three weeks to get it all cleared up and of course I had not yet started my leave, but I had been over here just over a month and I should have been back in Italy.

As my unit was not over here, I had to report to the nearest Military Unit which was here in Shepton, being the Military Prison, so I thought that I had better show myself or they would be wondering where I am. I went in there and spoke to one of the officers about my situation. He said, 'Right, I'll get it sorted out. Where are you staying, what is your home address? I'll let you know in writing.' Eventually it came to me, saying that my leave would start now that I had been discharged from hospital, so I carried on. In fact, they had given me more than I thought I would get, I also had to go back to the Prison Authorities and get some money as that was running short. When my leave was up, I had to report to some place in London to get my papers to get back to Italy but, when I got there, the Captain there said, 'They have said that you need not come back here now as you are getting near to the day of your discharge.' I said to him, 'But I have left a lot of important kit behind and I really need it, there are things in a locked box that I had accumulated during my service in North Africa and Italy. Some are war souvenirs I must have them.' This Captain said, 'Don't you worry, Sergeant, I will send a message to them to get this forwarded.' But, to this day, I have never received any of it. So, someone somewhere has been lucky to have my hoard of savings, that to me was a disgrace after all that I had been through to obtain them.

I was then posted to Plymouth Crown Hill Barracks, the train journey down there was pleasant enough. On arrival at the station, I was greeted with what they call a 'Tiddy Oggy', I think that is how they spelt it. It is a Cornish Pasty filled up with potatoes, meat and very nice, even hot. 'Any charge?' The lady said, 'No, of course not. We are the W.I. organisation, we have been here nearly all the time that the war has been on.' Another marvellous organisation, God Bless our British Ladies, they certainly did good work to please the Military.

So, I arrived at the barracks. The place was packed with troops who were all waiting to be demobilised and sent home to their families. It was another place that needed some organising, the discipline was not all that good, it was beginning to lapse, as they were nearly civilians again. I did nothing there, conditions were not so good. I caught conjunctivitis from dirty blankets so you can guess things were not what they used to be. Some troops were stealing blankets and sheets and selling them to the civilians outside the camp. This was because there was very little in the shops and people were asking the troops if they could get hold of some blankets for them, it was a temptation and a means of making some spare money but had to be stopped.

I was soon notified that I was on Group 21 for demobilisation, which was in a few weeks time, I was not happy about this situation. I was a regular soldier, I was only 29 years old and I was progressing well in my point of view. I had been sick this last eighteen months and was not in a unit, just wearing the uniform of the Hampshire Regiment and to be thrown out without any notification of a pension, being either a War Disability or a Service Pension did not agree with my way of thinking. I put two and two together and said to myself, do something about it, but what? I knew if I was not happy about things that I could defer for one year and sort things out to my satisfaction. This I did, I got in the queue on the day for discharge but as I got to the desk where there was an officer and a sergeant dealing with this task, I said to him 'I wish to defer.' He said 'You can't do that.' I said, 'I beg your pardon, yes I can.' The sergeant next to me said, 'Oh yes he can, Sir.' 'Well, I was not aware of that order,' he said. 'In that case why have you not mentioned it before now.' I said, 'Because I have just made up my mind.' 'Very well,' he said. So, he kept my papers and said, 'We will sort this out with H.Q.' That is what happened, I deferred for one year to sort everything out, which was well worth the effort I can tell you, but I had a lot of fiddling about to do.

I was out of the camp very soon, first I had to go on yet another medical at Newton Abbot. From there they sent me to a convalescent camp at Norton Fitzwarren, near Taunton. I was there for eleven weeks, it had been occupied by the Americans during the war and they had spent a lot of money on this place.

For instance, they had installed some nice central heating, so I had a nice warm bunk room on my own, living a life of luxury, doing nothing but sitting around and visiting the Sergeants' Mess or going to Taunton. They were not long in sorting me out for a small job whilst I was there. I was having a nice afternoon rest one day when there was a soft tap on my door. I shouted out, 'Whoever you are, please come in,' and in walked a Captain that I had never seen before. He said, 'Please don't get up, I'll just sit here on the end of your bed if you don't mind. I would like to have a talk with you.' 'Well, this sounds interesting, what have you got for me?' I said. 'Well, we know you are here on convalescence and you don't seem that ill, you are able to walk about,' he said. 'Well maybe, but I get trouble with this thrombosis leg of mine, I can't stand on it too long,' I said to him. 'Well,' he said, 'What I have to offer you during your stay here is not too strenuous I'm sure, but if it does upset the works you are to say so. It is really entirely up to you, but if you can do it, we will appreciate it.' 'Well, what is it? May I say, whatever it is, before I say yes I should see the M.O. to see what he thinks about it and if he will pass me as O.K.' 'Right,' he said, 'That's fair enough. What we want is a Sergeant like you to run the Mess, or help to run the Mess, especially in Officers' Mess Functions. It's not a hard job and you will of course be rewarded in addition to your normal pay. You are able to manage that I should think, don't you?' I said 'Yes, if he passes me as physically fit to do it.' He said, 'Good, thank you.' I replied, 'I can tell you that I am going to miss this nice warm bunk.' 'Yes' he said, 'But when you see the quarters that we have for you, you will not miss this all that much.' I saw the M.O. and he said, 'Yes, you should be all right, if you do get trouble, you will just come and see me and it will be sorted out and you taken off the job.'

A few days later I went along to see the Mess President, he showed me the job to be done and what it entailed, it was all similar to the Sergeants Mess, so I had no worries. I was to start on the job straight away. The next thing that I wanted was my quarters. He detailed one of the A.T.S. girls to show me my room. It was on one of the upper rooms, I should say it was about six times as large as the bunk that I had just left, with all good furniture in it, a good size bed with good material coverings and a good lighting system. In fact, everything that a General would need to make him comfortable. The girl was very nice, a good job that I was a married man, she as well as the other girl waitresses gave me a nice welcome, they said, 'Welcome Sergeant, it's good to have a boss at last as we have been trying to manage on our own for many months'. I thought I was going to like it here, what a difference from sleeping up in the mountains in the Casino area, wet slit trenches, water up to one's waist, no heat and no comfort. But then, I had other thoughts about my service in the army, no further responsibility, no more promotion, which meant more money privileges etc., etc. My life in the army as a career was practically over. I was down graded to Category 'C' and excused wearing boots, side arms etc.

The routine soon came to me. First thing in the morning one of the girl waitresses brought me an early mug of tea (sometimes with an early morning greeting, if you get my meaning), then the usual wash and shave, a bathroom to myself. Then, down to my breakfast and I made sure that everyone was about their duties, they did not need much telling as they were already experienced staff, they could tell me a thing or two. Although breakfast was no problem, no one had to wait for anyone like dinner in the evenings. Then I had to see that the place was kept clean, the bar had a good stock, the barman's duties arranged in a routine system. The evening's entertainment was the duty of the Entertainment Committee, not mine, except to see that all went well and that there were sufficient staff to cope with it all. The evening meals were slightly different, the usual system was to wait for the Senior Officer which was usually the Commanding Officer, if not him the next Senior. Once he was seated the meal commenced. The table was already laid out in good order, most times the Regimental Silver was laid out, but in this case not much of that was done because there was a mixture of regiments attached here, they were not all one unit. They were probably like me, stranded soldiers, wounded or with some other form of illness or accident that had down graded them during their service.

There were other times when some outside entertainment was arranged, like shooting. I joined them one afternoon to help get rid of too many rooks that were pestering the area. It was a good afternoon for us, but unfortunate for the rooks. We gave them all to the cooks who had the rotten job of cooking them for us all and not bad either, ever had rook pie? Very good with the pastry and rich gravy. I watched the cooks perform on that session, all they did was to stick a prong up his whatsit, burn off the feathers, pull out the innards and wash them and line them up in a very large tray, pour fat or gravy over them all and stick it in the oven for about an hour, it came out smelling just fine and tasted even better. The afternoon was not wasted, we shot them by the way with a two-two rifle, so there was no suffering, you rook lovers.

As you may guess this job like all the others had to come to an end. I did enjoy it, it was an experience which came in handy later on in life.

I had other orders now as I had been at one time an instructor, I was posted to Leichfield, Staffordshire, Wittington Barracks. It was a large Training Depot, at the moment just General Training Regiment. I went not in the least looking forward to this because I knew very well that I would not be able to do the job any more, I just was not fit enough. But, like many other times someone gets the details wrong of each individual.

When I arrived there, that was it, they wanted me as such but, I had to tell them the reason why I was here and that I was wounded and unfit and I was just waiting now for my disability results. They were annoyed about that, but it was not my fault if they had received the wrong information about me, they could see that I still wore the badge of the then Hampshire Regiment. I had to tell them all my history once again. Whilst I was waiting for my results I was given a job as C.Q.M.S. helping out in the stores supplies, not much of a job, not so interesting as being with one's own unit. I knew full well that this was the end of the line for me as a serving soldier, it was unfortunate for me that I was wounded and it was too bad for me not to be able to soldier on in any unit. There is a standard of fitness which is required and I did not fit into any of these, I was only twenty-eight years old when I was hit, so that only gave me ten years actual service with my Regiment. I was then a C.Q.M.S. (or Colour Sergeant) and I know full well that I could have gone on further. It would have left me to serve another thirty odd years and who is to know how I would have progressed but, there it is, I could not prove that.

My life in the army and with this regiment was a good one. I had bad times and pleasant times, met many good men in all ranks, some I didn't get on with.'

The early days I suppose were the worst, coming into a different type of living and having to knuckle down to discipline which is harsher than that in civilian life. Simple things like, 'Stand to attention when you are talking to me and don't answer back in an insulting way. Take that sour look off your face. Don't look so aggressive. Look straight to your front. Get a move on, don't hang about. Don't forget to salute to the person that is entitled to one. Don't breathe. Don't bat an eyelid. What have you got to say, if you have something to say, well? Shut up. I do all the thinking not you, you have nothing to think with. You are idle, what are you?' How could you stand all this going on, well it came to me that the only way to get out of it was get some promotion and get away from that type of thinking, in other words, join them. Once you get up a rank, you found things a little more pleasant, the higher one gets, the better it gets. In some ways, there are times when one does not like certain responsibilities especially when it affects lives, there it is, it has to be done.

We as sergeants very often come up against an awkward Senior Officer, who is aware of your own efficiency but does not like to show his own lack of efficiency. Consequently, he stands up to you and will show off his rank, which causes bad feeling. I have often had this experience during my service. I had an unfortunate way of not giving in and try to prove that I was correct in my own decisions. That would of course create trouble, we all wonder at times what kind of people are the ones that give us the opportunity for promotion and are they always right in their decision?

I had at one time the unfortunate task of having to put a Lance Sergeant under arrest for lack of good order and discipline. It happened in England before we were sent into action, it was when we were stationed in Kent at the crucial time when we were expecting the Germans to attack us on the coastal line defence. If they had attacked, he and his platoon would have been annihilated because they were all asleep, that was real neglect on his part. The result of this was he was no longer a Lance Sergeant, despite the fact that he was a very nice fellow, but gross inefficiency is not to be tolerated especially in the time of war.

My stay here at Leichfield was not for long. I was given a last medical and down graded as Class 'C' and was about to be discharged as medically unfit for further services with His Majesty's Army. So to Civilian Street it was for me. But, before I was sent off for demobilisation I had one more problem that I had to settle in my office. It was a case of having to deal with one of the soldier's wives, he was in detention here in the barracks. He was with a lot of other soldiers who were nearly all deserters, they had refused to fight for their country, that was their decision to make, but they were all subject to military discipline. Because he was a deserter his wife had to suffer the consequences of not receiving any pay. Somehow she arrived in my office ready to do battle with me, as if it was my fault, I obey orders not make them, I told her. She came in full of hostility as I have said, she started picking up things and throwing at me, I had to pin her arms to her side and with my other arm get on the 'phone and send for the Regimental Police to remove her. My first experience of having a woman showing her temper, what she would like to do with me and the army was nobody's business. As they took her away, she was still threatening me with vengeance. When she had gone I breathed a sigh of relief. Her husband had to report to me because he refused to wear his army boots. I said to the Corporal who reported this to me, 'Right bring him down to my office, I'll deal with him, I'll make him wear his boots.' But those words I was to eat, like his wife he came to my office full of fight. He was already serving so many years for desertion, so what if we did give him a few more months, he could not care less. 'What's the idea of not wanting to wear your boots?' I said to him. He said to me, 'Get stuffed. Go jump in the river.' I said 'Carry on, the more abuse, the more the punishment, the longer it will take for your wife to get any of your money'. So he said 'F... her. She is already going with some other fellow so why should I worry about her.' I was thinking to myself, why should I get myself involved with all his problems, get rid of him. So I said to him, 'Alright, if you refuse to wear your boots so be it, go about bare foot, and see how long your feet will stand up to the strain.' So he left to return to his cell bare foot, I did not see him again, as I was about to leave. But I always think about that sort of person and the way they behave, what good do they get out of life being like that? Against everyone and everything, born aggressive I suppose and just can't help it, so forget them, it's just not my way of thinking. I think it is unfortunate that we have to have these Laws, Rules and Regulations, but it is all due to people's behaviour, if we did not have them the good people would have to suffer too much because of their bad behaviour. I myself have always tried to behave myself and not go against the rules, merely because I have no wish to get myself into trouble and if you do go against them, you are punished, so why do the wrong thing? If I can have something without paying for it, why steal it? Especially if it has been someone else's good effort to obtain it again, why steal it? It's just not the right way to go about things. If I had my life to plan again, would I do the same things? I wonder, if I was of the same mind I suppose I would because I had no experience of anything else. If it was possible I would probably enter the service in a different way, I had the possible entry conditions to have gone in to Officer Training School, but failed to make good use of it, that was a fault of mine, failed to ask about the possibility. One lives and learns, but at times leaves it too late to take action at the right time.

CHAPTER THIRTY

Demobilisation – Civilian Life

I was to be demobilised somewhere near Aldershot and put on a civilian suit. I was not happy about it, why should I have been one of those to get in the way of an enemy shell and suffer for it the rest of my life? I know I was not the only one, there were many more, but I had not been in the army very long. As I have mentioned before, I was thirty years old when they finally sent me out in January 1947, I had very few plans as to what to do for a living. I had a young wife and a child to take care of now and that was some responsibility, what would I do?

As I was not too good on my legs at that time, my job would have to be a sitting job, in any case academic wise, I suppose I was not too bad so therefore it meant office work of some kind. Before I left the army I applied for some training as a typist and went to college. You had to pass out at touch typing, had to be at forty words a minute with two errors only, this I managed. I had to sit in this class with forty other girls to learn, yes, the only man in this class, but all went well.

Now that was over, home I went, my home at that time was with my mother and father-in-law, so it meant I would have to do something about getting our own accommodation. I pestered the Council to try and get me somewhere to live as promised by the new Labour Government. 'You ex-Service Men, we promise to obtain you a home to live in after your good service to your country.' Well we would put that to the test. After a few months they put us in a house that was requisitioned by the Local Council during the war. It was quite a nice house but after a few months the owners wished to have it back. In the meantime they had built some new Council Houses and we had to move out of this one we had and into the new house. It was very nice and new and so we settled in that for just a few years, it meant a lot of work in the garden, removing all the field walls that the workmen had just bulldozed into the soil. It took me about a year to do and I probably moved about three tons of brick and managed to get some sort of garden going, growing my own vegetables.

I managed to obtain a job as a clerk with an insurance company, dealing with peoples' arrears, but I did not like this job or the dude that was running the office, so I left as soon as possible. I found working in civilian life most difficult as well as uninteresting, in the army we did see a bit of the world as well as a variety of occupations.

I next noticed a paragraph in the local paper that a typist male or female was required at some Government Department known as Civil Aviation. So down I went to this place in the Anglo Bavarian Buildings, Shepton Mallet and had an interview with the officer in charge. We shook hands and I introduced myself. He asked me what I had been doing since I had left school, so I told him all, including my service and rank and in the army and the places I had been. He was most interested but did not think that this job as a typist would be suitable for a fellow like me. As I said, I had to start some place, why not here? 'If you are interested, then let's see what you can do as regards to typing, there is the machine,' he said to me. I slipped in a piece of paper, he gave me something to copy and away I went as I had just been instructed on my course, which was touch typing. He said 'Eh, hang on a minute, you are not looking at what you are typing.' I said, 'I am touch typing.' 'Show me,' he said, 'Well, that's something. Right when do you want to start?' 'As soon as you wish,' I said. 'You have the job,' he said. 'Yes, can you start on Monday? As this is the end of the week. On the way out tell all those that are waiting to leave their names and addresses and that the position has been filled.' So, out I went and told them this and they all looked at me and got up and went, all girls by the way. I wonder what they thought of me, taking a girl's job but, I'll tell you now, it was not for long as he later on took on a girl, in fact one of those who was waiting.

Next Monday, I started typing for the firm. In addition to that I had to control the telephone system, there were these eyelids that clicked down when the 'phone rang and all you had to do was slip in another lead to the extension that they asked for or that I knew that they wanted. After a few weeks of this he approached me one day and said, 'Don't you think that you have had enough of that?' I said, 'Yes, but it's a job.' 'Well how would you like to work in the office as a clerical assistant. The job entails keeping store accounts, you have been a Quarter Master, so it should not be any problem for you,' he said. So I finished off that week and the next week a girl took over from me, that also felt better, it was a girl's job in any case but it got my foot in the door.

I started and found the job more interesting, keeping store accounts. As the stores were issued, I kept records. In addition to this I was on provisioning, which was ordering supplies, all for the benefit of aviation like Heathrow (London Airport). I kept at this for a few years and after a while I became a clerical officer, so more pay etc. In this office there were a few others who were nearly all ex-service men and women so you can imagine that we all got on well together.

While this was going on we had another son, we called him Eric, after a school chum of mine, in fact two of them both called Eric. One was Eric Woodsford and the other Eric Harris, they both served in the forces during the war and both at that time lived in Netley, Southampton. They are still around and enjoying life, they are like me in their seventies, we are not able to see much of each other these days for various reasons.

Having worked for the Civil Aviation about four years, I had an opportunity to take another job with Clarks Shoe Factory, all this for much more money. It came about by my meeting the manager and one or two others of their staff when playing tennis. We got chatting about a few subjects and one of them was work, he said to me, 'What kind of work do you do?' I said, 'I am a Clerk in the Civil Service.' 'How much do you earn a week?' I said whatever it was in those days, about seven pounds a week. 'Well' he said, 'You could treble that by working with us as a cutter (cutting out the leather patterns for shoe making). I have a vacancy for one more if you are interested.' After a bit of thought and discussion with my wife I decided to take the job, seeing that it was to improve our standard of living.

The day came for me to resign from the Civil Service, hoping I was taking the right action and then I joined Clarks Shoe Factory at Shepton Mallet. When I got there and told him my age which was about thirty-three they said, 'I'm sorry, but you are too old for this job.' This came as a surprise. 'Too old?' I said 'At thirty-three.' 'Well according to our Rules and Regulations you are.' 'Well, this is rather disheartening, as I have just resigned from my job to take this, on the Manager's recommendations, I have already spoken to him about it.' There was a quiet moment and the Personnel Officer disappeared for a while, obviously to speak to the manager about this. It seems that he thought I was younger and forgot to ask me my age. 'Anyhow,' he said, 'We will give you the normal test and if you pass it the job is yours. How does that suit you?' I said, 'Fine.' So, off I went for the test and passed it, they were a little surprised about this because of the colour test and the feel with the fingers which get involved with cutting leather, feeling for flaws in the leather.

As he had said the money did rise, but there were other snags after a while. I started getting trouble with this injured leg of mine, it could not tolerate my standing on it too long, so I was in doubt about keeping this job. But I kept at it and put up with it, waiting to see how it stood up to it as the days went by. One day, after about six months the manager sent for me and offered me a job out in Australia, to be a foreman supervisor in one of their factories. The unfortunate snag here, was that I had to go out in advance for a while, get settled in the house provided and then send for my wife and children, for them to travel out there without me. This did not meet with Audrey's approval, what with that and that her mother did not like to lose her, this upset Audrey as well, so I had to turn it down, to the disapproval of the manager saying that I more or less had lost an opportunity of a lifetime. Well, the love of the family has to come first I suppose, so this move was cancelled. Who knows whether we made the right decision or not? Anyhow, I carried on with this cutting for a while and had to make up my mind whether to stick at it or not. But the Doctor told me to get off it and take a sitting job, so I had to write to the Civil Service again and ask for my job back. I thought it a bit of a cheek and that the answer would be sorry but no, they accepted what I told them and took me back, not as a Clerical Officer at first but as a Clerical Assistant, so I took it but, it was not long before I was back to a C.O. So I was back in the Civil Service.

During my time there I was also offered another job in addition to this one. My wife and I both applied for the job as Stewards to the Conservative Club in Shepton Mallet, went for the interview and got the job, so we now had two jobs. Audrey used to run it during the daytime and then I would join her in the evenings and weekend, that is how we managed. With this extra money coming in we managed to save some with the future intention of taking a pub, but something else cropped up to stop that. Her Uncle and Aunt Speeds were thinking about retiring from their little shop, where they sold groceries and pet foods etc. and Audrey was interested in it.

We came out of the Conservative Club and took the shop. Again, we took a risk, not really knowing if we were making the right move. It was another experience but I did not care for it much, a very inconvenient shop to work, so old fashioned. A lot of the stores were situated up two flights of stairs and then some of it was down in the cellar where rats were pretty frequent and that kept Audrey out at times. If she did go down there she would turn the lights up and down and bang the boxes to frighten them away if they were there. We even hired a killer cat once and this cat killed about a dozen in one evening as well as half eating one of them. We could not keep this cat with customers about, he was too savage and I had some job catching it to take it back to the farm where we borrowed it from. I had to put on a very thick pair of working gloves to get hold of it, it would bury its teeth into the glove and even penetrate the gloves, and then I had to shove it in a strong sack. It would then go mad in the sack to try and get out, I can see it now plunging about in the sack, in all directions. I put it in the car and drove it back to the farm, all the way it was going mad in the sack. When I took it back the farmer said, 'I told you it was a killer'. He took it back to the barn untied the sack and let it loose. You should have seen it when it got loose, it shot up to the barn roof like lightning, spitting venom all the time. I bet he did not have many rats on his farm, just as mad as a real tiger.

Trade wise in the town, I dare say we did fairly well, but nothing terrific, as these big multi stores were beginning to come into force at those times. We stuck it for about three years, but during our term of service here I was offered another job with a Canadian Firm with a Leather Company somewhere in Lake Michigan. Unfortunately for me, there was a time limit on it. I was having difficulty selling the shop and as time was running out it looked as if I was going to lose out on that job and that is how it ended up, me being the loser. It was about three weeks after that I managed to sell it, but too late, another good job gone. We don't always get good luck in this life, opportunity is a good thing when it happens.

Another voluntary job that I did at Shepton Mallet was as Branch Secretary for the Royal British Legion, that kept me busy as well. It was a good thing that I was still young enough to cope with all this, I won't go into all of this because it involved a lot of work helping out ex-service men and women. We had parades like all other branches in the U.K. on Armistice Day each year in the month of November. It involved most of the town folk of Shepton gathering around the Cenotaph and then the service in the local Church of England. I also started the Miniature Armistice Show in the local cinema. The money made all went to the aid of ex-service men and women.

But all this in Shepton had to come to an end as I was posted to Boscombe Down which is an experimental establishment mainly to cover aircraft for the Military. As well as Civil Servants there were some R.A.F. Servicemen and women there also at times, some army and some Americans, all had some connection with aircraft. I was stationed up there for ten years. I lived in various places around that area in those ten years, a bungalow in Boscombe Village, a maisonette in Downsway as well as another bungalow. Then we spotted an olde worlde cottage out in the country that we liked, at a little village called Wood Yates on the Blandford Road. We liked it there but we began to realise that it was too far out of town and away from friends. For another change, we took a larger house that had been half renovated. I bought it as it was with still a fair amount of building material about, so I spent many months working on this to put it in good order. To help Audrey's parents out we prepared some accommodation for them to live in, but unfortunately it did not turn out as we expected. Audrey's mother became ill and eventually she was admitted into hospital out at Oddstock and that was where she died, must have been about 1968. Her father Cyril decided to go back to Shepton Mallet and he bought a small cottage up at Downsway.

We also had a very sad occasion when we were living in Salisbury, we lost our very close friends Alice and Ted Jackson. They were both killed in a motor car accident, December 16th 1969. It was a terrible blow to us, their son Ian survived the accident and is getting on fine in life, the last time that we saw him.

I must go back to this house that I was talking about just now, the one that I renovated. This was situated right out at Tilshead on the way to Shrewton, a typical army training area. This house was called Mill House, not far from the local village pub the Red Lion. We even had a well here, but I filled it up with rubble as it was too near the road and could have been dangerous for somebody. Most likely, water still runs underneath that road, because at times if they had a lot of rain the street used to get flooded, I don't know if they still have that trouble. I even built a garage there. Like all the other houses I bought it was sold. This one I sold to a serving Major in the Royal Artillery, I wonder if he is still there or one of his relatives.

I moved from there because I was transferred to Bristol to work in the Civil Service Costing Section, M.O.D. We were all busy sorting out the costing of this Concorde that was going strong in this year of 1970. We had an office in Park Street called Embassy House, we were on the top floor, had one more office with Rolls Royce Dept at Patchway and another at Rolls Royce, Coventry. As you know, it was a joint contract with the French Airways and it turned out to be a successful aircraft but expensive to run. It seems to be still very popular, no doubt since my days, there have been many modifications on it.

It was now 1972. I for various reasons decided with my dear Audrey's approval to resign prematurely from the Civil Service, having completed enough service to obtain a pension from them at the age of sixty, but as I had about three years to go, my pension would be frozen. We decided to take a pub and one was offered to us at Crickham, near Wedmore. It was run down so it was a challenge to us to get it going. We both had had previous experience of Club life and also of business so we had little trouble in having good ideas. The locals called the place The Trotters because many years ago at the back of this pub, where there is plenty of land, they used to sell trotting horses. I made a suggestion to Courages to change the name to The Trotters for good and they agreed. We had a house to sell out at Pilning Village, we had very little trouble selling the place as we had made that one nice to live in, as all the others, but all this selling and waiting to get the proper approval from Courages to move in takes time going through solicitors etc. While we were waiting we had to get out of the house and stay with some friends for a while but there is a limit of time that one can do that, it's not fair on them. You can overstay those sort of things, so we had to rent a flat in Bristol. We did not like the area but we had to stick it out. After about six weeks of this temporary accommodation and having our furniture stored as well it was becoming expensive, so we were pleased when we received a letter from Courages that we could move in and get cracking.

The only wrong move that we made at the time was the selling of our house, we were not to know that the price of houses was about to rise at least three times the current value. When we came to sell our pub and had to buy another house we had to find more money or take out another mortgage.

The buying of the tenancy cost us nearly all our money. We had to refurnish the place as well as buy carpets and stock and paying the rent for the place that we lived in. As I said all the things that we required to run this pub just about ran us dry, but we worked hard and also set up a restaurant and employed a very good and honest loving lass from Cheddar by the name of Iris Barrett. The only thing that she did not want was me in the way, like hanging about in the kitchen, she must have had some bad experience of this somewhere before. Anyhow, I agreed as long as I got my prawn sandwich at eight o'clock each evening. All went well, the cooking and organisation, we are still friends as of today although I don't see much of her, Audrey does of course.

We had a good pub going, men and women's darts teams, a good tug of war team, all lads from Crickham and Wedmore area, in fact they had a summer competition that year of 1973. Our team which was run by Peter Hooper trained well and worked hard at winning and this they did. The day that the finals took place in our pub's grounds the place went mad, we had a good day's trade on that day as well as running the restaurant. The pub was doing well and Audrey and I wanted to improve it even more, by having a skittle alley, we were losing trade because we had no room for one. I went around looking for a mobile building that I could fix up along the side of the pub, I found one at a price that I could afford. The next job was to apply to Courages for permission to have it placed alongside. This they agreed to do but the stipulation was for their benefit, which we thought was improper and a silly move, that if we sold the tenancy it would then belong to them. This I did not agree with, the new tenants, whoever they might be could pay us for the trouble for organising this building, it was going to improve the sale of their beers. It was not good thinking on their part. I was not happy the way they were thinking, I decided or I should say we decided it was time we moved on and get ourselves another pub. With the experience that we had gained having this one, it would be no bother to us although nothing was at hand at that time. We also decided that we would return to the Salisbury area as we were well acquainted there as well as having friends and relatives nearby, so back we went.

CHAPTER THIRTY-ONE

Amesbury, Tidworth, Larkhill

For a while we stayed at a bungalow belonging to Joan Pinkham, who was then the proprietor of The Antrobus Arms Hotel in Amesbury. We knew them before, when we lived in Salisbury, so she kindly rented her bungalow to us for just a short period. Joan's daughter Geraldine and my son Eric are now partners and are living in Spain, Garcian.

During our stay in this bungalow, we started looking for a house or a cottage. We eventually found an old cottage in Flower Lane, Amesbury, that needed a lot of renovation but we negotiated with the owner and settled on a reasonable price. We also managed to get some help from Salisbury Council and once again made this into a nice home.

Whilst all this renovation was going on we started once again looking for a job, at least it was my responsibility to get one, not so easy at my time of life, but I managed to get two or three which lasted me until I finally retired. Audrey was helping our son Eric run his shop which was antiques and bric-a-brac.

My first start was to be a supervisor milkman, I thought I would try this out, but my leg let me down, it was too much for me so I resigned.

I then took over a club which was in a state of bankruptcy to help out in winding it up, but it just so happened that the club started to pick up again, unfortunately it was all too late so that job did not last long.

Where should I go now? I went to a place that I have never been before in my life, that was the Employment Exchange, they asked for my qualifications, so I told them all. 'Well, let's see now, how do you like the idea of a Manager position with the Officers Club at Tidworth Garrison? The Manager up there requires another helper and it seems that you would be suitable for that position.' Up I went and was interviewed and found to be just the person that they wanted, having had the knowledge of Mess procedure. I joined them within a few days. It meant wearing evening dress all the time but that did not worry me, I enjoyed it. The other Manager was a retired Major, I think from the Inniskillen Regiment, an Irish Regiment. With me as an ex-Senior N.C.O. and W.O. we got on pretty well together. There was a lot to learn in the club procedure, on some evenings we could seat about five hundred officers and their wives and the meal and entertainment would keep going until about 06.00 hrs in the morning.

That meant that we and the staff got very tired, but by sharing the duties we managed very well. We had the staff to cope with all this, even some on reserve which we could call upon as and when necessary. We also had the privilege of having a General or two visit us at times, even Royalty like Princess Anne, showing off her skills as horse rider. Those were the days when she was a little bit awkward with people and had a way with her that could rub one up the wrong way, but she got over that eventually.

The parties were at times a bit hectic, I had to admit that, some forgot that they were gentlemen. On the whole I enjoyed the job. We probably had about twenty-four staff, mainly girls, some even wives from the services in the area, it helped them out financially as well and they were all pleasant to work with. We did have some minor problems with sickness which worried us at times whether we would be able to cope with tonight's dinner.

Like all jobs these days, nothing seemed to be permanent, they had some other scheme that the club was to be taken over as an Officers Mess, so that meant a change of staff. We became redundant and were given a golden handshake. After about two years I was out and looking again for work, but I was still able to convince them that I could do something.

I next heard that there was another job going for a Manager to the Officers' Mess at Larkhill, Royal Artillery so I dashed up there. But I was too late for it and got beaten to the post by an officer, who was one of theirs and was retiring.

During my interview up at Larkhill about that time, I was spotted by their local Chaplain, who was looking for a Verger to help run his Garrison Church. He did not speak to me then but when I got home I had a telephone call from him and he said, 'I saw you a few minutes ago up here when you were applying for that Mess job. The staff suggested I ask you as you are an ex-Service man. Will you come up here and have a talk with me, with the prospect of taking this job? The pay and hours are very good.' Of course I had to say 'Yes.' What, me a Verger? I can't imagine that somehow. I had to make up my mind quickly I said, 'Right, I'll come up straight away. Where do you want to see me?' He said, 'Up here, at the Garrison Church.' Up I go, and what a charming man, the Reverend Major Fred Preston. He put the job over so well that I could hardly refuse, the hours were from about 09.30 until 16.00 hrs each day, nothing on Saturday but Sunday mornings. Yes of course, they had the usual Church Parade, also some evenings when the youngsters had choir practice, I attended some funerals, weddings, christenings and cleaned and looked after the place.

I was more or less my own boss, I needed no supervision, so I enjoyed that from 1978 until 1981 when I had to retire as I was then sixty-five years old.

I still did not really retire, I found out that a local furniture company by the name of Pickfords required a salesman to get business for them in furniture removing either in England or even overseas. A caravan was placed for me on alternate days either at Larkhill or Bulford Camp a few miles away. I stayed with them for about one year, another job that I enjoyed, I met some nice people, nearly all ex-Service men and women. I must say that all my life I had very little trouble obtaining employment, so what did I have that attracted me to them, was it looks or intelligence?

I forgot to mention just now that when I finished the job as a verger at the Garrison Church, the major that was in charge of the Military Band was about to retire. I knew him and I was about to retire so he asked me about the job. He said that it would be just the job for him, especially as he was having trouble with one of his legs as well and there was not too much standing about. He said that when I went up to the office not to forget to put in a good word for him. This I did, I passed on this information and they were glad of it, it saved them the trouble of advertising and interviewing, as they knew him as well. He got the job and that pleased him, his name has slipped my memory, maybe he would not like me to mention it in any case.

So ends that part of my life of working, no more work for me, apart from D.I.Y. stuff that I can cope with at home and that covers a lot of ground as well.

My main two occupations were of course the Army and the Civil Service, both working for the Government, so pension wise I have done fairly well and it was therefore worth my efforts to have been with them. The Civil Service I must say, treated me pretty well and bore in mind my service with the army and the fact that I am a War Disabled Person.

You might ask how does my disability affect me after all this time and what troubles still have ever since I received this wound. To tell you the truth, it is with me all the time, it never lets me forget. At my office one day at Shepton Mallet, when working for the Civil Aviation, I had a haemorrhage from the mouth. This caused quite an incident in the office and it must have worried the staff as well as myself. I did manage to clear it up from my desk before I took myself to Shepton Hospital, I drove myself up there whilst it was still haemorrhaging. On arrival at the hospital I did not hesitate, I knew where I was bound for and I took myself straight into the Treatment Room without knocking. It just so happened that the doctor was attending a young girl on the treatment bench as I butted in so rudely, I could not announce myself as I had a mouthful. He could see the plight I was in therefore did not reprimand me for my rudeness. His attention to the girl could not have been urgent because he just handed her over to a nurse there to deal with and attended to me without any delay. He laid me flat on this bench and made me keep still, can't really remember what he did exactly. I was taken up stairs and placed on a bed and he gave me an injection to keep me quiet. I went off to sleep and was there for a couple of hours. When I woke up, I had to explain to him what had happened. I told him what happened in the office, that I had coughed up this blood and that it was congealed and quite a lot of it. He said, 'Have you been having trouble with this before?' I said, 'Yes, for some while now I have been coughing up this, but only small amounts.' I told him about my war injuries and so he dug into a few things that may have caused the trouble. He then said, 'You had better come into the hospital tomorrow and have an X-Ray. In the meantime go home and rest and do nothing strenuous.' I thought well, that won't be hard.

This all led up to me having to see a specialist in Bristol, they looked me over and then gave me a barium meal, the putting of some liquid through a tube down my throat and into my lung to try and locate what was causing the haemorrhaging. This was not very pleasant, I did not like the tube down my throat. They eventually stopped putting this down then took out the flexible pipe, but left the rigid one in for a while. They said that they had to do that or else I would have choked, so I had to put up with this in my throat for about ten minutes and what a relief when they took it out. For three days I had a sore throat. They discovered that I had a very small piece of metal lodged in the lower part of my lung and that this was causing the problem, this had worked its way up from the kidney area where I was wounded. This meant that I had to go to Southampton Hospital and have it out. This again was most uncomfortable, another tube down the throat, no fluid this time, just another rigid tube and they threaded a kind of feeler wire gadget down through the middle of this. I could see it happening on the X-Ray machine, it eventually located the small piece of metal and cauterized the scar that was causing the bleeding. It never bled again. What happened to the small piece of metal? Well, the doctor said, 'You probably coughed it up some time or other, or swallowed it and passed it out through your motions.'

My other troubles were with the left leg, which swells up a lot due to the thrombosis, this also causes a sickly pain and hurts the veins in my leg. I had to use my right leg as a crutch for many years and still do today, that is why according to my judgement, I have a lot of pain in that leg today. I now have arthritis in this leg affecting the knee and ankle and I am having treatment for that now, it will not get better, but I think it gives some relief otherwise I am relying on the tablets that are prescribed by my own doctor. I can count my blessings, it could have been worse, I see many in a much worse condition than myself. In addition to these problems, I also have a loss of hearing, this started early in my life, about twenty years ago. It was mainly caused by the explosion when I was hit, now to add to it I have the old old story of age.

CHAPTER THIRTY-TWO

Family – Holidays

Starting with my own family first, John has been left school for some time now. His first position in life was my idea, to put him in the Boys Army, thinking that because I liked it so would he but that was my first mistake. He hated it and was pleased to get out, I'm not sure how long he did stay in, but no more than about three years, he just made it on to Man's Service, unlike me it was not his cup of tea as they say. He took a long time to settle down after that but eventually had a position in Saudi Arabia, in the welding line. He spent a few years there and came home once or twice for a break. He got married a couple of times, those did not work out, now he is settled down with Pauline, who has been previously married and has two children, one being Sam and her daughter Leila. They are young teenagers and doing well at their schooling. In addition, they have two younger bothers Timothy and Peter, both now going to school and seem promising, bustling and healthy lads. We wish them all a good, happy and successful life. Pauline is lucky to have her parents fairly near her, Don and Margaret Andrews, retired now of course like Audrey and myself. They see them more often than us, we do manage to see them a few times during the year, around this time of the year especially, as we are coming up to Christmas. They have a busier time than us, as they have many relatives in this area, been living in that area for many years, they are retired farmers, a pity we did not meet them earlier on in life. I must say that John did have his own business not so long ago, he had a partner as well. They were renovating old Morris Cars and gave them a fresh life. It was a car that was very popular and still is if they can get hold of them. They had this business for a few

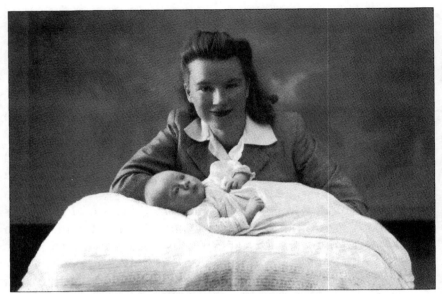

My lovely wife Audrey, with her first born, John. Shepton Mallet, 1943.

years, but they have decided to sell up and are now onto other developments relating to cars, like security locks and it seems to be progressing well.

Eric, our youngest son, at one time had an antique business in Amesbury where Audrey worked with him in the shop, as Audrey is very interested in antiques. That is one reason why Eric liked her about, she became very useful with her knowledge. But after a few years he decided to visit Spain for a holiday and whilst he was over there he found some property to buy fairly reasonably and between him and Gerry, his partner, he decided to settle out there. He came back and sold his business and out he went, took Gerry and her daughter Kimberley out there and over the years built his own villa and a very good job he made of it. They live in a village up in the mountains at a place called Gaucine not to far from Ronda. Coming in from Gibraltar, it can be seen direct north as the crow flies, it is about forty miles by road, probably near to fifty miles. They have found various ways of earning a living out there. Gerry teaches Spanish to the English speaking people and English to the Spanish speaking people. They also bake English bread and rolls and at times manage to organise walking holidays, not a hectic business, but enough for them I should think. Whatever it is, they seem happy enough at it. They have another lovely young daughter called Shoko, who is now about eleven years old and is becoming useful to them in many ways. She has had the task of having to learn two languages and is coping with it very well. Up to now we have been making the journey out there every year, that is for the last eleven to twelve years, but from now onwards I don't know if I will be able to because of my own health, it bothers me now. We have to seriously think about the medical situation out there which is not to our satisfaction, it's all right for the younger generation, but not for older people, so maybe we should give up travelling. We have not really made up our minds, but we have enjoyed going out there in that nice weather and scenery and seeing them making good progress, also to see some of Eric's handmade furniture. It is of Spanish style and very well made. He makes other things in that line as well and they take it all to market once a week, down on the coast somewhere near Estopona. A hazardous journey I should think, but they are used to it having made that journey many times, one needs to be a mechanic as well! They do at times make their way over here, so we do see one another at times, we are also on the 'phone.

What of my own generation, my brothers and sisters? Lorna was about eighteen months older than me, she died a few years ago. I have always kept in touch. She first of all married Ken Inglis from the Nottingham area, going back before the last war, 1931 I think. They lived at Hawhurst, Kent for a while and also in London, Streatham. They had three sons, Lorna named the first two after me, because we got on well together as kids. There was Douglas, who is now a doctor and living in Wales and John who is a Professor working in Oxford and living in the same town and the youngest one Stewart, living in Paignton, Cornwall. I have not seen much of any of them during my life until recently we had the pleasure of seeing both Douglas and

Our sons, John and Eric. Taken at Widdeats Road House, 1991.

John with their wives. Douglas married Janet and John married Urick, a lovely German girl.

My eldest brother Roland now lives in Northampton and has done for many years. He is about seven years older than I am but I should think a lot fitter as he was unhurt by the Germans during the war. I understand that at Dunkirk he was hit on the head by some flying object, probably the result of the air bombing on the beaches. According to Roland, a sailor heaved him out of the water and most likely saved his life as he was knocked out but suffered very little effects from the experience. He was with the R.E. (Royal Engineers), trade ordnance and maps etc., we couldn't do without them. On discharge from the army he was employed with his local Council of Northampton as a Surveyor, a Public Servant as I called them. He had a good hobby of mountain climbing which kept him fit. Today (1993) he is eighty-four years old and still going strong, I hope he has many good days left. He is more or less on his own as he and his wife were divorced many years ago, he has children now grown up. The only one I know fairly well is his daughter,

Rosemary, I met her down here a few months ago last July, 1993. Ernest I have not seen since he was a boy of about six and I am not sure where he is, probably still in the Northampton area.

Lorna whilst living in South Africa with Jack Coatsworth, her second husband, died in 1990. She had been ill for many years, mainly diabetes, she lived rather an unhappy life with her medical problems but Jack has seen that she has been put to rest peacefully. I am missing her despite the fact that I have not seen her since waving them both off from Southampton Docks back in 1975. She probably had about eighteen years out there with Jack. Jack by the way, has remarried again and all is well with them both.

Norman was my second eldest brother. He was about three and a half years older than me, he died in February 1994 after an operation on his shoulder that he injured one day when out playing his favourite hobby, golf. He fell on his shoulder and it was hurting him so much that they decided to operate and see what could be done about it, it caused him to have a heart attack, which was fatal. He is also now at rest in the Budleigh area. Norman like me, in his early days worked in the grocery trade with a firm called Pages in Ogle Road, Southampton. I'm not sure what he did, probably in the office, he stuck that for a few years and then like me again decided to join the services. He chose the Navy, having had a fair education at Queens College, Southampton with his brother Roland, he therefore was able to go in as a Junior Petty Officer as a writer. He spent some of his service at Lee-on-Solent and also out in Malta before the war, in fact, I think he was married out there. He married Edie Rowthorn and from this marriage had two sons, the oldest was David and the youngest was Peter. Norman towards the end of the war was posted to Australia, with the object of helping the Navy to finish the war with the Japanese, but he said when he arrived there he was surplus to requirements, so he did not do very much to help. He said that the Navy had offered him a Commission but he was not happy with the conditions that they had offered to him, so he decided to come out of the service, he was then a Chief Petty Officer in the Writing Branch. He had about thirteen and a half years service in. He then obtained a job with Hawkins Bros. a Building Company in the Portsmouth and Southampton area. He was their Secretary and Director for the rest of his working life and did very well for himself, quite successful. He had problems at times with his married life, a lot of that I am not aware of but it turned out with separation and divorce. He then eventually married Brenda and when he retired they settled down in Budleigh Salterton, a nice peaceful retiring area, visited by many people during the summer. Now sad to say, Brenda is on her own, we see her sometimes, but she has to live her own way of life, we hope to keep in touch,

We still have friends of old, but for health reasons don't see a lot of them. We are retired and they are still working, I am talking about Brenda and Gerald Rodway, they still live in Shepton Mallet, he now runs his own taxi business, so it keeps him busy. The medical reasons are mainly my fault not theirs. We still do have Phil Chapman, who is now also on her own as she lost Ron her husband last year as well, he had a massive heart attack during the time that they were on holiday.

We met Ron and Phil many years ago on an aeroplane when we all took a trip to Italy, must have been about twenty-four years ago. Those were the days when aircraft seats were not booked in advance, consequently, when the doors opened for people to make their way to the aircraft it was a scramble, first served effort. If you were slow you did not get the seat that you required, but we managed it fairly well, we sat near each other and had to laugh about it, not much of a system in those days. Nevertheless, they were good times, I think better than it is today, despite the better organisation. The trouble today is that there are too many people about, so it's long waits and delays, or something has gone wrong with the security, maybe a bomb or two about, not such happy days. We enjoyed our holiday in Italy, I think it was a place called Catolaca, cheap in those days, so it seems, but I suppose it seems like it now because the cost of living has gone up so much.

Norman's boys both did very well for themselves. David managed to get a commission in the Royal Air Force, I won't go into too much detail about it, but over the years he managed to reach a high Rank of Air Vice Marshall, shows what a good education does for some. His other son Peter is now a bank manager for Barclays Bank and is at the moment living in Jersey.

One or two old friends of the war days from our regiment, The Royal Hampshire Regiment, are still around. Norman and Betty Bryant, we were young sergeants together for a few years, at one time we used to see each other at our Sergeants Past and Present Dinners at Winchester. We still do see each other, but he does not attend the dinners. When we are well enough and feel that way inclined, we visit one another, we also keep in touch. He got himself captured when we first landed in North Africa, not his fault, and spent the rest of the war years in a German prison.

There is also Jock Barfoot, who was best man at my wedding, he was a C.Q.M.S. when in North Africa. He also got himself rounded up and spent some time in a P.O.W. Camp, he must be well into his eighties by now, I see him not so often. Many others are now up with the angels.

My first granddaughter Ruth I don't see much of as she lives way up north in Scotland. She must be about twenty-eight years old now, she lives in a place called Lockinver-by-Lairg, in the winter time I guess she has snow up to the roof tops. She has two sons and a daughter, we have seen them about twice I think. As you must realise, we as a family are well spread out, it's been like that nearly all our lives, I mean even when we were youngsters.

I have had some good holidays abroad, like the U.S.A. This was made possible by the fact of having a sister living out there, she became an American Citizen, not long after the 1939/45 War, obviously because of her marrying an American. We did not manage to get out there until she and her husband Joi retired from working in Saudi Arabia, they were out there for many years as well as other places, but mainly in Arabia. Our first visit was in 1979, where we were met at Kennedy International Airport, 23rd July 1979. Being our first trip to the U.S.A., they must have decided to make it a big affair and nearly all of them made the effort to come and meet us, it was quite an event. They were all there, from Pamela downwards, Elvia, her eldest and only daughter and her children, her daughter Tabetha, then her young son Tristian. They had a long drive up from Bristol Virginia, a matter of three hundred miles. The weather when we arrived was nice and warm, but stormy. We ran into one on the way down to their house, we did not finish the whole journey down in that day, so we stayed overnight just outside Washington at a Motel. We got up early in the morning and moved on down, all crowded in Elvia's car, she was driving.

We visited many places of interest, such as Washington D.C. itself, so much to see there, like the White House and various Museums, Arlington Cemetery, where a lot of their Military are buried over the years. We made a special effort to walk along and see where they had laid to rest their President, J.F. Kennedy, who was assassinated in 1963, also his brother Robert, who is buried just above him. We also saw the Washington Memorial from the car window on the way out of town.

Once we arrived at Elvia's House, we were welcomed with the Union Jack as well as the Stars and Stripes stuck up in front of her house. This was a nice place and we enjoyed their wonderful hospitality all the time we were out there.

It was not long before we were on our way again for a journey down south, we were off to Florida. It was another long journey and we eventually arrived at some apartments that we found and decided that this looked a nice place to stay, Treasure Island. This we did and enjoyed it very much. The weather could not have been better, the beach was not of sand but minutely crushed up shells, so small that it gave the appearance that it was sand until you picked it up in your hands and studied it. At about midday you could hardly put your bare foot on the shore it was so hot, you had to skip across it quickly to gain access to the sea and cool down. The fish just gave themselves up, they were so easy to catch, but I caught nothing that was worth eating, so I just put them back into the sea again. Whilst we were in this area, we visited St. Augustine, another old Spanish town, this was on the Atlantic coast side.

Let's also not forget our fantastic visit to Orlando, to visit Disney World. The wonders of this place are hard to express, many things of interest. We spent the whole day there until late at night and still did not see it all. In one's lifetime, one must make the effort and visit this place. We know full well that there is a copy of this near us now situated in Paris, but they say that it does not have the same atmosphere, I don't know, I have not been to that one.

When the vacation was over for us in Florida we had a nice journey back and many sights to see en route. As I have said before, both Audrey and I have visited America on four occasions and have practically covered from New York right down the East coast down to Florida, which covers the States of Virginia, North Carolina and Georgia. We have been to Williamsburgh, Washington, Bristol, Alexandria, Norfolk, Charlotte, Charleston, Savannah, St. Augustine, Orlando, Tampa, St. Petersborough, St. Myers, Everglades, Appalachian Mountains, Raleigh, Gatlinburgh and many other smaller places, not forgetting the White Mountains up in the hills where the Hill Billys live and enjoyed their company. We joined in with their local fairs and fun, all good visits, well worth visiting that country. Whoever you might be who takes the trouble to read this don't go out of this world until you have had a good look around over there, you really are missing something. The majority of Americans will welcome you so long as you behave yourself, I've got to admit that I could not have made these visits without the help of Pam and Joi.

They have now settled in a place called Salem, South Virginia, nearly on the border of North Carolina, not far from where her son Terry lives.

We must not forget the holidays that Audrey and I had back here in the U.K. Apart from our own country, we have visited Italy quite a few times. It was one of the first places that I wanted to take Audrey when I came home from that last war, as we spent many months trying to clear out the German Army. Despite the fighting part we could not forget the beauty of the country and its climate.

We visited France a few times, motored from Lidd to Le Touquet and flew the car over on a Bristol Freighter, going back in the 50's, a long drive right down to Nice, Monte Carlo and St. Raphael, a journey of about 780 miles each way. This was the first time that we took our two sons who were then old enough to appreciate the country. We know that they enjoyed that very much, we had no worry about them when they were playing about in the sea as they could both swim. They were gone nearly all day and always came back starving.

We visited Switzerland, Germany and Holland and journeyed down to Venice, Spain and travelled many miles either by coach or drove ourselves, all a great experience and well worth the effort of going. One needs to enjoy these sort of holidays when one is young and fit, now we look back and remember the pleasant times that we had.

Travelling by air in the early days I think was much more enjoyable than it is today, now there are just too many people flying and it is no longer a novelty, too many delays and so many excuses, you can't believe whether it be true or not. They are probably better aircraft which get you there quicker and safer, but to some too many security worries.

CHAPTER THIRTY-THREE

Reminiscences

I would like to go back a while and think of the things that happened. Unusual things that perhaps only happen once in our lives. What one did or planned, if you had that time over again, would you go about it in a different way? Some events that would never occur again because of the situation as it was at that time, it could be interesting to discuss those happenings.

Story Number One
There was one man who, after he had been with us for a while, we found out was a deserter from the Royal Navy. We thought he had some sort of previous experience because of the way he behaved and also that he was a few years older than ourselves. He was one of these men who thought he was pretty smart, with his fiddling as we called it, always trying to raffle some object or other, like watches or wallets, anything that he managed to get hold of cheap, or else they were stolen goods. I was one who would have nothing to do with him and his con ways. He eventually got himself into trouble and was charged, most likely with fraud or receiving stolen goods. It was then because of this the authorities found out that he was on the Navy list of wanted deserters, so he was taken away and never seen again. From all this, I was beginning to learn a bit about what life was all about, the types that are about.

We had another who was to us quite a normal and likeable man, but one day he started to do silly things, like putting his equipment on backwards. He failed to do up his bootlaces on his boots and he would shoulder his rifle on the wrong shoulder or stand to attention when he was ordered to stand at ease. He would not wash or comb his hair, you name it he was doing it.

He was what we called 'working his ticket', in other words doing his best to get out of the army without having to buy himself out. He was hoping to get discharged for not being medically fit to serve in His Majesty's Service. He at times caused a lot of laughter amongst the ranks, which did not please his Sergeant Instructor, he kept this up so long and he was put on so many charges that eventually he was discharged. We later found out the proper reason for him carrying on like this, his father had died suddenly and his mother had been left to try and run the business and she could not manage this on her own. He must have said to his mother, 'Don't you worry Mum, I'll get out of the army and come and help you.' This he did and very well too, he was one up on the army, he was not so crazy as they thought.

Story Number Two

We had a young room orderly in our barracks at Rawlpindi. This meant he had access to the small arms and ammunition because that was part of his job for the day, to take care of all this and to clean some of the ammunition which was put on inspection. On a nice quiet afternoon when nearly everyone was having a rest, something came in his mind to load one of these pistols and shoot the place up, not at the men, but things in the room, like the clock or someone's mess tin on his locker, mirrors and windows. He was laughing his head off as he did so, he was promptly attacked and put under control, as well as put under close arrest. What were his reasons for doing this? When he had to come before his Company Commander he asked him 'What was your reason for this stupid act?' He merely said, 'Sir, I just felt like it that's all, I was browned off and wanted some excitement.' 'Well you will have some of that now, because you are off to do some detention,' he was told. He was sent to a Military prison for twenty-eight days, breaking up stones with a small hammer. He did his sentence and rejoined his company and carried on with his soldiering, I don't think they gave him that job again. But the whole reason for this action was never analyzed, probably put it down to the sun being too hot, no more was said about it. Strange to me why they just let that problem of his fade away. We never did hear it mentioned, there must have been some explanation somewhere.

Story Number Three
Another shooting, this time fatal.
On another quiet Saturday afternoon, a certain private was getting himself ready to go on guard. This of course included the cleaning of his rifle, so that each man was issued with ten rounds of .303 cal, but it was not loaded into the rifle until the man was on sentry go. There were a few men in this barrack room, just lying back on their beds, resting or reading, nearly all in shorts as it was hot. The punkahs were going to help cool them down, when out of the blue, we heard a shot. I was in the next room up, so what few were about rushed round there to see what was happening and we saw this man standing there with his rifle, in a state of shock, and opposite his bed, was a dead soldier. What he had done, was to bring his rifle up in the aim at this young soldier, he was reading a book, he had aimed at this book which was also in line with his heart. The bullet went threw the book with ease and his body and then ricocheted around the wall of the room. He of course, was arrested at once and placed in the Guard Room Cell to await trial. He appeared to have a look of no concern, just as if he had done nothing wrong. It seemed that there was something mentally wrong with him. As far as we know he had no reason to shoot this man, in the past they had always got on well together. It must have been a difficult case, all we heard was that he was sentenced to ten years for unpremeditated murder to be served in England so he was gone and never heard of again.

Story Number Four
Camping in India.
This is some experience, one can be pestered with insects. You know we used to get a blanket allowance whilst out camping. You could wake up in the morning and find a good quarter of

your blanket eaten away by the white ants. They were only small but good munchers, they had a liking for wool and soft woods, never known them to touch flesh. To get a new blanket, you just had to take it to the Quarter Master and show him and he would replace it. I woke up one morning and started to tidy up my bed, which was only a ground sheet and a couple of blankets, the pillow was my haversack, part of our equipment. Anyhow under the pillow as we called it, was mother centipede with a crowd of her offspring. She had crept under there during the night because of the warmth of my body and given birth to this lot. Now these can give you a nasty sting, so down came the tent mallet on those, no mercy given. We could get some nasty spiders at times as well, there were so many types that we did not trust so, if seen, they were pursued and promptly done away with.

Let's not forget the snakes, the boot lace snake was the one we did not like. It was so small and yet so deadly, those were little black ones, not much longer than about five inches in length.

Then there were ants, ones that bite and sting, but I must say that we did not get much trouble with those. In any case, before we pitched our tents, we would always have a good look around to make sure that we were not in their line of nesting or along their trail. As you may know at certain times of the year a certain big black ant used to go on a big hunt, that would include a few million of them and they would attack practically anything that moved. They have even been known to kill a sheep, they do it by their sheer mass of numbers and if you were camping you could actually hear them coming by a rushing noise or crashing noise. Whatever, you knew that something was coming, so took off without question.

Story Number Five
Leeches.

Still out camping, which of course meant that we were on manoeuvres, still in India. One day, when we had finished off a mock battle and were all very hot and sticky. We spotted a lake which looked very tempting to get into, so permission was given for us to have a bathe. If we had only known what was in front of us, we would not have gone in, but we were all full of having a nice cool swim, stark naked of course. Some dived in with no thought of anything else but cold water. I was not the first one in, so I was not much of a victim, when some of them started shouting leeches and I could see a lot of them rushing out of the water with some big leeches stuck on their skin having a good drink of their blood. I was lucky really, I only had one on me, this was on my leg, so someone shouted out, 'Don't pull them off, you only leave part of them on you to still keep drinking. Some of you go get your cigarettes, light up and burn them off.' So, there was a big rush of lighting up and puffing and a big task of getting them off. The Medical Officer was kept busy for a while sealing off these small places where the leeches had punctured the skin, but no great damage was done. It sure did teach us a lesson, to test the water in future. This lake had some sort of weed in it, that attracts leeches. There is also a certain over hanging weed that attracts these creatures, when you pass under it, they drop on you and set into your skin, so there is a warning.

Story Number Six
Bird Eating Spider
I had rather a hideous experience just once only, witnessing a spider grab hold of a small bird, when we were stationed down on the Central Provinces at Kamptee. I have mentioned this place in the main story.

Next or very close to the barracks was a jungle where at times we would carry out certain training. It was during a break, I was lying back resting, some of us were having a bit of a nod, I did for a while, just resting not asleep. I was just casually looking around the jungle and noticed a few very small birds hopping about on some branches. One or two for a moment perched on a branch, within a second it was grabbed by something so fast. I thought it might have been a spider, but I jumped up quickly to see what was going on and I saw this spider, quite large, already had it at its mercy, killed it I suppose with its venom and then took off.

We are all aware that the years have gone by too quickly, but this time of the year is the remembrance of our fallen Comrades. It is something I know that we shall never forget, but what of the younger generation, it is impossible to rub off some of our experience into their minds, as they were not around to take part, so therefore, their feelings must differ from ours. They are probably sympathetic and have some idea what wars are about by the fact of watching films on T.V. etc., but even that is not fully explained. I suppose it's just an impossibility, because the War Correspondents, although they get as close as possible to the fighting, are not living that kind of life continually like we did, in fact it would not be right to show some of the things that did occur.

We know full well that there are people about who object to all this fuss about the wars and the marching with full bands and flags flying. It is not the glory of war that we celebrate, but the people that were killed and wounded. This includes the civilians that were killed in their own homes, who were unable to take part. We had a menace to get rid of so that we could live a respectable life. I wonder where we would be if they had not helped to get rid of them, it's like a thorn in one's side, you don't like it, so you get rid of it.

Before finishing up my story of the past and some of the present, let's try and put something together about the present and the future.

The older ones especially can see how people have changed in their way of thinking. Let's mention behaviour, starting from an early age, how difficult it is to summarise it all. I suppose up to the young age of six, they can be controlled by their parents and the majority like them to be polite to grown ups and to be respectful, but it seems once they start to go to school their behaviour becomes more difficult to control. The watching of bad T.V. shows which cover violence and the showing of children being insolent to their teachers, seems to give them ideas to bully at school. Also the lack of teachers keeping an eye on their behaviour, because they do not have time to observe, one thing leads to another. It could be because their parents are not home much, because of work, then again it could be that their parents are unemployed and they lose all self respect.

What is so annoying, is when a son or daughter has worked hard at school and has managed to get some degrees and then attempts to obtain employment and it is impossible or it may be a long term effort. That to me is disappointing and very wrong, it does not give others the incentive to even try to pass for any qualifications. Also, what career should one take that is not going to stand you off after a few years of being employed, that must also be a worry for some. It's happening both in the Military Service and the Civil Service, when are they going to make these positions more secure? What else can we say is the cause of the world problems? It's a subject that can be discussed for many hours, even then I doubt if we can find a respectable answer to it all.

None of us is perfect, maybe some think they are, I for one do not think I am, but at least I can say that if there were no Police Force that would not bother me, as I have never had them calling on me because I have broken some law. I might have some times during my life, but I'm not aware of it, there are many people like me, who as far as they know live just an untroubled life in respect of being a law abiding citizen.

So here we are, both Audrey and I, living in Cheddar, famous for its Cheddar Gorge, where probably millions of people have visited the scenery up in these hills of the Mendips. A visit worth your while, to spend a few hours there, especially in the spring or summer. Even winter time we get people who are interested in walking, well there are twenty-six miles of it and what could be better after a long walk, to come down and visit some of the local attractive pubs in the background, which sometimes get missed, but look around a little deeper and you will find some.

Audrey has many friends and associations in the village, as well as the well known W.I. Ladies, they get together and enjoy themselves. Me, I have at one time held office with the Royal British Legion both at Shepton Mallet as well as Cheddar. I enjoy a game of skittles with the members at times, also a game of snooker. The rest of our own entertainment is to visit the local towns, like Bristol, Bath, Street, Glastonbury, Taunton and Wells City. We are also both members of the local Church of England, Audrey more so than me, I don't go so often now because I have lost my hearing, no matter what aids I have they are of no use, that's how bad it is. Anyhow, we are both enjoying our retirement here, a nice peaceful village, let's hope it stays that way.

Recollections and Reflections

Having putting the finishing touches to this story, I have decided to call it 'Hampshire Boy'.

Someone said to me, 'What if you had been lucky enough to have been able to have completed your service in the Army without any interruptions, like being medically discharged, how do you think you would have progressed?' A difficult question, I suppose I could base it on how some of my friends progressed who were of the same rank as me as of then, some with the same qualifications as myself. Then again, we have the same old question, depends who you meet and who is your chief. Whether one's in his favour or whatever. So, judging by my past promotion, which I considered fair, I know I could have at least reached at least a substantive rank of Warrant Officer. Also, having passed my academic qualification exams, it just remains then to have passed any other Carter Exams. There had been some evidence in the past for a while that a Commission could be forthcoming, but this could not come for me as my Service was finished at the time I was injured, but I felt it was there somewhere lingering in the background. Mainly because I was so long acting as Platoon Commander which is a Commissioned Officer's position, so they must have had some confidence in my abilities.

So, let's go ahead and see what I can make of myself using this little word 'If' I was able to carry on with my service.

In those days a Warrant Officer was able to serve in the army until he was in his early fifties, the same if he was a Commissioned Officer. If he managed to get a Commission from the Ranks, from W.O., he was automatically promoted to a Full Lieutenant and then with a little more service, so long as he had a good record, he would eventually become a Captain. I had plenty of time to complete another twenty years, making me around forty-eight years old, still young enough to find myself a career in civilian life.

The rest of my service, well it would be a guess where I would have been stationed, probably Germany for a few years as my Regiment was over there, also over in Ireland, and back in England at Netheravon on Salisbury Plains. Then again, most likely out in the Middle East again. I am unable to make much of a story to all this, just guess work.

My wife Audrey, would have probably enjoyed some service life, especially in the Mess Functions. I know that at one time she was looking forward to some service overseas with me, as I had so often spoken to her about overseas, but all that came to an end once I was medically discharged, it was a pity.

I know that I was not the only one who had to finish his service long before it was over and it was a great disappointment to us. Those who did not get wounded were the lucky ones, but at least we can be thankful that we are still on this earth and have managed to do something with our lives. When the day came for us to leave, we felt like fish out of water for quite a while, not knowing what we were going to do to earn a living, having very few qualifications to help us on our way. We thought, if we could make some progress in the army, surely we could make something of ourselves in civilian life and I guess we did not do so badly.

Having Audrey around me all these years, has made a very good life for me, I wish I could find the right words to fit her character. She must have found me hard to get on with at times, because I am far from perfect, but at least I did try.

A few words about our offspring, John and Eric, I must say if I had my time over again and knew what I know today, I would have taken more care of their upbringing. But, there it is, at my early age, I was green at that sort of thing and just did my best. As it is, they are both married and have their own families to take care of and are I hope enjoying their lives. Our only one regret is that we are all so far apart, that we are not able to see each other very much. We do see John more so because he is living near Salisbury but Eric is way down in the south of Spain.

Audrey on the verandah at Eric's house, Garcian, Spain.
Our last visit, April/May, 1994.

Audrey and I have managed to get down to see him in the past, at least once a year, but the time is coming now that we are both getting older, that this may soon not be possible.

I often think about myself, when I was about to come out of the army as to what kind of a father I would be. Let's be honest, what did I know about that subject in any case, really nothing at all. I just did things on the spur of the moment, none of us fathers took a course on fatherhood, we just got on with it. I had experience handling young men of my own age, but under different circumstances, just training men to kill and fight for their country. But, coming out into this civilian life and having to bring up children and to make them into good citizens how does one go about it? I can only go back to the way that I was brought up and as far as I can see I have nothing to worry about. If I did something that was wrong to my father's eyes and I have been previously warned about it, then it was my fault, so I was punished for it. I merely saw my father's belt coming off, which was to be laid across my bottom a few times,

251

My eldest son John, with me attending one of our Sergeants Past and Present Dinner functions, Winchester, September 1994.

just to remind me not to do it again. My behaviour was not criminal, just stupid things that I used to do, like tie tins on a dog's tail and see him run down the road with these tins clanging behind him. To me at that time, it was funny, but not to the dog, it would frighten him. I was only a kid and a bit of a lively one, so if I did these stupid things, I deserved to get a thrashing. It certainly did not make me hate my father because I was at fault, in fact, I think it did me good. I never stole or had the police knocking on the door so I guess that that was the way I was to treat my boys. It was hardly ever a belt that I laid across the bottom, but a piece of flat wood, never a cane, that left welts on their skin and believe me they had that a few times. They were a couple of lively lads, they alone hold the secrets as to what their behaviour was in their youth. Now in their manhood, I wonder what they think about their childhood and bringing up as children, I should think before they criticised me, they should give some thought as regards to their own behaviour. Let me say now if I had that time over again would I do the same? No, I don't think so, probably try more talking to them and asking them why they did these things that are not good and right, surely they know what is good and what is wrong. There is a proper way of doing things in life to make it easier for us all round, I certainly would use a little more tact.